D1193896

Union Institute
& University

Vermont College

Gift of
Richard Hathaway

GARY LIBRARY
Montpelier, Vermont

Christology in American Unitarianism

William Ellery Channing

Christology

in

American Unitarianism

*An Anthology of Outstanding Nineteenth
and Twentieth Century Unitarian Theologians,
with Commentary
and Historical Background*

Prescott Browning Wintersteen

*The Unitarian Universalist Christian Fellowship
Boston, Massachusetts*

To Elizabeth Abbot Smith, an earnest birthright Unitarian, whose loyalty and generosity have helped immeasurably to preserve Unitarian Christianity and to spread its enlightment to all who may seek it.

"I examined [the evidences of Christianity] with caution, and I think without prejudice; and I am convinced that this religion is truly divine. . . . My object is to discover the truth. I wish to know what Christ taught, not what men have made him teach. . . . I was certain that, as Christ came to save the world, every truth essential to salvation must be plainly unfolded in the Scriptures."

> William Ellery Channing at the outset of his ministry, in a letter to the Reverend Joseph McKean, youthful minister of the Church in Milton, Massachusetts. The church later became Unitarian (1834).

Contents

Illustrations

Foreword

A genetically traced and amply documented account of Christology in American Unitarianism is the enterprise of the ensuing book. The doctrines of the unity and unipersonality of the Godhead (unitarianism in the strictly theological sense and a humanized Christology) are closely interrelated in the history of Unitarianism as a movement from the sixteenth century. In a word, without a high doctrine of the Person and Work (pre-eminently: the Atonement) of Jesus as a Messiah and Son of God the Father there would never have evolved a doctrine of the Triune God. Yet historically a high Christology, more liturgical and devotional than systematically verbalized, *preceded* the trinitarian formulations by the two major ecumenical councils in the fourth century, Nicaea in 325 and I Constantinople in 381. With respect to *dogmatic* formulation, however, Christology only subsequently engaged the Church Fathers in councils: pre-eminently in the fifth century, at Ephesus in 431 and at Chalcedon in 451, with additional clarification at II Constantinople in 553.

When one compares the distinctive doctrines of catholic/orthodox Christianity with those of Judaism, Islam, or others it was the centrality of Jesus as the Christ in the worship, the daily lives, and in the martyrdoms of early Christians that sets it off. Existentially, "practically," Christology antedated full-fledged doctrinal explanations by Christians who stubbornly professed to be monotheists, while they appeared to Jewish and pagan critics to be worshiping three divine beings, God, Christ, and the Holy Spirit.

Without retracing a millennium and a half of the history of dogmas, something must still be said historically about the reassertion of unitarianism and a doctrine about Jesus Christ in American Unitarianism with its evolving or, more accurately, devolving Christology, and this should be seen in the general context of world Calvinism, apart from Lutheranism and other forms of Christianity, that emerged in the sixteenth century.

Unitarianism, as distinguished from the explicit trinitarianism of all the surviving ancient communions of Christians and from that of most Reformation and post-Reformation communions and denominations, has cropped out in denominational form conspicuously from within the context of Calvinism: within the Reformed Church of Transylvania already in the sixteenth century, in the Helvetic Church in Poland-Lithuania at about the same time, in the seventeenth and eighteenth centuries in the nonconformist churches of England and Ireland, and even in latitudinarian Anglicanism, in the Remonstrant Church in the Netherlands, and in New England Puritanism become Congregationalism in the nineteenth century. This does not exhaust the list but supplies the geographical scope for the oft-repeated observation that Calvinism, which was in John Calvin himself, wholly trinitarian, has an inherent tendency to become unitarian. The explanation is on the surface, at least, readily forthcoming.

Both Martin Luther and John Calvin, the latter a really second-generation Reformer, stressed predestination and the invisible Church of grace unto salvation.

The sometime Augustinian friar of Wittenberg derived his insights from the Old Testament (of which he was in our modern sense a professor at the University of Wittenberg), from Paul pre-eminently among the New Testament writers, and from the Patristic namesake of his original order, Bishop Augustine of Hippo.

It is generally recognized in retrospect that Augustine, the greatest and by far the most influential of the four Latin Doctors of the Church, was never as highly developed and nuanced in his Christology as were his Greek patristic predecessors, contemporaries, and those who continued at the christological problematic up to the Fifth Ecumenical Council in 553 under Justinian and intensively for more than two centuries thereafter, even though it is also generally recognized that Augustine gave the definitive Latin patristic formulation to the dogma of the Trinity. Now central to these few words of Introduction is the fact that Augustine was the ranking Church Father, whether Latin or Greek, on all the subtleties of predestination and grace. Indeed, on predestination he came towards the end close to affirming double predestination, that is, the view that God, to be sure the Triune God, in his eternal decrees, even before the fall of Adam, had already predetermined which out of the mass of human perdition — the descendants of Adam and Eve — He would condemn and which He would save. Pauline texts provided Augustine with terms which would eventually become the technical language of supralapsarian (pre-Fall) reprobation and election. Clearly, in the theological system of Augustine, as he finally reconsidered all that he had written, Jesus could not have died on the cross for *all* men, though that might have been theoretically the divine intention and the intention of the Man Jesus.

In any theological system where election by predestination, especially by predestination before the fall of Adam and thus before the crucifixion of the Second or Last Adam, the Work of Christ on Calvary can best serve as an epiphany or historically dramatic explication of God's primordial intention for the elect. To be sure, Augustine himself never drew such a picture of Jesus' life, birth, and teaching, always taking the gospels very seriously and all that Jesus preached and performed sacramentally. And so it was with medieval Latin Christendom for whom Augustine was the *Doctor Ecclesiae* by excellence. This same medieval Christendom developed out of Pauline and Patristic material a distinctive theory of the Work (as distinguished from the Person of Christ), known after its chief formulator, Archbishop Anselm of Canterbury (d. 1109), as the Anselmian or satisfaction theory, according to which Christ in his human nature satisfied in penal pain God for the original sin of humanity, a work sufficient to satisfy God's demand for plenitude of justice in that Christ's human work was, as it were, multiplied by the infinity of his presupposed Deity. At the time of the Reformation, Chalcedonian Christology and the Anselmian Theory of the Atonement were upheld in general by both the Augustinian professor of Wittenberg and the theocrat of Geneva, who together continued more or less intact the fabric of traditional parochial practice and piety and stoutly affirmed the creeds of the Ancient Church, even while insisting more firmly than any council hitherto on predestination to election and salvation by faith alone on the basis of Scripture alone.

But Calvin was more consequent in his reform; and, while he gave a much more prominent place in his *Institutes* to sanctification as distinguished from justification than Luther would ever have permitted himself, because Luther had had to fight the battle of what he called the Roman Catholic merit system of works-righteousness over against God's free grace — and Calvin was also more concerned than Luther about sanctification in the sense of justice in state and society than Luther — nevertheless, on the Trinity and on Christology Calvin did move more freely than Luther, at least, at first. Then, when seeming to be satisfied with the formulation of the Apostles' Creed without the philosophical-philological safeguards of the great conciliar creeds of the fourth and fifth centuries, he was accused of being himself weak on the dogma of the Trinity; and that charge may well have partly motivated his handling of the case of Michael Servetus, in the burning of whom on the issue of Trinitarianism, Geneva could make it clear to Lutherans and Catholics alike that Calvinism, for all its liturgical and other forms of radicalism, remained Catholic in creed. But for Calvin, more than for Augustine, more than for Anselm, more than for Luther, the Work of Christ on Calvary was subsumed under, and even submerged into, the primordial salvific act of God in the predestination of the elect and the reprobation of the "foreknown," even though, of course, in Calvin, as earlier in Augustine, it was a basic postulate that no individual believer and church member could be sure of another's being of the elect or of the reprobate; and Calvin retained the basic outlines of the Anselmian Theory, applying Christ's Work of merit (the utter suffering of the utterly innocent) to the elect *alone*. Yet even here, without so intending perhaps, Calvin so stressed sanctification in personal holiness and in public righteousness that he encouraged facile followers to try to find clues to presumptive election in their piety, prosperity, and even power.

Moreover, Calvinists or to speak more generally, the Reformed, carrying Luther's conception of the Bible still further, in contrast to the Catholics (and the sixteenth-century sectarians, like the Anabaptists), explicitly held to the view that there had been one covenant in two dispensations: one for the ancient Elect or Chosen People and one for the New, partly invisible, Elect mingled in their earthly pilgrimage or in the earthly City (Augustine) with the reprobate (who might well be quite nice people for all that, simply not of the elect!). The clearest outward demonstration of the Lutheran and particularly the Reformed understanding of the Bible as a homogeneous salvific book, embodying one covenant, was the insistence that the circumcision of the elect Israelite was repeated *mutatis mutandis* in the baptism of the Christian *infant*. Luther and Calvin were opposed to adult or believers' baptism (except adult converts), called by them Anabaptism. And although the Catholics, too, practiced infant baptism, their liturgical calendar kept alive in them the distinction between the feast of the Circumcision and that of Epiphany (January 6, the feast of Christ's baptism); and in any case they held to two Testaments not one in two dispensations, like the magisterial or classical Reformers.

In all this and more American Unitarians were heirs of the Congregational Calvinist Puritan tradition. The Pilgrims of Plymouth and the Puritans of the Bay Colony and the sister colonies did not believe in believers' baptism. Puritans/Congregationalists had, on this issue, treated Baptist Roger Williams in the seventeenth century and Isaac Backus in the eighteenth century pretty hard. But they did believe in predestination, although by the close of the eighteenth century this view had softened in three important respects (C. Conrad Wright).

Predestination itself was wideley understood in New England in the modified direction which goes by the name of Arminianism in reference to a movement within the Dutch Calvinist Church that had become Remonstrant (the clerical and other leaders having been exiled from 1618 to 1627). For the Arminians, once the divine decree for election could be perceived as promulgated at least *after* the fall of Adam, the way was opened, as the strict Calvinists had feared, to further modification of predestination toward the eventual presumption of election in all who lived worthy lives and attended upon the services of the churches of the Standing Order.

The second respect in which predestination had been muted was that New

England Congregationalists, destined soon to be called by their opponents "Unitarians," had come to soften their judgment about the reprobate. In fact, there was a sharp falling off of a sense of the universality and gravity of the misconduct of Adam and Eve, or at least of their most recent Eastern Massachusetts descendants! Here fits the famous quip about the difference between Unitarians in New England and the Universalists, who arose in the same area and elsewhere at a somewhat earlier date and commonly from a different class of the population and who soon became also unitarian in theology: "The Universalists believe that God is too good to damn men; the Unitarians, that men are too good to be damned." Most facets of traditional Christology disappear when salvation is severed from damnation and especially when salvation comes to be interpreted as immortality accessible to all (the distinguishing postulate of universalism).

The third respect in which New England Congregationalism had come to modify its Christology and related doctrines before the formal emergence of Unitarianism was the adoption by liberal Jonathan Mayhew and Charles Chauncy (see Conrad Wright, *The Beginnings of Unitarianism in America,* 1955, pp. 218-21) and by Samuel Hopkins (d. 1803) and Dr. Jonathan Edwards, Jr. (d. 1801) of the Governmental Theory of the Atonement, which the Dutch Remonstrant jurist-theologian, Hugo Grotius, formulated ponderously in his *Defense of the "Catholic" Faith Concerning the Satisfaction of Christ* (1617), directed in the full title against the Sienese-Florentine-Racovian Unitarian, Faustus Socinus (d. 1604). Grotius, however, unwittingly made so many concessions to Unitarian Socinus that he in effect substantially altered the Anselmian ("Catholic") Theory by making God the Father and Christ the Son *mutually* involved in a *token* act of justice in a concerted concern for benevolence as well as exemplary justice for the good of the human race. It is of interest that William Ellery Channing in his youth was influenced by the Hopkinsian "disinterested benevolence of God" (cf. Herbert Schneider, 1931, and Conrad Wright, 1970).

The "Arminian" Congregationalists who thought of themselves in 1825, when they formed their first Association that was to eventuate in a full-fledged denomination (to be merged with the Universalists in the mid-twentieth century), as "Liberal Christians" (William Ellery Channing's phase), were not happy at first in being labeled "Arians" and "Unitarians" by the orthodox Trinitarian Congregational critics; but the schism in the Standing Order of Massachusetts trinitarian Congregationalists and Unitarian congregationalists, was by then already well under way.

Dr. Prescott Wintersteen traces the devolution of Christology in the second grouping, which had allies beyond New England in Pennsylvania and elsewhere and in Old England as well, and which eventually spread across the continent in the Yankee Exodus to become a major intellectual force in the history of the American religious experience and religio-cultural-philanthropic enterprise, all out of proportion to the size of the emerging denomination.

As Unitarianism became fairly rapidly explicit, Christology in Unitarian thought had more to do with the Person than the Work (Atonement) of Christ. William Ellery Channing in his sermon, *Unitarianism Most Favorable to Piety*, expressly disavowed as horrendous the idea of a Grotian gallows erected at the center of the cosmos. Early American Unitarians were intensely interested, instead, in the miracles of Jesus, although the preeminent miracle of the Gospels, the Virgin birth, was recognized as theologically linked to the doctrine of the fall of Adam and the apostolic-patristic effort to exculpate Jesus as the Second Adam from the sin and guilt of the first Adam. And they recognized that Augustine had been particularly responsible for connecting original sin and its transmission of guilt with procreation.

Unitarians became very much interested in Jesus as Teacher and Exemplar. Strangely, though they were often charged with being Socinians (heirs of Polish Unitarians of the sixteenth century), whose *Bibliotheca Fratrum Polonorum* was to be found in several New England libraries in the late eighteenth and early nineteenth centuries, they did not seem to be much interested in that Unitarian counterpart of the Trinity prominent in the writings of the Polish Brethren and basic in the structure of the Racovian Catechism (Raków, 1605) and dedicated in 1609 in its Latin form (needless to say in vain!) to James I of England: namely, the *triplex munus Christi*. This conception of the threefold office of Christ as Priest, Prophet (teacher), and King derived from Desiderius Erasmus, by way of Martin Bucer in Strassburg, and was recognized as useful by Calvin himself; and it went on to become the common heritage of all Western Christians, including Roman Catholics. It is surprising that early American Unitarians did not exploit this Calvinistic, not to say Socinian, sanction for a fresh attempt to arrange their christological research and aspiration. The virtual absence of traces of this threefold office in early Unitarianism goes far to substantiate the axiom of Conrad Wright that the father of American Unitarians was John Calvin — by way of Hugo Grotius — and not Faustus Socinus.

Dr. Wintersteen shows what other lines they pursued.

As a modified doctrine of predestination (which for a while set Unitarians apart from the Universalists) imperceptibly gave way to feeling for the providential progress of mankind ("onward and upward"), despite evil and setback, the crux of the christological problem became for Unitarians, in the context of Transcendentalism, the uniqueness of Jesus among the founders and seers in various religious traditions. In the course of American Unitarian christological thinking it has been said (H. Richard Niebuhr) that Unitarians came to understand God the Father as indeed sole Deity but with the lineaments of Jesus Christ, made experiential for them through the Holy Spirit of God that had been at work in the youthful Hopkinsianism of Channing. The sense of the Spirit of God was very prominent in Unitarianism; and any understanding of the successive efforts at christological formulation in ever changing contexts must take into account the experiential and not merely the alleged "rationalistic" character of Unitarianism, whether under more conservative influence or under that of Transcendentialism.

Despite the disintegration of the venerable and elaborate frame made up on four sides: of predestination, original sin, conciliar dogma concerning Christ as one Person in two Natures, and the Anselmian/Calvinist Grotian Theory of Substitionary, then Governmental Atonement, Unitarians still had a vivid, variegated canvas of Christ, the more so for the reason that they made of him a model. They studied closely his life, death, teaching, actions, and resurrection, and at length they found in him a successor of the prophets, still unique however in the manner of his life and instruction. Moreover, eschewing the credal formulations and the postulates of the Reformers, the Unitarians who dealt with Jesus were freed to make use of a good deal of scriptural material that had not easily fitted into the post-biblical dogmatic formulations of the Church and also of pre-conciliar and patristic statements that now gave freshened, though venerable sanction to what they were trying to say, along with the rich philosophical-religious material coming principally out of German universities, of which Unitarian divines kept themselves abreast well into the nineteenth century.

Dr. Wintersteen has carried his account of American Unitarian Christology from William Ellery Channing to Charles E. Park and beyond, that of both preachers and professors of Bible (Harvard and Meadville) well into the twentieth century. The chapters on various divines were originally given as the Minns Lectures, and they have the distinction of having been presented before audiences in Japan as well as in the United States. As a Church historian concerned with theology and hence specifically with Christology, as a roommate of the author when we were in seminary together at Meadville and at the University of Chicago, hence as a career-long friend, I am honored to be asked to introduce the following book by Dr. Wintersteen, a retired Navy chaplain, who knew well what holy communion meant to those to whom he ministered in World War II. A graduate of Harvard College and of Harvard Divinity School, honorary Doctor of Divinity, resourceful ecumenical minister of the First Parish in Milton, Massachusetts, Dr. Wintersteen has with courage and concern tackled in these pages a difficult aspect of American Unitarian history of abiding importance to all in the Unitarian Universalist denomination and beyond.

George H. Williams

Hollis Professor of Divinity
Harvard University

Preface

Before plunging *in medias res*, I shall steal a moment for personal comment. It may afford the reader something of an insight into the author's religious background and so reveal the basis for his motivation.

I was brought up a Unitarian and never questioned my remaining a Unitarian. In those early years of my life, when I might have begun to look about and discover that there were other churches in town, it never occurred to me to ask why I was a Unitarian or why others were what they were. The fact that our church was what would be called at a later period the *status* church in town probably made no difference to my not entering into a comparative evaluation of churches; it may, of course, have contributed subconsciously to my contentment. I am speaking of the six years' period from the time I arrived in town with my family, at the age of nine, until I went away to a boarding school, at the age of fifteen.

It is appropriate to mention that my father was the minister of the Unitarian Church in town (as well as of the Unitarian Church in the next town). He had been an active layman in the Methodist Church, in fact a lay reader. Upon his discovery of Unitarianism he was so seized by its principle of freedom in religious thinking, that he resigned his job with the New York Central Railroad and began his studies for the Unitarian ministry. I mention this circumstance because it accounts for the familiarity with the name and figure of Jesus which characterized my father's teaching and preaching. At the same time, it is significant that in leaving the Methodist Church, my father did not abandon Jesus and certain religious practices and conventions, as have many come-outers. For example, the Last Supper was observed in our church as a regular practice, once a month.

In view of this background of religious focus, it was a surprise to me to learn that Jesus was not always the central figure in a Unitarian's religion. As

I look back to the prayers and sermons of my earliest ministry, I find what appears to be a wholly unselfconscious reference to Jesus, indeed, to *Jesus Christ*. In view of my home indoctrination and of my brief apprenticeship under Dr. Charles Edwards Park, at First Church in Boston, an unwavering Christo-centric Unitarian, this circumstance was natural. It must have been, then, after I had become a chaplain in the United States Navy, beginning that service in anticipation of the United States' involvement in World War II, when I became acutely conscious of the alledgedly weak or abandoned place of Jesus in religion for many Unitarians. I was repeatedly advised of it by my orthodox chaplain associates. On the one hand, I did not believe it; on the other hand, I resented the accompanying conclusion by them that there-fore, as a Unitarian, I was not and could not be a Christian, nor, therefore, a generally useful chaplain. For one who had been raised with never a thought that his religion was not centered in Jesus nor completely adequate and valid, such allegations were a shock. I felt it was regrettable that much of the Christian world did not understand the truth about the Unitarians and Jesus.

As my experience with other Unitarians widened, however, and as the years rolled on, bringing changes in emphases, I learned that it was true that some Unitarians had abandoned Jesus, if not God, as well. I felt that the record could well be set straight, both for those of other faiths and for younger Unitarians and Universalists, who may not have been trained with teachings of Jesus, the Christ. It would be only candid to confess that I believe now, as I grew up believing, that Jesus not only is, but should be, at the heart of our religion.

The theme of this book may be said to be the life, death, and resurrection of Jesus Christ in American Unitarianism, and a *double entendre* is purposely allowed. Both theological and historical views are held of the life, the death, and the resurrection of Jesus. Let us put them in one category for our purpose. But in using the expression life, death and the resurrection of Jesus in Ameri-can Unitarianism, I am also alluding to the role Jesus has played, or has been deprived of playing, in the religion of Unitarians. What happened to his place, his changing role and significance, is thought of in our scheme here as his life and is definitely related to shifts and trends in Unitarian emphasis. His death is spoken of in the sense of his widespread dismissal from Unitarian religious thinking. His resurrection is conceived of as speculation with regard to a renewed emphasis upon Jesus in Unitarian religious thought.

It goes without saying that a discussion of the theological and historical views of Jesus Christ in Unitarianism must involve references to orthodox classical Christian concepts, beliefs, and declarations.

As a final word of introduction, I would say that the present age, for all its high science and materialism, finds man no less responsible for his spiritual sustenance than man in simpler ages before it. Man's search for assurance, reality, and purpose goes on and on, and every instrument, every device, every conjectural force or historical reality which can be brought into play should be recognized, accepted, utilized, and enjoyed. If men in other times have looked to Jesus Christ for their enlightenment and leadership, so men of these times must do, if they are not to deprive themselves of the most essential element in their search.

A number of acknowledgments are in order: to the Minns Lectureship Committee, under the chairmanship of Mrs. James H. Jackson, for providing the basic occasion for gathering and presenting the material which became the Minns Lectures and furnished the greater part of the material contained in this book; to Dean Krister Stendahl, of the Harvard Divinity School, who expressed his desire to see an introduction to the Christology of Channing and the Unitarian Christians, for the benefit of persons unfamiliar with the history of American Unitarianism; to Conrad Wright, Professor of American Church History at Harvard Divinity School, who offered suggestions of sources of information, including his own writings, and kindly granted permission for quotations from his works; to George H. Williams, Hollis Professor of Divinity at Harvard Divinity School, who graciously wrote the Foreword; to the Unitarian Universalist Christian Fellowship for assuming the role of publisher; to Richard E. Myers, Editor of the Universalist Unitarian Christian for editorial assistance; to Mr. Alan L. Seaburg, Curator of Manuscripts, the Andover-Harvard Theological Library, Harvard Divinity School, and Mr. Carl G. Seaburg, Director of Information, the Unitarian Universalist Association, for furnishing the photographs of principal persons whose works are discussed in the text; and to Mrs. Elizabeth F. Bruehl and Mrs. Rosemary S. Way for typing, proofreading, and otherwise assisting with both the lecture and the book materials. A special word of appreciation is due my patient and forebearing wife Dorothy, who indulged me the summer days and other times which went into the research and writing of this project. To all these individuals and many others who contributed directly and indirectly to the publication of this book I offer my humble thanks.

Christology in American Unitarianism

Introduction

Although it is not the compass of these chapters to trace the history of Jesus and the religion called Christian in any detail, the briefest sort of recollection may, nevertheless, be of some use in establishing a perspective of the growth of Christian belief and dogma regarding Jesus Christ.

About the year now reckoned as 6 B.C., in the village of Nazareth, in the northern province of Galilee, in the county called Palestine, during the reign of King Herod, when Augustus was ruler of the Roman Empire, a son was born to a builder named Joseph and his wife Mary. The son was named Jesus. He lived for about 33 years and died from the cruel punishment of crucifixion. He had offended the high priests of his native religion and was seen as a threat to civil order by the Emperor's local governor, Pontius Pilate. Brief recollections of his life have survived, together with things he is reported to have said, during the less than three years' period when he was active as a philosophizing and reforming religious teacher. His original purpose was to straighten out the entangled religion of the people about him. One might say he was the original puritan. His followers quickly recognized his extraordinary powers, however, and he was soon the annointed one of God, the Christ, and the long awaited Messiah, although not the political military leader traditionally expected.

Out of Jesus' purified Judiasm grew a new religion of hope with a personal, individual appeal, which led to a rapid spread of it in the civilized world, through the enthusiasm of its converts. Here was a religion with a God in heaven who had no truck with emperors, and an emphasis on living life well, through the observance of such virtues as love, honesty, sympathy, humility, and helpfulness. In the end, immortality awaited the faithful. Evidently the world needed this kind of religion. Jesus was, from the beginning, a central figure. He not only taught men about God, he was an intermediary between man and God, and in a short time he became God himself. Not only that, he was declared to be the founder of a church, The Church. In a beguiling Greek pun, it was claimed that the new church was founded upon the apostle Peter, that is, upon rock Petros, Petra (Matthew 16:18).

As with any organization, there were from the beginning, those who wished to run things and build an empire. In fact, the church did become a great political power. In the meantime, controversies regarding doctrine abounded. They were dealt with in councils, and those who refused to go along with the decisions of the church authorities suffered ostracism, exile, imprisonment, or death. Christians became martyrs for the Martyr they espoused, first under the sentences of the Roman government and later under the sentences of the governing factions of the new church.

Monks and priests devoted their lives to the contemplation of God, man, and Christ, and extraordinary conclusions were reached regarding all three. God was primitive and anthropomorphic; man was susceptible to evil and the machinations of the Devil, and, later, was thought to be inherently evil; and Christ was God, Judge, and Ruler.

Eventually the great central power of the Church was challenged, and ultimately the Church was divided into two main sections, called Catholic and Protestant.

Throughout the centuries following the creation of a church based on the religious views of Jesus, there were always those who maintained a truer view of who Jesus was and what he intended to do, but the large majority went along with an institutional growth which created something quite different. This is not to say that what Christians have made of Jesus' religion is altogether lacking in elements germaine and appropriate to that of Jesus himself; it is merely to say that what they created was *sui generis*, and not in Jesus' pattern.

Both the seeds and stimuli for their growth which are reflected in the blossoming of American Unitarian Christianity are to be found in the formulation of early affirmations of belief, and reactions to them, such as the Apostles Creed (circa A.D. 160), the Arian controversy (318 to A.D. 380), the Nicene Creed adopted at the Council of Nicaea (A.D. 325), the Council of Chalcedon (A.D. 451), and the Athanasian Creed (circa A.D. 460). Likewise, in the years before, during, and after Calvin and Luther and the Protestant Reformation, the true nature of Jesus Christ was debated, the orthodox views of it contested, and alternate positions claimed and sometimes sustained, in Europe. Early Unitarian views were especially prominent in Poland and Transylvania.

The spirit of individualism fostered by the Renaissance found expression in the religious controversies of the sixteenth century. Resistance to orthodoxy in the early centuries of Christianity, when there were still those who fancied they knew what were the true characteristics of Jesus' religion, may be attributed to an abiding reluctance to see the new religion distorted. After the desert of the Middle Ages, the spirit and verve required to think independently of the enforced formulae which governed Christian beliefs and practices had to be re-developed. The worth and potential of the individual person, which had been the concern of Jesus himself, had to be rediscovered and reaffirmed.

Protestantism became the champion of the individual, while the Catholic Church maintained that the Church as an institution was the visible representative of Christ and therefore the proper source and repository of authority and truth. It was inevitable, in view of the persistent characteristics of persons to divide themselves into the two groups of those who desire conformity and those who prefer independence, that within Protestantism itself differences should arise with respect to the true nature of Christ and of the religion which bore his name.

It is contended, and rightly, that the new world of America gave birth to a liberal tendency in religion out of its own need and stimuli; although some of the liberal thinking of England and the Continent cannot but have contributed to the character and body of American liberal theology. As the Renaissance reawakened individualism, so, in a different and more explicit way, the American Revolution awakened individualism in a new country, an individualism which was not limited to political views and economic enterprises, but which extended to religious thinking, as well.

Thus, in the century preceding the formulation of a Unitarian association in 1825, we find reactors against Calvinism adopting what Professor Conrad Wright of Harvard Divinity School has called "a new set of basic assumptions about human nature and human destiny." Professor Wright's presentation of the characteristics of the liberal school is so lucid and succinct, I quote it here in part, with his permission:

"The doctrinal position of the liberals combined three tendencies which may be logically distinguished: Arminianism, supernatural rationalism, and anti-Trinitarianism. Arminianism asserted that men are born with the capacity both for sin and for righteousness; that they can respond to the impulse toward holiness as well as the temptation to do evil; and that life is a process of trial and discipline by which, with the assistance God gives to all, the bondage to sin may be gradually overcome. This assertion of human ability contrasts with the Calvinist belief that the innate bent of all men is toward sin, that God has decreed everlasting happiness to some and eternal torment to others, and that salvation comes as the unmerited gift of God's Holy Spirit.

"Supernatural rationalism, accepted by many Calvinists as well as by the liberals, was virtually the orthodox theology of the Age of Reason (eighteenth century). It asserted that the unassisted reason can establish the essentials of natural religion: the existence of God, the obligations of morality, and a divine order of rewards and punishments. But unlike Deism, it insisted that natural religion must be supplemented with a special revelation of God's will. The Bible is such a revelation, which reinforces natural religion by stating its obligations more clearly and impressively; and it proclaims the gospel of redemption through the perfect obedience of Christ, which unassisted reason could never have discovered. The authority of the Bible rests on internal and external evidences, particularly the miracles of Christ, which attest that he was a divinely inspired messenger. Human reason must examine and assess such evidences, and determine the true meaning of obscure or disputed passages of Scripture. But while reason is essential, it must not substitute its own speculations for gospel truth. The Arminians condemned equally the orthodox insistence on creeds and confessions of faith of human origin, and the deistic confidence in natural reason unassisted by divine revelation.

"Finally, the liberals tended to be anti-Trinitarian, largely because they were not convinced that the doctrine of the Trinity is scriptural. Most of them were Arians, believing that Christ, while not a part of the Godhead, is a being of a far higher rank in Creation than mere man. They were not 'Unitarian' as that term was then understood, since only a small minority believed in the simple humanity of Jesus."[1]

All these categories of theological position are related to Jesus Christ. It may be said that Arminianism is primarily a view of man, an elevation of man to a position of initiative and worth, but herein it is directly in line with Jesus' own idea of man. What must be remembered is that whereas it is not quite true to say with the cynical writer of the Book of Ecclesiastes, as though it were a statement of fact to be taken literally, "there is nothing new under the sun," certain positions and emphases became identified with the names of persons who reintroduced them or of positions redefined. Holders of the Calvinistic belief in the secondary position of man, so to speak, of course would use such a term as Arminian rather than to identify the position with Jesus, because it would be in conflict with the thesis they were supporting. They would do nothing deliberately to cut themselves off from identifying themselves with him. For most of those who would enhance the status of man, there was a concomitant view, a corollary so to speak, with reference to the nature of Christ. This view was called Arianism, after a 4th Century presbyter (or priest), named Arius. Arianism was the belief that Christ, though a being far above man, was yet less than God; that he was created before the creation of the world; and that his nature was different from that of either God or man.

Perhaps one can say that the same spirit which evoked individualism in the Renaissance and sparked the demand for individual respect and independence before the War of the Revolution engendered this championing of status for man in Christian theology and the insistence upon the de-deifying of Christ. A struggle between proponents and opponents of the man-upward and the Jesus-downward views was precipitated by the period of extreme evangelism in the decade 1735 to 1745, known as the Great Awakening. The narrow Calvinistic evangelism of Jonathan Edwards and George Whitefield, from England, put to the test the budding views of man and Jesus we have just reviewed and spurred active response. Such a juxtaposition of emphases is not unfamiliar. Today, as then, the espousal of a "new" or "fresh" or "liberal" view is quickly matched by a "reactionary" or "right-wing" flurry to combat it. Every live age has its darers, its frontiersmen, on the one hand, and those who prefer to stay home, or to retreat farther into the cave, away from the fresh air and light of the doorway, on the other hand.

The Christ who emerged for the generation of Channing's launching into the ministry and for the others of his time, was described in part by Professor Conrad Wright in this way. "The function of Christ was not merely to make atonement by his obedience for the disobedience by men. Centuries of devout Christians have produced a much richer interpretation of his mission than that, and the Arminians had no reason to reject most of the traditional doctrine. They described him, in familiar terms, as prophet, priest, and king. As prophet, he is the chief source of our knowledge of God's revealed will. He teaches both by his doctrine and by his example: 'He came to give mankind the most perfect and engaging example of obedience to the will of God; of all piety and righteousness, humility and charity, temperance and patience; — a living example in frail human flesh.'[2,3] Since 'examples teach more effectually than precepts,' he has 'set us the most shining example of that holy religion, which he came to preach and establish in the world.'[4] Samuel Webster spoke of him as [priest,] 'a Mediator between God and us, and a powerful advocate at the Father's right Hand.'[5] As king, Christ is the ruler of his church, its sole law giver and the judge of transgressions. It was he who 'sent forth ministers to propagate it,' and 'fixed constitutions and ordinances, to derive on it all the advantages of religious society.' "[6]

What was happening in the world politically and socially in the early years of the nineteenth century?

Napoleon had been consecrated as emperor of the French by Pope Pius VII in 1804. The British won the battle of Trafalgar, and the French and Spanish fleets were vanquished. While England became mistress of the seas, Napoleon expanded the land area of his control, but by 1812, with his retreat from Russia, Napoleon's star was on the wane. Austria, with allies and enjoying the support of the English, attacked Napoleon the next year, and by April of the following year, 1814, Napoleon gave up the world for the island principality of Elba. The following year he tried unsuccessfully to regain his throne and was defeated at the battle of Waterloo. A declaration of Christian principles was signed by nearly all the European rulers to achieve The Holy Alliance. Meanwhile, England was undergoing political and economic troubles, which lasted from 1815 to 1834. During this period Catholics were granted suffrage and the right to sit in Parliament, and in Ireland the people objected to enforced support of the Established (Episcopal) Church through tithes. A new era began in 1837, with the accession of Queen Victoria to the throne.

The United States was developing governmental procedures, acquiring land (for example, the Louisiana Purchase), and exploring the northwest. In 1807 Robert Fulton's steamboat traveled from New York to Albany in 32 hours, and African slave trade was prohibited beginning January 1, 1808. Thomas Jefferson had hoped to stave off war with England, but in 1812, under President Monroe, the United States became involved in a war with England. The country was very busy. The establishment of the Second Bank of the United States, tariff laws, a treaty with Spain resulting in the acquisition of Florida, court decisions regarding centralization of power in states and against democratic attacks upon private property, the Missouri Compromise, a land law, the Monroe Doctrine, the completion of the Erie Canal, and the creation of the first public railroad — these were signs and symptoms of the new country's growing up. The common man was receiving more attention through state voting laws and the establishment of the Working-men's Party in 1829. In 1830 the Mormon Church was organized. William Lloyd Garrison began his explosive advocacy of the abolition of slavery in 1831. Speculation and reckless expansion led to a panic and crash in 1837, and the first women's college, Mt. Holyoke Seminary, was opened in the same year. Trade unionism began to grow, and there was political reaction against Jacksonian Democracy. In the five years from 1834 to 1839 McCormick invented a reaping machine, Colt invented the six-shooter, and Goodyear discovered the process of vulcanization.

In such a period man sees himself accomplishing. For Christians, it was a period of emancipation. During this natural process of growth and transistion, it could well have been asked what was happening to belief in God and to the Christian concept of Jesus Christ. In general, new problems arose and were solved, mostly on the basis of existing values and old and tried principles. At the scene of Unitarian development, Boston was entering what has been called its "Periclean Age."[7] To a pride in its role in the War of Independence, development of characteristics of classic Greek democracy, and a polished development in the individual (obviously only on the financial level where it could be maintained), persons in the vicinity of Boston were adding a discovery of Europe, especially of Germany, as a source of ideas and intellectual styles. Through the extensive efforts of George Ticknor, a Unitarian, a public library was founded, destined to be within a generation or so the largest free circulating library in the world. Literary frontiers and communications were not limited to the United States, and Boston was the scene of active publishing of literary works and the home of such standard-setting periodicals as the *North American Review* and *The Dial,* the Transcendentalist magazine.

Admittedly, these historical, political, and social factors do not themsleves say anything specifically about the role of Jesus in Unitarianism, but I beg to point out that the Unitarian who was thinking about Jesus and delineating his role was not living incommunicado, in a perfect isolation from the world about him. The fact that history was being made rapidly both abroad and at home can hardly be overlooked. In the sketchy resume just offered, man can be seen taking a very large hand in shaping his destiny, and this is a factor significant to a display of initiative in religious thinking. Channing came along at a time of emancipation of man's spirit. He stood at the doorway of the predictable course of development and transition in all the affairs of his living. In cutting loose from the home base (England) and progressing through hints of idealism and the curbs of experimental hard-knocks, the citizens of the new kind of world were bound to adapt the configurations and conformities with which they started to the new conditions into which they found their single steps had taken them. With respect to Jesus Christ, Channing recognized his essential merit and purest delineation, and in doing so appeared to say something new, yet to remain faithfully within what he considered the old format.

Chapter 1

William Ellery Channing's Pure Christianity

Let us begin now by turning our attention to the period when Unitarianism was assuming shape and identity and to a central figure of that religious development, William Ellery Channing. Who was William Ellery Channing? Unitarians should have no illusion that there is a widespread interest in and understanding of his religious points of view, nor of any other prominent figures in the relatively brief history of Unitarianism in the United States. In two out of three classes of high school students I met with recently, it was understood by at least one person present, who made the affirmation uncontested by any classmates, that Unitarians do not believe in God (let alone in Jesus Christ!). To most persons, the handsome statue of this great figure on the edge of the Boston Public Garden means nothing.

Those who possess enough knowledge of Unitarianism to have become curious about its history in America have heard of Channing, however, and would be interested to learn more of him. It must be remembered, of course, that our subject is not Unitarianism or Channing, but the place of Jesus Christ in Unitarianism.

What was the general climate of Channing's time? A growing sense of identity and assurance in the Colonies had led to increasing resistance to the Crown. By 1775 Thomas Paine dared to publicize his *Common Sense,* and courage born of desperation and pride led soon to the Declaration of Independence of the United Colonies. Three years before Channing was born, the Articles of Confederation were prepared. The Confederacy was to be known as the United States of America. It would be twelve years before the present system of government would be formed, but the new country was on its own, and approaching its problems with initiative and resourcefulness.

Thomas Jefferson became the third president of the United States in the second year of Channing's ministry, following John Adams. These were both men of social idealism and religious liberalism.

During this period there was a continuing exchange of ideas with persons in England and France, although the influence of France was more that of induced popular reaction to the changing fortunes of that country than intellectual. The Colonies had enjoyed France's assistance during the War of Independence, and France followed the example of the new government in the new world, with its own political revolution. In contrast to the tone which pervaded the new United States, however, the excesses and crudities of France during this period of evolution evoked a reaction of disgust in Americans. One observer declared "[T]he French Revolution had broken up the foundations of religion and morals, as well as government, and continued to rage for some years with its utmost fury, spreading its disastrous influence throughout the civilized world, and pouring upon our country a flood of infidel and licentious principles."[1] This state of affairs not only influenced Channing's college generation but also was a continuing source of concern to him years later. In 1831 Channing was asking, "From what means or efforts may a better state of things be hoped in France? What can be done for religion in that country?"[2] Again, "I neither expect nor desire Christianity to revive in France under its old forms. Something better is needed. Christianity, I conceive, is to be re-established by clear developments of its original, essential truths."[3] Here Channing revealed his purpose for the United States, as well.

Both the idealism of the exciting new country and the sordid life in an old country with a new government contributed to an emergent state of mind. John Adams eloquently put into words the thoughts which would characterize leading American minds at this time:

"Let us dare to read, think, speak and write. Let every order and degree among the people rouse their attention and animate their resolution. Let them all become attentive to the grounds and principles of government, ecclesiastical and civil . . . Let the pulpit resound with the doctrines and sentiments of religious liberty. Let us hear the danger of thralldom to our consciences from ignorance, extreme poverty, and dependence, in short, from civil and political slavery. Let us see delineated before us the true map of man. Let us hear the dignity of his nature, and the noble rank he holds among the works of God . . . and that God Almighty has promulgated from heaven, liberty, peace, and good will to man! . . . "In a word, let every sluice of knowledge be opened and set a-flowing . . . The prospect now before us in America, ought in the same manner to engage the attention of every man of learning, to matters of power and of right, that we may be neither led nor driven blindfolded to irretrievable destruction."[4] Such was the fervor of John Adams.

On the social and intellectual level in the United States, but most especially in Channing's world of New England, there were additional environmental factors. The colonies had but recently gained their independence of

Great Britain, when Channing was born, in 1780. 1620 was the better part of 200 years back. The manners and trappings of England and the Continent were in evidence. Bold or desperate frontier thinking was increasingly meshed with the thinking of the city and the salon. There were already, so to speak, two societies, as indeed there are two or more levels of thinking and living in any seasoned culture. "Eighteenth century Boston was a leading commercial centre, where social life modelled itself on that of London, with a miniature court around the governor, and where large fortunes and elegant manners were the normal objects of ambition. It was in its measure a worldly and epicurean city, with a worldly and rational ideology . . .."[5]

Although it would be imprecise to refer to the Boston of this era as "Puritan," in the seventeenth century sense, yet that term suggests itself because the Bostonian character reflected a significant concern with such subjects as "values," "standards," and "moral taste." Education and the practice of a sense of responsibility were also characteristic. Perhaps it should be said that Bostonians shared these characteristics with certain English counterparts like Coleridge and Carlyle. There was a literary air about the city at the time of Channing, and writing was a self-conscious art taken seriously. Theology was the other distinguishing excellence of Boston. Harvard University, though located in Cambridge across the river, was considered not only a part of the Boston cultural and intellectual scene, but a mirror that matched Boston's own mirror, in the way of one reflecting the other. Unitarian theology was early found at Harvard, from the top administrative level down through the student body.

In this connection, it may be said that Channing's ordination and installation as minister of the Federal Street Church, in Boston, in 1803, coincided with the culmination of the remarkable development of liberal theological thinking and its inevitably accompanying controversy of the previous hundred years. The appointment, in 1805, of a liberal, a Unitarian, the Reverend Henry Ware of Hingham, as Hollis professor of Divinity at Harvard, was characteristic of the time. In the following year, another liberal, Samuel Weber, was named president of Harvard. The Unitarians had arrived, and a great new influence in Christian theology and Christology would now take shape. This was the stage setting when Channing appeared as the representative Unitarian of his time and the first individual whose conception of the place for Jesus Christ is to receive our attention.

As the customary popular pictorial representation of Jesus has most often made him a delicate, sensitive-appearing, almost effeminate man, so does the most familiar representation of Channing take notice of his short, slight, stature, with narrow shoulders and a thin face, and deep-set eyes. There is some suggestion that he may also have possessed a fastidiousness, which reflected a delicacy of taste. In other words, he was anything but hale, hearty, and robust. Having said this much of Channing's physical characteristics and temperament, however, not enough has been said to convey an accurate likeness. In his childhood and youth, Channing was strong and full of vigor, even physically aggressive, and prone to seek adversaries for wrestling matches, while in his later years, the power of his words and the force of his thoughts, launched against the ears and minds of his listeners, revealed a temper of high spirit, and an earnestness for truth and setting the record straight, that belied his physical appearance and ignored the chronic illness which kept him weak and fettered for most of his adult life.

An account narrated in the biography written by his nephew, William Henry Channing, reveals a source of lasting influence on his religious thinking. "His father, with the view of giving him a drive, took William in his chaise one day, as he was going to hear a famous preacher in the neighborhood. Impressed with the notion that he might learn glad tidings from the unseen world, he listened attentively to the sermon. With glowing rhetoric, the lost state of man was described, his abandonment to evil, helplessness, dependence upon sovereign grace, and the need of earnest prayer as the condition of receiving divine aid. In the view of the speaker, a curse seemed to rest upon the earth, and darkness and horror to veil the face of nature. William, for his part, supposed that henceforth those who believed would abandon all other things to seek this salvation, and that amusement and earthly business would no longer occupy a moment. The service over, they went out of the church, and his father, in answer to the remark of some person, said, with a decisive tone: 'Sound doctrine, Sir.' 'It is all *true* then,' was the boy's inward reflection. A heavy weight fell on his heart. He wanted to speak to his father; he expected his father would speak to him in relation to this tremendous crisis of things. They entered the chaise and drove along, but, absorbed in awful thoughts, he could not raise his voice. At length they reached home; but instead of calling the family together, and telling them of the appalling intelligence which the preacher had given, his father quietly read a newspaper. All things went on as usual. At first, he was surprised; but not being given to talking, he asked no explanations. Soon, however, the question rose, . . . 'Could what he had heard be true? No! his father did not believe it; people did not believe it! It was *not* true!' He felt he had been trifled with; that the preacher had deceived him; and from that time he became inclined to distrust everything oratorical, and to measure exactly the meaning of words; he had received a profound lesson on the worth of sincerity."[6]

Even as a child and very young man, Channing was "grave and reflective" and "fond of lonely rambles on the beach" near their home in those years when he still lived in Newport, Rhode Island. His disposition was kind and gentle, as well toward animals as toward human beings. One may wonder at the similarity of Albert Schweitzer's reverence for life and Channing's, as revealed in a letter written by Channing soon after he was graduated from college: " 'Thanks that I can say I have never killed a bird. I would not crush the meanest insect which crawls upon the ground. They have the same right to life that I have, they receive it from the same Father, and I will not mar the works of God by wanton cruelty.' "[7]

The true religion of Jesus would satisfy this sensitive soul, but harsh evangelical Calvinism like that of Jonathan Edwards repulsed him. Channing was sent to New London, Connecticut when he was twelve years old, to prepare for college, under the guidance of an uncle, the Reverend Henry Channing. A revival was sweeping New London at the time, and Dr. Channing later attributed his entrance upon "a decidedly religious life" to this period.

Later, while in college, he experienced a spiritual rebirth which came upon him as he was reading passages in which the author "asserts man's capacity for disinterested affection and considers virtue as the sacrifice of private interests and the bearing of private evils for the public good, or as self-devotion to absolute, universal good ... There suddenly burst upon his mind that view of the dignity of human nature which was even after to 'uphold and cherish' him, and thenceforth to be 'the fountain light of all his day, the master light of all his seeing . . ..' "[8] Channing's consciousness was awakened to "an exhaustless tendency in the human soul to moral perfection." At the same time he was led to a concentration of "his energies upon the thought of social progress."[9]

When we read of Channing's finding his true course in life and peruse his own accounts of his development, we tend to forget how young a man he was at this time of discovery. He was graduated from college at the age of eighteen, and he was still eighteen years of age when he wrote to a classmate of a choice of career. "I shall be a minister, a sheperd of the flock of Jesus, a reformer of a vicious, and instructor of an ignorant world. I look forward to a better country, and, while I am journeying toward it myself, I wish to lead others the same way. I know that you revere religion; and I wish that in your political career you would sometimes look beyond the strife, crimes, and intrigues of nations, to the harmony and blessedness of the Christian society in another state. We shall take different courses in life, but we shall meet in the grave. We shall bow before the same tribunal, and, I trust, shall rejoice forever in the same heaven, and join in the same celebration of Almighty love. You will think I have grown quite ministerial, but believe me, I cherished the same sentiments in college as I do now. In my view, religion is but another name for happiness, and I am most cheerful when I am most religious."[10]

Following college, Channing felt he must no longer look to others for support. In order to pursue his professional studies, therefore, he accepted a position as a tutor in a prominent family in Richmond, Virginia.

In narrating this period in Channing's life, his biographer writes: "He had also gained from the Stoics, and from his own pure standard of virtue, ascetic desires of curbing the animal nature, and of hardening himself for difficult duties. For the end of overcoming effeminacy, he accustomed himself to sleep on the bare floor, and would spring up at any hour of waking to walk about in the cold. With the same view he made experiments in diet, and was rigidly abstemious, while he neglected exercise from too close application. The result of these night-studies and of his general ignorance of the natural laws was, that an originally fine constitution was broken, and the seeds of disease were planted in his system which years of scrupulous regard to health could never root out."[11]

Channing returned to Newport in July of 1800. It was a miserable voyage, and he suffered from exposure. His friends were surprised and dismayed to see what a change had taken place in him physically since his departure.

Let us spend a minute of two looking at written expressions which came out of this period of continued preparation for his newly chosen profession. In a letter to the Reverend Joseph McKean, recently settled over the First Parish in Milton, Massachusetts, Channing wrote, in part, "I examined [the evidences of Christianity] with caution, and I think without prejudice; and I am convinced that this religion is truly divine . . . My object is to discover the truth. I wish to know what Christ taught, not what men have made him teach . . . I was certain that, as Christ came to save the world, every truth essential to salvation must be plainly unfolded in the Scriptures."[12]

Years later Channing was to write of his religious views at this time, " 'There was a time . . . when I verged towards Calvinism, for ill health and depression gave me a dark view of things. But the doctrine of the Trinity held me back. When I was studying my profession, and religion was the subject of deepest personal concern with me, I followed Doddridge through his "Rise and Progress" till he brought me to a prayer to Jesus Christ. There I stopped, and wrote to a friend that my spiritual guide was gone where I could not follow him. I was never in any sense a Trinitarian.' "[13]

Contemporary Unitarians, if they refer to the prophet of Nazareth at all, call him Jesus. One seldom hears him referred to as Jesus Christ or as Christ, alone. In my own church the Covenant is repeated every Sunday, and the full cognomen is used, just as it would have been in 1834, when the Parish divided into two parts, the Unitarian and the Trinitarian. The Covenant is the familiar one, "In the love of truth, and in the spirit of Jesus Christ, we unite for the worship of God and the service of man."[14] But this is not a typical practice, and it would surprise many present day Unitarians. It is traditional, however, and not remarkable, that in the index of the *Works of William E. Channing, D.D.,* published in 1875 by the American Unitarian Association, the only reference to Jesus Christ is under "Christ." There is no entry under Jesus. We shall be speaking, then, of Channing's views regarding Jesus Christ, sometimes called by him Christ and, occasionally, Jesus.

To search out the truth as to the kind of religion Jesus had in mind was

Channing's purpose, and then to let that purified Christianity stand on its own legs, rather than on those subsequently supplied to it by latter day disciples. He had a firm intention, and he reacted with asperity to unjust criticism from those who feared the light of truth; yet his tone was consistently positive, patient, and appreciative of doctrines he felt were in error. Channing's most famous sermon, "Unitarian Christianity," commonly referred to as the Baltimore Sermon because it was delivered in that city, sets forth Unitarian beliefs about Christ and Christianity. Its text could not be more characteristic of his concept of the role and style of Unitarian thinking: "Prove all things; hold fast that which is good." (I Thessalonians, 5:21)

"We would not . . . be understood as wishing to exclude from religion warmth, and even transport," said Channing. "We believe that Christianity is intended to act powerfully in our whole nature, on the heart as well as the understanding and the conscience. We conceive of heaven as a state where the love of God will be exalted into an unbounded fervor and joy; and we desire, in our pilgrimage here, to drink into the spirit of that better world." Channing then goes on to say that whereas he values warmth in religion, it should be a refined and elevated warmth which comes of moral living and exalts the understanding. He was opposed to a "feverish, forced, fluctuating zeal, which has little power over the life."[15]

In his earnest and persistent desire to get to the heart of the true Christ and to keep on the track of genuine Christianity, Channing vigorously objected to the importunity of those Christians who presume to make creeds for Christ's church and to cast out those who were quietly thinking for themselves. "An enemy to every religion, if asked to describe a Christian, would, with some show of reason, depict him as an idolator of his own distinguishing opinions, covered with badges of party, shutting his eyes on the virtues and his ears on the arguments of his opponents, arrogating all excellence to his own sect and all saving power to his own creed, sheltering under the name of pious zeal the love of domination, the conceit of infallibility, and the spirit of intolerance, and trampling on men's rights under the pretence of saving their souls."[16]

If the authority of man's institutionalized church is to be eschewed, what, then, is the source of authority? Channing's unequivocal answer was the Bible. The Bible, however, is to be read with discrimination and critically. "[T]he Bible is a book written for men, in the language of men, and . . . its meaning is to be sought in the same manner as that of other books." "[A]ll books and all conversation require in the reader or hearer the constant exercise of reason . . ." "We profess not to know a book which demands more frequent exercise of reason than the Bible."[17] He added, however, "Whatever doctrines seem to us to be clearly taught in the Scriptures, we will receive without reserve or exception."[18]

In a sermon quaintly entitled, "Unitarian Christianity Most Favorable to Piety," Channing set forth nine substantiating arguments, which may be succinctly summarized in his own words in the following manner:

"Unitarianism is a system most favorable to piety, because it presents to the mind, one, and only one, Infinite Person, to whom supreme homage is to be paid . . . . Unitarianism promotes piety, by the high place which it assigns to piety in the character and work of Jesus Christ."[19]

But what did Channing say about Jesus Christ? What were his beliefs regarding him? Was Christ central or peripheral in Channing's religious thinking? One can summarize in one's own language, but frequently more is told, and more precisely, by quoting Channing's powerful words.

First off, note the centrality of Jesus' position: "Jesus Christ is the only master of Christians, and whatever he taught, either during his personal ministry or by his inspired Apostles, we regard as of divine authority, and profess to make the rule of our lives."[20]

But, "The only master of Christians" is not God. "We believe in the doctrine of God's UNITY . . ." wrote Channing in his Baltimore Sermon, and "we believe in the unity of Jesus Christ." The Trinity, he observed, makes of Jesus two beings — "an enormous tax on human credulity."[21] For one who espoused the cause of reason in religion, this was an unwarranted requirement of belief.

If there is one single most frequent allegation, or assertion, about Unitarians' belief regarding Jesus Christ, it is that Unitarians deny his divinity. Channing's words are crystal in their clarity. In his sermon entitled "Objections to Unitarian Christianity Considered" (1819), he said: "[W]e do not deny it . . . We believe firmly in the divinity of Christ's mission and office, that he spoke with divine authority, and was a bright image of the divine perfections. We believe that God dwelt in him, manifested himself through him, taught men by him, and communicated to him his spirit without measure. We believe that Jesus Christ was the most glorious display, expression, and representative of God to mankind, so that in seeing and knowing him, we see and know the invisible Father; so that when Christ came, God visited the world and dwelt with men more conspicuously than at any former period. In Christ's words we hear God speaking; in his miracles we behold God acting; in his character and life we see an unsullied image of God's purity and love."[22] A few sentences farther on Channing writes: "Trinitarianism teaches that Jesus Christ is the supreme and infinite God, and that he and his Father are wholly one in affection, counsel, and will, but are strictly and literally one and the same being. Now to us this doctrine is most unspiritual and irrational. We say that the Son cannot be the same being with his own Father; that he, who was sent into the world to save it, cannot be the living God who sent him. The language of Jesus is explicit and unqualified. 'I came not to do my own will.' — 'I came not for myself.' — 'I came from God.' Now we affirm, and this is our chief heresy, that Jesus was not and could not be the God from whom he came, but was another being; and it amazes us that any can resist this simple truth. . . . [Jesus] always expressed towards God the reverence of a Son. He habitually distinguished himself from God. He referred to God all his powers. He said, without limitation or reserve, 'The Father is greater than I.' — 'Of myself I can do nothing.' "[23]

Channing concluded, "We believe that [Jesus] was sent by the Father to effect a moral or spiritual deliverance of mankind; that is, to rescue men from sin and its consequences and to bring them to a state of everlasting purity and happiness."[24]

As for Christ's origin, Channing sided with other liberal thinkers in declaring, "as the Scriptures have not taught us the manner in which the Son derived his existence from his Father, it is presumptuous to affirm that the Son was created, or that there was a time when he did not exist. On these subjects the word of God has not given us light, and therefore we ought to be silent."[25]

"The agency of Christ is at present silent and concealed; but the time is approaching, when the veil which conceals our Lord will be removed, when he will be revealed, with the angels who now obey him, in the glory of the Father, when his power will be felt through the regions of the dead, when all who have lived will receive new life at his hands, and when all will surround his judgment-seat. Then will be seen, and felt, and acknowledged by all, the exalted authority of Jesus Christ . . . At that day men will be as angels, and will be associated in a measure with angels; and then will be understood that striking language of Paul, that it is the purpose of God to 'gather together in one all things in Christ.' "[26]

Was, then, Jesus human? Channing replies: "He, and he alone, is the perfect man, an unerring standard."[27] If Jesus was not God but "a more than human being," as Channing averred, what were his recognizable characteristics? "The character of Christ may be studied for various purposes," wrote Channing. "It is singularly fitted to call forth the heart, to awaken love, admiration, and moral delight . . . . The character of Christ is a strong confirmation of the truth of his religion . . . . Taken as a whole, [it] could not have entered the thoughts of man, could not have been imagined or feigned; . . . it bears every mark of genuineness and truth; . . . it ought, therefore, to be acknowledged as real and of divine origin."[28] A little farther on Channing writes: "I ask you whether the character of Jesus be not the most extraordinary in history, and wholly inexplicable on human principles."[29]

And yet Channing likened Jesus to other leaders when he wrote: "[The] relation of Jesus Christ to the human race is not altogether without example. On the contrary, it is God's common method to connect one being with others, for the sake of imparting to them the blessings we need. All the good which we have received has flowed to us, not immediately from the Father, but from other beings, who have received power, authority, wisdom, and love from God, that they might be sources of good to us and all around us."[30]

That the "human" Christ transcended man in Channing's thoughts could not, nevertheless, have been expressed more clearly than in these eloquent sentences: "It may be objected to the views which have now been given as to the power to which Christ is exalted for human salvation, that we do not see such sensible effects as might be expected from this universal sovereign. To this I answer, that a being so far exalted above us must have innumerable modes of operation which we cannot discern or comprehend. His agency may continually be mingled with human events, and yet we not discern it. No being acts, if I may use the words, with so much silence and secrecy as the Infinite Father. He is ever present, and ever operating, and yet we see him not, we hear him not; and his Son Jesus Christ, who is the image of his power as well as of all his perfections, may act in the same unseen, yet efficacious manner. The narrowness of our vision is sufficient to account for our not distinguishing more sensibly the operation of Jesus Christ in human affairs . . ."[31]

At this point it is appropriate to introduce Channing's views of miracles. In his Dudleian lecture, given at Harvard in 1821, we find him saying: "Christianity is not only confirmed by miracles, but is in itself, in its very essence, a miraculous religion. It is not a system which the human mind might have gathered in the ordinary exercise of its powers from the ordinary course of nature."[32] He goes on at length to differentiate between the orderly processes of nature and God's providential acts which are "higher than nature." Elsewhere he wrote: "If the Supreme Being proposed only such ends as mechanism can produce, then He might have framed a machinery so perfect and sure as to need no suspension of its ordinary movements. But He has an incomparably nobler end. His great purpose is to educate, to rescue from evil, to carry forward forever the free, rational mind or soul; and who that understands what a free mind is, and what a variety of teaching and discipline it requires, will presume to affirm that no lights or aids but such as come to it through an invariable order of nature, are necessary to unfold it?"[33]

Having stated his position with respect to God and miracles, Channing went on to discuss the miracles of Christ. He said they "were not wrought by a man whose character in other respects was ordinary. They were acts of a being, whose mind was as singular as his works, who spoke and acted with more than human authority, whose moral qualities and sublime purposes were in accordance with superhuman powers. Christ's miracles are in unison with his whole character, and bear a proportion to it like that which we observe in the most harmonious productions of nature; and in this way receive from it great confirmation."[34]

With respect to "the direct evidence of miracles," Channing wrote: "I would only observe that they may all be resolved into this single principle; namely, that the Christian miracles were originally believed under such circumstances that this belief can only be explained by their actual occurrence." And, he averred: ". . . Christianity was received at first on the ground of miracles, and . . . its first preachers and converts proved the depth and strength of their conviction of these facts by attesting them in sufferings and in death, [as] we know from the most ancient records which relate to this religion, both Christian and heathen; and, in fact, this conviction can alone explain their adherence to Christianity.[35]

The question of Jesus' genuineness occupied Channing. That question is seldom if ever raised in these days, but it must have been raised by skeptics in Channing's time. We have just heard Channing's assertion that Jesus' character could not have been feigned. Again, in declaring that Jesus was not an imposter, Channing says, "You never hear from Jesus that swelling, pompous, ostentatious language which almost necessarily springs from an attempt to sustain a character above our powers."[36]

Channing repeatedly introduced the subject of Jesus' serenity, which evidently held a special attraction for him. Another person, in a different mood or state of mind, might not have observed it or mentioned it at all, let alone have developed it as Channing did. "The truth is that, remarkable as was the character of Jesus, it was distinguished by nothing more than calmness and self-possession. This trait pervades his other excellencies. How calm was his piety!" Channing did not keep Jesus above the human level to the extent that the characteristics remarkable in human beings might be considered standard in "a more than human being." "His benevolence, . . . though singularly earnest and deep, was composed and serene. He never lost the possession of himself in his sympathy with others; was never hurried into the impatient and rash enterprises of an enthusiastic philanthropy; but did good with the tranquility and constancy which mark the providence of God."[37] One wonders what image of philanthropic impatience Channing had in his mind when he wrote these last words!

If these characteristics deserve approbation and, presumably, emulation, then it may be that Channing recognized the need of them in himself and others. What is more significant, he found their source in Jesus Christ, exemplar for men, and truly this is a justified and understandable discovery. Channing shrewdly pointed out that what happens is that we fail to take advantage of Jesus' example for us. "[O]ur long familiarity with Jesus blunts our minds to his singular excellence," he wrote.[38]

If patience and self-restraint characterized Jesus, so, too, did sympathy. What though his own status was different, he lived with his fellow men, as brother, friend, and servant of all. "The great principle on which his wonderful sympathy was founded, and which endeared to him his office of universal Saviour . . . was his conviction of the greatness of the human soul. He saw in man the impress and image of Divinity, and therefore thirsted for his redemption . . ."[39] Our own source of sympathy for the fallen, Channing declared in an address before the Council of the Massachusetts Temperance Society, in 1837, was not derived "from the schools of ancient philosophy, or from the temples of Greece and Rome." Rather, "We inherit it from Jesus Christ."

Not unrelated to sympathy is charity. Channing wrote: "Christ has expressly declared that [charity] is a necessary qualification for one of his followers . . ." Channing's study of the Bible led him to see "how Christian charity differed from what [he] used to call benevolence."[40]

We cannot conclude this resume of Channing's beliefs regarding Jesus Christ, without taking a look at his views of Jesus' death and of resurrection and immortality.

Regarding Jesus' death: "It is our belief that Christ's humiliation was real and entire, that the whole Saviour, and not a part of him, suffered, that his crucifixion was a scene of deep and unmixed agony. As we stand round his cross, our minds are not distracted, nor our sensibility weakened, by contemplating him as composed of incongruous and infinitely differing minds, and as having a balance of infinite felicity. We recognize in the dying Jesus but one mind. This, we think, renders his sufferings, and his patience and love in bearing them, incomparably more impressive and affecting than the system we oppose." The "system" Channing alludes to is the Trinitarian belief that Jesus, as the second person of the Trinity, was not wholly involved in his crucifixion. "According to their doctrine," wrote Channing, "Christ was comparatively no sufferer at all."[41]

What of the efficacy of Christ's death for mankind? Jesus accomplished his divine purpose of rescuing men from sin and its consequences, and bringing them to a state of everlasting purity and happiness, by a variety of methods. Channing recognized that there was a difference of opinion among Unitarians "in regard to the precise influence of [Christ's] death on our forgiveness . . . many of us . . . think that the Scriptures ascribe the remission of sins to Christ's death with an emphasis so peculiar that we ought to consider this event as having a special influence in removing punishment, though the Scriptures may not reveal the way in which it contributes to this end."[42]

Channing vigorously objected to the concept of the appeasement of an angry God or that Jesus' death produced a change in the mind of God toward man. It was not that Jesus evoked God's mercy, but that God in his mercy sent us Jesus to be our Saviour. Though Jesus came to rescue us from punishment, "he was sent on a still nobler errand, namely, to deliver us from sin itself, and to form us to a sublime and heavenly virtue. We regard him as a Saviour, chiefly as he is the light, physician, and guide of the dark, diseased, and wandering mind." Christ's efficacy was not merely salvation from sin, but went farther, that is, it was to leave its mark on the character of the saved. "Why pluck the sinner from hell," he asked, "if the hell be left to burn in his own breast? Why raise him to heaven, if he remain a stranger to its sanctity and love?" Channing's line of reasoning, his insistence on the importance of the acquisition of virtue, leads him away from concentration upon Jesus' death as the sole effective agency to the conclusion that the "doctrines, precepts, promises, and the whole life, character, suffering, and triumphs of Jesus [are] the means of purifying the mind, of changing it into the likeness of his celestial excellence."[43]

The death of Jesus cannot be discussed in the Christian context without continuing on to the subject of resurrection. According to Channing, not only did Jesus offer himself as "a spiritual deliverer, as the founder of a new empire of inward piety and universal charity", but he suggested "a more mysterious office. 'Many will say unto me in that day, Lord, Lord, have we not prophesied in thy name? and in thy name done many wonderful works? And then will I profess unto them, I never knew you, depart from me, ye that work iniquity.' " Channing asserted that he better understood these words when in them he hears Jesus foretelling, "after a painful death, he [will] rise again and ascend to heaven, and there, in a state of preeminent power and glory, . . . be the advocate and judge of the human race."[44]

Channing's first child, a girl, died within twenty-four hours of her birth. There is a touching account of this sad event, presented in Channing's own journal for October, 1816. It reveals his concept of life after death. The latter part of his entry follows: "Thursday afternoon I carried her to the tomb, in the full and certain hope of a blessed resurrection . . . I feel as if I had a child in a happier world, who will know her past history, who will know how earnest were my wishes to bless her, to guide her to all virtue and felicity; and I hope yet to meet her, and to know that my prayers were not in vain, and to see that my child is more excellent, more happy, than I could have rendered her."[45] Here was a natural application of the belief Channing ennunciated in his sermon at Baltimore: "[Christ's] resurrection is the foundation of our hope in immortality. His intercession gives us boldness to draw nigh to the throne of grace, and we look up to heaven with new desire when we think that, if we follow him here, we shall there see his benignant countenance, and enjoy his friendship forever."[46]

Elsewhere he wrote, "Jesus not only *was*, he is still the Son of God, the Saviour of the world. He exists now; he has entered that heaven to which he always looked forward on earth. There he lives and reigns . . . I confidently expect . . . to see him face to face. We have indeed no absent friend whom we shall so surely meet. Let us then . . . , by imitation of his virtues and obedience to his words, prepare ourselves to join him in those pure mansions where he is surrounding himself with the good and pure of our race and will communicate to them forever his own spirit, power, and joy."[47]

It is the common Christian assertion that Jesus purposely founded a new religion and established a church to promulgate and preserve it. Of this belief Channing wrote, "By his Church our Saviour does not mean a party, bearing the name of a human leader, distinguished by a form or an opinion, and, on the ground of this distinction, denying the name or character of Christians to all but themselves. He means by it the body of his friends and followers, *who truly imbibe his spirit,* no matter by what name they are called, in what house they worship, by what pecularities of mode and opinion they are distinguished, under what sky they live, or what language they speak. These are the true church, — men made better, made holy, virtuous, by his religion, — men who, hoping in his promises, keep his commands.

"Ever since Christ's church was established such a unity has existed, such characters have been formed by the gospel; and this influence it will exert through all ages. As we have said, we have reason to suppose, from what has been experienced, that great changes will take place in the present state of Christianity; and the time is, perhaps, coming, when all our present sects will live only in history. But the influences of the gospel will not therefore cease; the church will not die with the sects into which it is broken. On the contrary, we may hope that the vine of God will flourish more, when these branches are lopped off which exhaust its strength and bear little fruit. Men will then learn that Christianity is designed for practice, and not for contention; ceasing to censure others, they will aim to reform themselves. The simple gospel, divested of human addition, no longer disfigured by absurd explanation, will be the centre and bond of union to the world. Human churches, human establishments, — the effects and monuments of folly and ambition, — will fall. But the church of Christ — which is another name for piety, goodness, righteousness, peace, and love — shall endure forever . . ."[48]

At the center of that church he awaits us. Channing writes: "[W]e may all approach Jesus Christ . . . we may all unite ourselves in living bonds to Christ, — may love as he loved, may act from his principles, may suffer with his constancy, may enter into his purposes, may sympathize with his self-devotion to the cause of God and mankind, and, by likeness of spirit, may prepare ourselves to meet him as our everlasting friend."[49]

Channing spent the years of his ministry in endeavoring to teach pure Christianity. The effort was not in vain. Succeeding generations profited from his labors. Yet, in 1845, three years after he died, we find President Josiah Quincy of Harvard having to reply to the charge of the Calvinists regarding the characteristics of Unitarianism and its place at Harvard. "Harvard College is represented as a society combined and laboring for the propagation of Unitarianism; as an association of infidels, without belief in the awful mystery of Christ's incarnation, placing no reliance on his propitiatory death, and deriving no assurance of a future state for his glorious resurrection and ascension; denying his divine mission, not acknowledging him either as Mediator or Redeemer, but resting all their hopes of a future life and happiness on their own merits; 'not mentioning Christ in their prayers,' and 'openly denying the Lord who bought them.' "[50]

These persistent allegations would not die, even in the face of clear affirmations which continuously flowed from Channing's pen such as those with
respect to Jesus' words in the Bible. He wrote: "I feel myself listening to a
being such as never before and never since spoke in human language. I am
awed by the consciousness of greatness which these simple words express; and
when I connect this greatness with the proofs of Christ's miracles . . . , I am
compelled to explain with the centurion, 'Truly, this was the Son of God.' "[51]
[I]ndeed I know not what can be added to heighten the wonder, reverence,
and love, which are due to Jesus." "The Gospels must be true; they were
drawn from a living original; they were founded on reality. The character of
Jesus is not a fiction; he was what he claimed to be and what his followers
attested."[52]

Perhaps the controversy will never end regarding the characteristics and
intentions of Jesus, and the day never come which Channing looked forward
to in his early ministry, when "The name of *Christian* will absorb all other
names; and the spirit of love to God and man will take the place of unhal-
lowed zeal and bitter contention."[53]

We have reviewed in some detail the place of Jesus in early American
Unitarianism as represented by Channing, not for the purpose of reawaken-
ing old controversies, although it might be well for present-day Unitarians to
refresh their minds, or to learn for the first time the source of their Christian
tenets; not necessarily to acclaim again that eloquent expositor of biblical
Christianity, Channing, but to introduce the suggestion that the times when
Channing lived, which evoked his concept of the character of Jesus Christ,
were not altogether unlike our own, and that we may discover in some degree,
his Christ may well be ours, also. This subject will be explored further in the
last chapter.

Appendix A

Channing's Unitarianism as expressed in his sermon *"Unitarian Christianity
Most Favorable to Piety"*

"I. Unitarianism is a system most favorable to piety, because it presents to
the mind, one, and only one, Infinite Person, to whom supreme homage is to
be paid."

"II. Unitarianism is the system most favorable to piety, because it holds
forth and preserves inviolate the spirituality of God."

"III. Unitarianism is the system most favorable to piety, because it presents a distinct and intelligible object of worship, — a Being whose nature,
whilst inexpressibly sublime, is yet simple and suited to human apprehension."

"IV. Unitarianism promotes a fervent and enlightened piety by asserting the absolute and unbounded perfection of God's character."

"V. Unitarianism is peculiarly favorable to piety, because it accords with nature, with the world around and the world within us; and through this accordance it gives aid to nature, and receives aid from it, in impressing the mind with God."

"VI. Unitarianism favors piety by opening the mind to new and ever-enlarging views of God."

"VII. Unitarianism promotes piety, by the high place which it assigns to piety in the character and work of Jesus Christ."

"VIII . . . Unitarianism promotes piety by meeting the wants of man as a sinner . . . [Man] wants assurance of mercy in his Creater [and] . . . pledges that God is love in its purest form . . ."

"IX. . . . Unitarianism promotes piety because it is a rational religion."[54]

Appendix B

Extracts from *"Objections to Unitarian Christianity Considered."*

"1. . . . We do not deny [the divinity of Christ] . . . . We believe firmly in the divinity of Christ's mission and office, that he spoke with divine authority, and was a bright image of the divine perfections . . . [W]e do not believe him to be the Supreme God himself. We maintain that Christ and God are *distinct beings,* two beings, not one and the same being . . ."

"Trinitarianism teaches that Jesus Christ is the Supreme and Infinite God, and that he and his Father are not only one in affection, counsel, and will, but are strictly and literally one and the same being. Now to us this doctrine is most unspiritual and irrational. We say that the Son cannot be the same being with his own Father; that he, who was sent into the world to save it, cannot be the living God who sent him. The language of Jesus is explicit and unqualified. 'I came not to do mine own will.' — 'I came not from myself,' — 'I came from God.' Now we affirm, and this is our chief heresy, that Jesus was not and could not be the God from whom he comes, but was another being; and it amazes us that any can resist this simple truth. The doctrine that Jesus, who was born at Bethlehem; who ate and drank and slept; who suffered and was crucified; who came from God; who prayed to God; who did God's will; and who said, on leaving the world, 'I ascend to my Father and your Father, to my God and your God;' the doctrine that this Jesus was the supreme God himself, and the same being with his Father, this seems to us a contradiction to reason and Scripture so flagrant, that the simple statement is a sufficient refutation. We are often charged with degrading Christ; but if this reproach belong to any Christians, it falls, we fear, on those who accuse him of teaching a doctrine so contradictory, and so subversive of the supremacy of our Heavenly Father. Certainly our humble and devout Master has given no ground for this accusation. He always expressed towards God the reverence of a son. He habitually distinguished himself from God. He referred to God all his powers. He said, without limitation or reserve, 'The Father is greater than I.' — 'Of myself I can do nothing.' If to represent Christ as a being distinct from God, and as inferior to him, be to degrade him, then let our opponents lay the guilt where it belongs, not on us, but on our Master, whose language we borrow, in whose very words we express our sentiments, whose words we dare not trifle with and force from their plain sense. Our limits will not allow us to say more; but we ask common Christians, who have taken their opinions from the Bible rather than from human systems, to look honestly into their own minds, and to answer frankly, whether they have not understood and believed Christ's divinity in the sense maintained by us, rather than in that for which the Trinitarians contend."

2. Nothing in the Bible says that the sin of man is infinite and needs an infinite atonement.

3. Works are not enough, good as they are. "We always affirm that God's grace, benignity, free kindness, is needed by the most advanced Christians . . ."

4. In replying to the objection of others that Unitarians preach morality, and neglect "to inculcate inward purity, devotion, heavenly-mindedness, and love to Jesus Christ . . . ," Channing replies that this is a false charge and is a misuse of the word "moral."

5. In reply to the criticism that the Unitarian "system does not produce as much zeal, seriousness, and piety as other views of religion," Channing replies, "if the zeal . . . [is] faint, the fault is our own, not that of our doctrine." Channing says that with Jesus, we hate ostentation. And he goes on to declare that "religion is cheerful;" and he objects to "those overwhelming terrors and transports which many think essential to piety." And in conclusion on this point Channing declares, that out of respect for the position of others we do not undertake to spread our particular views.

6. Unitarianism does not reject revelation nor does it lead to infidelity. Channing cites several great persons who were Unitarians, including philosopher John Locke and the physicist Newton. He says we are foes of infidelity but Unitarianism fortifies faith and is convinced that Christianity must be purified.

7. In reply to the objection that Unitarian views give no consolation in times of sickness and death, Channing replies that this is a false objection. The emphasis is upon the mercy of God, "[which] unlocks infinite springs of consolation and joy, and gives . . . living, overflowing and unspeakable hope."[55]

Chapter 2

Foundation Stones of American Unitarianism: Norton, Ware, and Palfrey

We have begun our review of the place of Jesus Christ in American Unitarianism by jumping off with the first great exponent of the new religious denomination, William Ellery Channing. He was not the only able thinker and writer in the field, of course; and if one calls him the "first" in this particular sense, one must recognize that beginnings so subtly become accomplishments that it is usually difficult to tell where the one leaves off and the other begins. Further, I have no mission to favor Channing, but, rather, to get at the theme in the most direct way, and therefore have utilized him as one of the most effective exponents of the subject under exploration, namely, the place of Jesus Christ in American Unitarianism. Let us examine now the Christology of three of Channing's contemporaries, Andrews Norton, Henry Ware, Jr., and John Gorham Palfrey.

Andrews Norton

As Channing rippled the waters of the world of preaching, his contemporary, Andrews Norton, stirred the depths of theology in controversy with the orthodox. Norton was born in Hingham, Massachusetts, December 31, 1786. He was graduated from Harvard at the age of seventeen and continued in the study of theology. In 1809 he preached for a short time in Augusta, Maine, followed by a year at Bowdoin College, as a tutor. He returned to Harvard for another one year stint as tutor in mathematics. The following year he established an erudite journal called the General Repository and Review. It lived for two years. From 1813 to 1833 he served Harvard successively as Librarian, Lecturer on the Criticism and Interpretation of the Scriptures, and Dexter Professor of Sacred Literature, in the Divinity School. He resigned his Professorship at the early age of forty-seven, but he continued his scholarly pursuits until his death in 1853 at the age of sixty-seven. Of small and delicate physique, Norton possessed a towering and fearless intellect.

It may surprise the new reader of liberal Christology in America to observe how closely the early Unitarians hued to the approved, orthodox line. They were able to retain most of the beliefs and assertions with which they began. Their forte was new, reasonable interpretation of the Scriptures. The most notable exception was belief in the miracles purportedly performed by Christ: they were convinced that acceptance of these was central to Christian belief, and there was no explaining them away in rationalistic terms. Norton, Channing, and others vigorously opposed the younger liberals who had cut loose altogether from traditional Christianity.

The single most useful work of Andrews Norton with respect to Christology is his *A Statement of Reasons For Not Believing the Doctrines of Trinitarians, Concerning the Nature of God and the Person of Christ,* first published in 1856, three years after his death. On the subject of the divine authority of Jesus Christ and Christianity, Norton wrote in the preface of this work: "The whole proof of the doctrines of religion, as taught by Christ, consists wholly in the fact that he was a teacher from God. He did not reason; he affirmed. He adduced no arguments but his miracles. Considered as a self-taught philosopher, he did nothing to advance human knowledge, for he brought no new evidence for any opinion. But considered as a teacher from God, he has provided the authority of God for the foundation of our faith."[1]

Jesus' authority did not, however, make him one with God. Norton found the doctrine of the union of the divine and human natures in Christ, constituting but one person, more incredible than the Trinity itself. It was self-contradictory. God is infinite, he argued; man is finite. One being cannot be both. "No words can be more destitute of meaning . . . than such language as we sometimes find used, in which Christ is declared to be at once the Creator of the universe, and a man of sorrows; God omniscient and omnipotent, and a feeble man of imperfect knowledge."[2]

As further evidence of the absurdity of this doctrine, he observed: "[Christ] prays to that being whom he himself was. He declares himself to be ignorant of what (being God) he knew, and unable to perform what (being God) he could perform."[3]

Using many examples from the Scriptures themselves, Norton showed that passages cited to support the doctrine actually disproved it. His skill and technique in the use of this device are illustrated in this quotation: "In John v. 22, it is said, according to the common version, 'The Father judgeth no man; but hath committed all judgment unto the Son.' '*The Father judgeth no man,* that is, without the Son,' says a noted Orthodox commentator, Gill, 'which is a proof of their equality.' A proof of their equality! What, is it God to whom all judgment is committed by the Father?"[4]

The declarations of "our Saviour," said Norton, "the whole tenor of the Scriptures, and all the facts in the history of Christ," as well as the belief of the disciples themselves — all belie the doctrine of the union of divine and human natures in Christ.

Jesus observed the distinction between himself and God in the matter of prayer; he did not command his followers to pray to *him*. Norton observed, " The meaning of the terms rendered 'calling on the name of Christ,' would, I believe, be properly and fully expressed in English by the words, 'looking to Christ for deliverance,' that is, through the power of the Gospel." "Whatever you may ask the Father in my name, he will grant you," Jesus said, but if he commanded his followers to pray to him personally, they failed to do so. "The case was the same with them as with us;" Norton argued: "if it be not a duty to pray to Christ, it is a duty not to pray to him."[5]

It is illuminating to observe Norton's views as to why so many questions go unanswered in the Gospels when, "As a teacher from God, it was the proper and sole office of Christ to make known to men, on the authority of God, the fundamental truths of religion."[6] Norton says, "Under circumstances in which it is impossible to explain the whole truth, or in which it is certain that the whole truth cannot be understood and felt, in addressing men who are unaccustomed to exercising their understandings, and who from childhood have incorporated false conceptions with right principles of action, we may use their errors for their reformation; we may appeal to their feelings or their fears through their mistaken imaginations; we may employ one wrong opinion to counteract others more pernicious; and in reasoning, exhortation, or reproof, we may thus avail ourselves of their more innocent prejudices in opposition to their passions and vices. But in doing this, we are precluded from directly assailing those prejudices; though we may at the same time be establishing truths which will effect their gradual abolition. Such was, I believe, in some particulars, the mode of teaching adopted by Christ."[7] Norton adds: "We forget what opposition he had to encounter, how all his words and actions were watched with malignant eyes, how often his enemies came proposing questions to try what he would say, that they might find opportunity to injure him. [Norton's footnote here: "The Common Version says, 'to tempt him.']' We do not remember, that no error could be touched without affording some new occasion or pretence of hatred; and that whatever he spoke would be misunderstood, preverted, misrepresented, and made a ground for false inferences. We do not keep in mind the imperfect apprehensions of his disciples."[8]

To speak of Christ personally became a common practice of New Testament writers, when actually their reference was to Christ's religion. Norton applies this principle in treating of Jesus' return to his disciples after the crucifixion. Jesus tells them (John 14: 18,19): " 'I will not leave you fatherless. I am coming to you again. A little while only, and the world will see me no more; but you will see me. Inasmuch as I am blessed, you will be blessed also.' " Norton explains: "Here, as I have before had occasion to explain, our Saviour refers, not to any personal presence with his disciples, but to his presence with them in the power of his religion, his presence to their minds and hearts."[9]

On the subject of the pre-existence of Christ, one of the most difficult beliefs for twentieth century, rational Christians to embrace, Norton once more offers an ingenious clarification. "One of the main objections of the generality of the Jews to Christianity was its being a novelty, an innovation, subverting their former faith."[10] To meet this prejudice, the Christians adapted familiar theological language to their own modes of conception; for example, they asserted or implied that the sending of Christ to establish his religion had always been God's purpose. Norton refers to a passage in the Talmud, where it is recorded that the Messiah, the Son of David, was the last of seven things created before the world. In the Talmudic Book Cosri it is affirmed, " '[T]hey were prior in the intention of God' . . . the end for which the world was created; . . . the end being *in intention* precedent to the means."[11]

Norton goes on to reason that to avoid arousing the apprehension of the Roman rulers that a "daring rebel" was "exciting a nation to revolt," Jesus is quoted in several places as saying only, "I am," when he means, "I am the Messiah," as in Mark 13:6 and Luke 21:8. In those instances Jesus predicts, "Many will come in my name, saying *I am* . . ." In Matthew 24:5, however, the ellipsis is supplied: "Many will come in my name, saying, I am the Messiah." It may be that Christ deliberately spoke ambiguously, "for the purpose of at once intimating his claim to be the Messiah, and leaving his meaning in some degree uncertain."[12] Again, "The language used by Christ is of the same figurative character with that which we find at the commencement of the prophecy of Jeremiah, as addressed to him by God (i. 5): 'Before I formed thee in the womb, I knew thee; and before thou camest forth at thy birth, I sanctified thee, and I ordained thee a prophet to the nations.' "[13]

As for the Apostles, however, Norton has this to say: "[I]f the Apostles had regarded their Master as an incarnation of a great pre-existent spirit, far superior to man, they would not have left us to gather their belief from a doubtful interpretation of a few scattered passages. No fact concerning him, personally, would have been put forward in their writings with more prominence and distinctness. None would have been oftener brought into notice. None would have more strongly affected their imaginations and feelings. None would have been adapted more to affect their disciples. St. Matthew would not have written an account of his Master, as it must be conceded that he has, without anywhere expressly clearing the fact. The Apostles would have left us in as little doubt concerning their belief of it, as concerning their belief of his crucifixion and resurrection."[14]

Convinced of the resurrection, what can be said of the Apostles' expectations "concerning the visible return of their Master to earth"? Norton's thought is so clear that one is persuaded by it. He says that the first coming of the Messiah was so unlike what they had expected, that, "when he spoke of a future coming while the existing generation was still living, they transferred to this some of the expectations which had been long entertained respecting his appearance and kingdom."[15]

Again, Norton finds the Master's language on the subject of his return, the establishment of his kingdom, and his judgment of all men, to be figurative. The Apostles were simple men, however, and not equal to their Master and hence were unable to understand his subtleties. They were enlightened "by direct miraculous communications from [God]," but they fell victims to error "whenever . . . men's minds were left to their natural action, and the current of their opinions was suffered to pursue its ordinary course, — whenever infallibility was no longer secured by the power of God, — errors of some kind would necessarily mingle with men's religious faith."[16]

Again we see Norton holding on to tradition and justifying its retention by reference to intended meanings.

Finally, what did Norton think that Christ had in mind, when he referred to the kingdom of Heaven? "For myself," he said, "I conceive him to have intended by the 'kingdom of Heaven,' or, in other words, 'the kingdom of God,' that state of things in which men should recognize the authority of God as the supreme lawgiver, and submit themselves to his laws, as human subjects to those of a human government."[17] We see here expressed the idea that the "kingdom" can be a contemporary reality, without its being the *temporal* kingdom of the familiar, simple Jewish expectation.

Henry Ware, Jr.

From the erudite, thorough-thinking Norton, who established and strengthened the basis of what may be called *conservative* liberal thinking,[18] we pass now to an able preacher and teacher, who strongly favored the establishment of a small Unitarian organization, the Reverend Dr. Henry Ware, Jr. Dr. Ware was the son and namesake of the first Hollis Professor of Theology at Harvard Divinity School to be characterized a Unitarian. He was born in Hingham, Massachusetts in 1794 and died in Framingham, in 1843. He served as minister of the Second Church in Boston for a dozen years, from 1817 to 1829, when he resigned to accept the new Professorship of "Pulpit Eloquence and the Pastoral Care," at the Harvard Divinity School. He was succeeded at the Second Church by Ralph Waldo Emerson, then twenty-six years old and Dr. Ware's junior by nine years.

Henry Ware, Jr. was characterized by what may be called the older Unitarian piety of Norton and Channing. His interests were wide-ranging, going out to the frontiers of humanitarian concerns, but including therewith the systematic instruction of the young through books which he edited for Sunday School use, including his own *Life of the Saviour.* He also published a series of books which he entitled *Scenes and Characters Illustrating Christian Truth.* As an advocate of maintaining a Unitarian Association, he favored active interchange with like minds in England and Ireland.

Ware took a kindly but positive exception to Emerson's theological departures and wrote Emerson: "I must confess with regard to some of your views that they appear to me more than doubtful, their prevalance would tend to overthrow the authority and influence of Christianity. On this account I look with anxiety to the course your mind has been taking."[19] He felt God was a personality and not the universe, nor "beauty," nor "virtue," as with Emerson.[20]

Dr. Ware was most considerate of those who would know his beliefs about Jesus Christ. These were set forth in a series of eleven sermons, called *Discourses on the Offices and Character of Jesus Christ,* published in Boston in 1825, with a second edition in 1826. A quotation from John 10:36, printed on the title page, provides an immediate clue to Ware's Christology: "Whom the Father hath sanctified and sent." Ware never knew the suspicion of the reliability of the Fourth Gospel, which was in the minds of some later liberal biblical scholars and which, one might suggest, deprived them of some of the clearest insights and spiritual reinforcements preserved by the writer of the Gospel from early Christianity. The book was ascribed to the Reverend Francis Parkman who, eighteen years later, was to take part in Ware's funeral service in the Harvard Chapel. Ware wrote in his introductory remarks: "That they [these sermons] may aid believers in rightly appreciating their relation to the Saviour, and cultivating the sentiments and habits which it requires, is the writer's highest wish and ardent prayer."

Discourse I deals with the subject, "Christ the Foundation", and takes as its text First Corinthian 3:11: "For other foundation can no man lay than that is laid, which is Jesus Christ." "Jesus is the foundation of *the Church . . .* [its] chief corner stone," Ware affirms. "The church is that society or collection of the good, who have been brought home to God and been fitted for heaven, through the instrumentality of the dispensations of grace upon earth. It is a permanent body, existing alike in all ages. It is one body, though of many members. It must then have some common head, and common bond of union; and that is Christ. The members are united in him as the branches in the vine, and draw nourishment and support from one stock. If There be any other head, bond of union, source of nourishment and strength, it ceases to be the Church; and those individual members who abide not in him, are like branches severed from the vine, 'cast forth and withered.' Without him, they can do nothing. They can find neither life, nor light, nor support, nor the power to bring forth fruit."[21]

There is no foundation other than Christ, because *"the christian religion rests on his authority."* "The wisdom of man is an uncertain and insufficient guide. For Christianity is not something to be discovered by us; but is a revelation from heaven, sent for our acceptance, concerning which we have nothing to do, but to study and receive it. It affords no scope for invention or discovery. We may not add to it, nor take from it. We may speculate concerning it, but may not affix our speculations as a part of it."[22]

Jesus Christ may also be considered the foundation of the church, "because to believe in him as the predicted Messiah, is the *fundamental article of the christian faith*."[23]

"The term *Christ*, as is well known, is not the name of the person, but the title of office. It indicates the station or character, and is equivalent to the *Messiah*, or the *Anointed*. The proper name of our Lord's person is *Jesus*; by which he is designated throughout the Evangelists. The official title, *Christ*, did not become a proper name until after the resurrection. For until then the great undecided question among his countrymen was, whether he were truly the Christ or not. It was the belief that he was so, which distinguished his disciples from the other Jews, and they accordingly called him Jesus, the Christ — the Messiah — the Anointed; from which use it readily passed into a name, as in our text, and throughout the Epistles."[24]

Again, Jesus Christ is the foundation, "because he is *the source of all satisfactory religious knowledge*.

"Jesus called himself, 'the Light of the world;' and he is truly the fountain and depository of whatever light we possess on the great subject of religion. There is to us, strictly and properly speaking, no other . . . . It is true that we gather something of the existence, attributes, and providence of God from the works of nature; but how little should we be able to do it, without the aid of revelation? We find the great principles of morality and accountableness in 'the law written on our hearts;' but it is our previous acquaintance with the christian revelation, which enables us to see them so distinctly there, and they have been very obscurely discerned by those who have not the benefit of this aid . . . . For it is certain, that however great the wisdom of the world may have been, still 'the world by wisdom knew not God.' "[25]

Jesus Christ is the "foundation of *true morality*.."[26] The character of Jesus' morality differs from that which had prevailed in the world, because heretofore the appeal was to "the sensitive sentiment of honor," so that men should be moral "from selfishness and pride." "The moral principle of the world has thus been always unfixed and wavering; it has fluctuated with fashion and circumstances, and changed as humor or accident might dictate . . . . But Jesus speaks with authority — the authority of a commissioned messenger from the moral Governor and Judge of men. He communicates, from the instructions of Infinite Rectitude, the knowledge of duty, the boundaries of right and wrong, the definitions and motives of virtue, the promises and threats of retribution."[27]

"Christ is the only foundation of the *believer's hope*": hope of forgiveness and salvation, and hope of immortality. "How does the humble and self-distrusting believer, who stands trembling and abashed in the presence of infinite purity — find comfort in the encouraging accents of Christ's soothing voice, and the hope of acceptance at the throne of grace . . . . Thanks be to God for this unspeakable gift — this glorious hope, which, in every season of trial and every stormy strait of sorrow and fear, is 'an anchor to the soul, sure and steadfast.' "[28]

The subject of Discourse II is "Jesus The Messiah," with an introductory text consisting of the 15th and 16th verses of Matthew xvi: "He saith unto them, But whom say ye that I am? and Simon Peter answered and said, thou art the Christ, the son of the living God."

Jesus' role has always been a question which has provoked differing answers, even among Jesus' own disciples. Ware states his conclusion succinctly: "The passion for speculation, and the fondness for opinion, have found exercise even on this subject, and have thrown perplexity and debate on what is in itself plain and simple, and has been most clearly decided, in the only important particular, by the express authority of Scripture."[29]

The term *Messiah,* or *Christ,* was the distinguishing title accorded to Jesus, and under this title his coming was predicted, expected, and announced. Under it he was received, acknowledged, persecuted, preached to the nations, and believed on. As Messiah, Jesus could not have been literally a Priest, because he was not of the family of Levi, nor in any way attached to a temple, but he was literally a Prophet. As for the role of King, the Messiah was to sit on the throne of his father David, and before Pilate Jesus acknowledged he was a King, but his Kingdom was not of this world. Ware declares, "He is our master, and guide, and king, and we cannot escape the obligation to follow his instructions and obey his laws."[30]

In Discourse III, Ware discusses the "Sufficiency and Efficacy of Faith in the Messiah," and uses as his substantiating text I John v. 5: "Who is he that overcometh the world, but he that believeth that Jesus is the Son of God." His summary statement on the subject is: " 'Whosoever believeth that Jesus is the Christ, is born of God.' What further testimony could be desired to the efficacy of this faith? He who truly possesses it, is regenerate, is become one of the adopted family of God, one of the household of heaven; and thus in him the very purpose of the christian dispensation is accomplished."[31]

In Discourse IV, Ware discusses "Jesus The Mediator" and selects as his text I Timothy ii. 5: "For there is one God, and one Mediator between God and men — the man Christ Jesus." Of the title *Mediator,* Ware says: "[I]t has happened that the name is most usually given in the sense of a *peace-maker,* or one who effects reconciliation."[32] "When therefore we are told, that in the affairs of salvation, there is a 'Mediator between God and men,' we are taught what is perfectly coincident with the uniform method of divine procedure; we behold 'a beautiful analogy, in a very considerable and important point, between the settled method of God's natural providence, and the extraordinary operations of his grace.' As in the natural so in the spiritual world, we discern the agency of God only through the action of second causes."[33] "It was [Jesus'] direction to the apostles, that they should ask 'in his name.' The apostles enjoined it on the churches, to approach God in praise and prayer, in thanksgiving and confession, 'through him,' 'by him,' and 'in his name.' The injunction has ever been observed; and the constant devotions of believers ascend to God through Jesus Christ. They come to the mercy seat, not in their own name, but in that of the Mediator, and hope to be heard because they come through him."[34]

On the subject of praying "through Christ" or "in the name of Christ," Ware has this to say: "It is not intended, we may first of all remark, that we are not to come to God directly, and address him personally; but quite the contrary. 'Ye shall ask *me* nothing,' said our Lord; 'but whatsoever ye shall ask the Father in my name, he will give it you.' The express doctrine of his religion is, that men shall address the Father, and the Father only. And therefore, the offering of prayers through Christ, cannot be understood to mean that they are first to be presented to him, and by him presented to God. All the precepts and examples of scripture direct us to God himself, personally; and the phrase in question, as we shall presently see, bears a meaning which does not contradict them."[35] He says further, "We are to pray, as the disciples of Christ, guided by faith in him, and influenced by the devout dispositions which he requires; — 'through him,' because through the directions he has given for acceptable prayer, and the encouragement he has offered to sincere worshippers; 'in his name,' because by this authority, confiding in his warrant, commanded and invited by him, members of that family which he has brought nigh to God, and given access to the throne."[36] And he concludes, "There is no charm in the words, no talisman in the forms we utter, no mysterious efficacy by which they force their way upward, from whatever heart they may rise. We might as well pray in the name of Mahomet, as in that of Christ, if we do not pray as disciples of Christ — not nominally and outwardly, but heartily and consistently as his disciples."[37]

"Jesus The Saviour" is the subject of Discourse V, and the text is the 21st verse of Matthew I: "And thou shalt call his name Jesus; for he shall save his people from their sins." Ware treats this subject under three headings:

"I. Whom he is to save;
II. From what he is to save;
III. How he is to save;

or, in other words . . . *the subjects, the nature,* and *the method* of the salvation which [Jesus] came to effect."[38] The "sinners" who are to be saved are "all that have need of it," "all that are 'lost,' " " 'the world,' " "all men."[39]

From what are sinners and the world to be saved?: from their sins. This salvation "is not the abolition of punishment, but of sin."[40] The point is an important one, in the light of the Roman Catholic system of assigning and of relieving offenders of periods of expiation in Purgatory.

The manner of salvation is linked to the nature of salvation, which is "a moral salvation." "Our Lord must consequently have employed moral means. The misery from which man is to be delivered, originates in and depends upon the wrong state of his mind and affections. It is to be removed, it can be removed, by no arbitrary appointments of place or condition, by no exertion of absolute power, like the striking off of chains at a blow. It can be only by the operation of spiritual and moral remedies, suited to the spiritual and moral malady, which shall act gradually on the spirit, and restore it to health, vigor, and virtue."[41]

"[God] has not sent his Son to touch them [i.e., the free, intelligent, voluntary agents, existing in a state of probation while awaiting regeneration] with a wand, to re-create them by some inexplicable and unparticipated operation, like a spell or charm. But to 'sanctify them through the truth;' to 'justify them through faith;' to regenerate them 'by the word of God.' " It should be noted, further, that "Salvation is offered to men, but not forced upon them. It is left to depend upon the use which is made of those privileges and aids, which the grace of God has bestowed. It is thus entirely conditional. It is dependent on every man's free choice."[42] And, "Grace *provides the means.* Sinful and undeserving man, by an act of essential benignity, by the unmerited favor of divine love, is put in the condition to escape from sin, and reach the bliss of heaven. It is a general provision for the human race; not a plan for the recovery of a selected few, nor a favor bestowed upon individuals; but an impartial offer of mercy to all — which offer having been made, and the opportunity having been given, each one is then, separately, to 'work out his own salvation with fear and trembling.' "[43] Here we find the foundation of James Freeman Clarke's article of faith: Salvation by Character.

What are the means of salvation thus instituted by Jesus? "They are, in one word, the revelation which he has made of the doctrines and promises of true religion, and whatever provision exists for perpetuating and promoting its influence."[44]

It is difficult for the self-sufficient rationalist of this era to achieve the feeling of dependence upon Jesus' instrumentality which Ware so eloquently bespeaks when he says, "But if, slighting these means of guidance and salvation, we seek to pass forward unsupported and alone; how serious is the danger that we shall be lost in error, overcome by temptation, corrupted by the world, and miserable in the end. For where is there security, except where Christ has provided it? Where is there 'joy and peace,' except 'in the believing?' And 'how shall we escape, if we neglect so great salvation?' "[45]

Discourse VI deals with the subject, "Jesus The High Priest," and Ware's scriptural text is Hebrews ix. 26: "But now, once, in the end of the world, hath he appeared to put away sin by the sacrifice of himself." His observation is that it was Paul's aim to conciliate the Jews by speaking to them in familiar words regarding a new subject, hence heaven is equated to the temple, Jesus to the high priest, and Jesus himself, in a dual role, is the sacrifice, offering his blood instead of that of beasts. Of this sacrifice and its efficacy Ware says, in part:

"As the blood of the passover lamb upon the door posts was 'a token' to the inhabitants of the house, that they should be saved; so the blood of all the sacrifices was a 'token', or sign, that God's mercy was extended toward them. He had annexed to it this signification. And just so when he delivered his Son to death, it was for a *sign* — the most convincing and satisfactory which could be given — of his inexhaustible mercy, of his willingness to forgive and save; a sign, that as 'he did not spare his own Son, so he was ready with him freely to give us all things.' It was therefore well called a 'sacrifice.' It signified, what the Jewish sacrifices signified; that God, holy as he is, and abhorring all iniquity, is yet plenteous in redemption and ready to forgive; that he is waiting to be gracious, and encourages his prodigal children to return; that he is ready to enter with them into a new covenant, and allow them henceforth a new opportunity of approving themselves to him.

"Such is its resemblance to the sacrifices of the ancient covenant; a resemblance, which evidently does nothing to destroy the moral nature of the influence it exerts. Those availed in ritual blemishes by a positive ritual appointment; but in regard to moral guilt, only by their power to impress the mind, and move to penitence and holiness. And who is not aware that precisely in this mode the blood of Jesus avails to the cleansing and salvation of man? Who pretends that it shall reconcile to God, except through the faith, repentance, and obedience which it produces? that it shall bring to him any heart, which does not come with its own affections? any soul, which does not surrender itself to his love and law?"[46]

Once more we see Ware's conviction that salvation cannot be enjoyed without the participation of the individual suppliant.

In Discourse VII, Ware discusses "The Atonement By Jesus Christ," and begins with Romans v. 11: "And not only so, but we also joy in God, through our Lord Jesus Christ, by whom we have now received the atonement." This is the only use of the word atonement in the New Testament, Ware points out. It is, in fact, he declares, a mistranslation of the word which everywhere else is rendered *reconciliation.* Reconciliation, not atonement, is "the entire purpose of the Saviour's mission."[47] In this connection, Ware asserts that the Son lived and suffered for the salvation of men, not "to win the good will of God toward them."[48]

In Discourse VIII, Ware discusses "Jesus the Intercessor," and uses as his text Romans viii. 34: "It is Christ that died, yea rather, that is risen again, who is even at the right hand of God, who also maketh intercession for us." Again Ware points out an example of the use of a rare reference to create a

John Gorham Palfrey

Henry Ware, Jr.

Andrews Norton

wide claim: this scriptural reference to Jesus as intercessor is one of only two such references. He says, further, "In what his intercession consists, we are nowhere distinctly told."[49]

Intercession is not an unfamiliar concept, however. It appears in both Old and New Testament writings. Moses was an intercessor for his people, with God; David, Samuel, Elisha, Solomon — all offered intercessory prayers. In the New Testament, the apostles prayed for their brethren and request prayers for themselves, in return, while "Paul directs that 'intercessions be made for all men.' "[50] The point to observe here is that "No being exists alone. All lean upon each other. Every individual is made to help others, and to receive help from others."[51] If this is the case for all, "how much more must it be so to the voice of his chosen, his anointed, his dearly beloved Son?"[52]

"We then, instead of the cold incredulous assent which we now give to the doctrine of Christ's intercession, should feel that nothing could be more natural, or more agreeable to his character and office. If our fellow-men carry with them the recollections of earth, and the desire to benefit their friends; how much more must He, the whole object of whose life was to fit men for that world; who left upon earth a mighty work but just commenced; who left the church he had just founded struggling for its existence, and the dearest desires of whose heart can be accomplished only by its growth and prosperity. The work which he began is still going on, as important, as interesting, as glorious, as ever. He cannot be separated from it."[53]

There are those who object that no consequences of Jesus' intercession are discernible. "This objection proceeds upon the supposition, that the intercession of the Mediator must necessarily be all-prevailing; that such must of course be its virtue, as to occasion at once the perfect accomplishment of his great work. But we have no authority for such a supposition. It is without sufficient reason or warrant, that we fancy the Deity pledged to grant immediately, unreservedly, and perceptibly, the petitions of the intercessor." Jesus was granted the power to raise Lazarus from the dead, but "it must be observed, that there is a great difference between such operations on the bodies of men, and the influence of religion on their souls. The souls of men are subject only to a *moral* influence. There can be no reformation or holiness by compulsion."[54] What can be said of the lack of evidence of "the complete efficacy" of Jesus' intercession? "The truth is, that nothing at present has its full and perfect effect. Every thing is in tendency, rather than in result."[55]

Once more Ware asserts: "[Our Lord] appears at the throne of grace in behalf of his friends — not because God needs to be entreated and rendered willing to grant blessing; but because, already waiting to be gracious, he has appointed this method of dispensing blessing."[56] Ware concludes: "[T]he christian, perhaps, owes much of the efficacy of his faith and the serenity of his spirit, the peace and joy which he has in believing, his deliverance in temptation, and his consolation in trouble, and whatever holy influences he may rejoice in, to the intercession of his Lord. At any rate, one consequence is certain. The doctrine has a tendency to excite gratitude, and to promote the growth of religious affections."[57] Such is the substance of Ware's argument on the subject of intercession.

"Christ The Judge Of The World" is the subject of Discourse IX. The text is John v. 22: "For the Father judgeth no man, but hath committed all judgment to the Son." Christ may be called the Judge of the world, in the sense that what he causes to be done is said to have been done by him. "[W]e may understand Christ to be called the Judge of the world, because he provides the rules and publishes the laws by which judgment shall proceed. He himself authorizes this interpretation, when he says, 'If any man hear my words and believe not, I judge him not; he hath one that judgeth him; *the word that I have spoken,* the same shall judge him at the last day.' It seems also to corroborate this interpretation, that he promises his disciples, that they shall sit on twelve thrones, judging the twelve tribes of Israel; and also that Paul says, 'Know ye not that the saints shall judge the world? Know ye not that we shall judge angels?' Now we do not for a moment suppose that the apostles shall be actually seated on twelve thrones, and take part in the distribution of rewards and punishments to God's creatures; much less that all christians shall be so employed; for they are all to be themselves subject to judgment. And still less do we imagine, that they shall be exalted to pass sentence upon angels. We do not hesitate to understand by this language, that the doctrine they hold is the rule by which all shall be judged, that the gospel they profess is the standard by which sentence shall be passed. And why are we not warranted in adopting the same exposition in the instance of our Lord? Why not use as a key to the other expressions his own declaration, that it is 'the word which he hath spoken, that shall judge them at the last day?' "[58]

Jesus' authority is derived from the Father, but that does not make him Almighty God himself. But why should Jesus be the Judge, instead of God? "We may undoubtedly find one reason in the circumstance to which we have already alluded — that it is the general method of God's administration to provide for and rule his creation by the agency of intermediate ministers. From this method we do not know that there is any departure. To maintain a uniformity with the general system, we may readily suppose to be one reason of this judicial appointment. As he had led his people by Moses and Joshua, and taught them by the prophets, and chastened them by the heathen, and enlightened men by a special messenger, and reconciled and saved them by a chosen mediator; so he would in like manner judge the world by his Son. It is one instance among multitudes of what is the established ordinance of the divine government."[59]

Ware sees us all as ultimately appearing before the judgment seat. A "right spirit of subjection and submission" to Jesus is necessary: to refuse it is "an evidence of disrespect toward the Sovereign himself." "But this is not our only duty," Ware continues. "If Christ is to sit on the judgment seat, we are to stand before it, and give account of every work which we have done, and of every secret thought, whether it be good or whether it be evil. For that day we are to prepare. The thought of it should have influence upon the whole habitual frame of our minds, and the entire character of our lives. It should make sin our abhorrence and holiness our delight. It should excite us to diligence in the work of obedience and faith, that we may be found blameless and accepted at last. It should lead us to familiar acquaintance with the word according to which our destiny shall be determined, and to the devout performance of every duty it enjoins; that so we may be welcomed to the joy of our Lord, and not be cast out with the rejected and impenitent."[60]

Discourse X is entitled, "On Honoring The Son." Ware's text is John v. 22: "That all men should honor the Son, even as they honor the Father." His view is simply stated: We are to honor the Son as we honor the Father. The ground of honors due the Father is the divine *"moral* perfections — his essential holiness, his perfect rectitude, unerring wisdom, unwavering truth and faithfulness, impartial justice, infinite goodness and mercy. He is clothed with righteousness, purity and love — the kind Creator, the observing Governor, the gracious Father; earnestly desiring first the perfect virtue, and then the perfect happiness, of every living being."[61]

With respect to Jesus, he is to be honored "on account of the offices to which God has exalted him; his own authority or right is never alleged as a ground of it, as it always is in the case of God himself."[62] We are to show honor to the Son "by the exercise of *faith* in him" and by our *love, gratitude,* and *obedience* to him.

In the final sermon, Discourse XI, Ware discusses "The Example of our Lord," and takes as his text Hebrews xii. 2: "Looking unto Jesus, the Author and Finisher of our Faith." Why should we not literally make our Lord our "Pattern?" "[I]f we may be . . . moved and animated by the example of imperfect men, who after all have followed their holy Master only at a distance; what might not be the effect of bringing home to our minds, and setting before us in our lives, the perfect example of that blessed Master himself? I fear, brethren, that we place him too far from us. I fear that we too much neglect to bring him near, and keep him before us, and realize the manner of his conversation and life; and that he requires us, not only to do according to his commandment, but according to his example."[63]

We shall be well served in time of need to keep Jesus' agony in the Garden alive in our consciousness. Ware feelingly admonishes the Christian: "Go, as he did, and pray — not once, but twice and thrice; and God will answer you too, by 'an angel from heaven to strengthen you' — not indeed in a visible form, but in an inward peace. It is no sin to mourn and weep. Jesus wept. The sin lies in refusing to look for comfort, in obstinately murmuring against the hand of God, in complaining of his severity. Jesus even prayed that 'the cup might pass from him.' But not repiningly, not rebelliously. He added, with filial submission, 'Nevertheless, not my will, but thine, be done.' Brethren, this example is of infinite worth to us. Dwell upon it in the day of your sorrow. Imitate it in the hour of your trouble. You will not fail to attain something of the peace which the Saviour promised to his followers, and which God gives to all those, 'whose hearts are stayed on him, and who trust in him.' "[64]

This long exposition of the Christology of Henry Ware, Jr., is presented on the grounds that it is a rare example of a systematic presentation of the conservative brand of liberal religious thinking in America, in the first quarter of the nineteenth century.

John Gorham Palfrey

We come now to the third and last of this group of distinguished Unitarian figures, John Gorham Palfrey, who lived from 1796 to 1881. The opening paragraphs of the Preface of Frank Otto Gatell's *John Gorham Palfrey and the New England Conscience* afford a quick insight into the man. "When eighty-five-year-old John Gorham Palfrey died in his Cambridge study in 1881, the literary, social, and hereditary aristocracy of New England mourned the event. A man of moral substance, a man who represented, as much as any single individual could, the victory of New England Conscience, had closed a blameless and exemplary life. Palfrey's career was a monument to the Puritan ideal of rectitude, and his survivors could take pride in themselves as part of the same stock. Such was the feeling of the time, and Palfrey's family, his daughters in particular, had no desire to disturb the bland consensus of eulogy, however much it distorted the reality of their father's life. "Could he have registered an opinion, Palfrey would have admitted candidly that he had been anything but a success. He had desired too many unattainable things. But the New England of 1881 saw only the myth of the 'Good Doctor Palfrey,' forgetting the disappointments of previous decades, and declared with certainty that Palfrey's memory would live forever — if nothing else, his massive and definitive *History of New England* would never allow generations that followed to forget this kindly, honest, and representative New Englander."[65] The author goes on to add that the generations which followed did not remember him extensively in their histories.

Our interest in Palfrey rests in his roles of minister and teacher. He was the minister of the prestigious Brattle Street Church in Boston, from 1817 to 1831. At the very outset, on the day of his ordination as minister of the church, his theology was challenged by pastors and delegates from twenty Boston churches. The gist of his reply may be briefly summarized: There is one God, who is personally involved with the affairs of men. He exercises his power in these affairs through direct revelations. Of Jesus Christ, Palfrey said: " 'I rest my faith in the truth of the divine authority of Jesus on various proofs which seem to me irrefragable; on those of miracle & prophecy; of miracles which I believe none but God or one acting under his commission could have wrought . . . Secondarily on . . . the pure morality which he taught [and] the rapid progress of his religion.' "[66] Interpretation of the Bible according to his own lights was the prerogative of each person, said Palfrey, and "Only an understanding of the Scripture could fortify a man in a life of affliction, deter him from sin, or fit him for heaven."[67]

In contrast to Norton and Ware, Palfrey's views of Jesus Christ are not so exclusively and specifically delineated. One must look within his writings to find by inference what his Christology was. For example, we may deduce his unitarianism from the following statement included in a sermon he preached in 1824, "The Prospects and the Claims of Pure Christianity: A Sermon Preached at the Dedication of the Twelfth Church in Boston, October 13, 1824." He endorses "that system of scriptural belief which prevails in the old Congregational Churches of his place, — the system whose prominent features are well known to be the *personal unity and parental character of God,* and the *intelligible import and moral design of Christianity."*

Although Palfrey declares, "The chain with which errors in religion have bound themselves to men's interests and passions needs to be broken link by link," he reveals in the same sermon his disposition to a preservation of Christianity as he has known it. The same position was evident years later, when, as Dean of the Harvard Divinity School, he objected to the implications contained in the highly controversial address Emerson delivered before the Harvard Divinity School student body. Palfrey said: "While we profess so much satisfaction that we have been led to adopt the faith of Christ in its primitive simplicity, let me ask the question whether we are sufficiently in the habit of regarding it as a *trust*; whether we perceive distinctly enough that an obligation lies upon us to pray, give, and labour for its diffusion?" And he went on to conclude: "[L]ittle as the condition of the world seemed to favour the diffusion of Christian truth, to doubt that it would one day prevail would have been a distrust of providence; for he who made Christianity for man no doubt fitted it for his cordial reception in some period of his progress." Indeed, within this religion, responsible for its survival and ultimate growth, was a "primitive integrity and power."

In 1831 Palfrey became Professor of Sacred Literature in the Harvard Divinity School, with the added role of Dean. Evidently to dispel apprehensions of conservative members of the School, alumni, and other interested persons, he sought to clear himself of any suspicion of unbecoming liberalism by proclaiming, upon taking office, "I, John Gorham Palfrey . . . believe in the Christian religion, and have a fine persuasion of its truth . . . . I will not only labour to advance the knowledge of the department committed to my charge, but . . . will in every other Subject consult the prosperity of this University."[68]

During the period of his eight years at the Divinity School, Palfrey provided the most advanced criticism of the time in the field of "the Jewish scriptures and Antiquities." His conclusion regarding Christianity was included in the 28th Annual Report of the American Unitarian Association for 1853. Therein a defense was erected against charges of infidelity and rationalism by the Orthodox. Palfrey said, in part: "[T]he evidence of Christianity is identical with the evidence of the miraculous character of Jesus," and "his miraculous powers were the highest evidence that he came from God."[69]

The influence of this remarkable man, who went on from his posts in the Harvard Divinity School to become lecturer, state legislator and secretary, representative in Congress, postmaster of Boston, and historian, was bound to be felt in the expression of his theological and Christological views, on both planned and unplanned occasions, over a wide range of contacts, and, no doubt, strengthened the liberal views of the Unitarians for many years.

Chapter 3

Jesus in
Ralph Waldo Emerson's
Transcendentalism;
Theodore Parker's Practical Christianity

We come now to a new era, begun even while Channing, Norton, Ware, and Palfrey still preached and wrote, when the role of Jesus and his characteristics were consciously and deliberately recast into a new, and at first shocking, identity.

The first notable figure in this drama of mutation was Ralph Waldo Emerson, and his literary instrument was an address at Harvard in 1838, called afterward The Divinity School Address. Emerson earlier had resigned from the ministry of the Second Church in Boston, because he could not conscientiously conduct the service of the Lord's Supper. By the time of the Divinity School Address, he had achieved an objectivity with respect to Christianity unknown to his Christocentric father, the Reverend William Emerson, who had been minister of First Church in Boston and, as secretary of the Society for Promoting Christian Knowledge, Piety, and Charity, was the publisher of the *Christian Monitor*. Emerson's message now was the gospel of Transcendentalism. It was a reaction against the dependence upon the Bible and external authority. Channing loved to find his guides and justifications in the Bible, but Transcendentalists believed all men, not only those who set down the scriptural words of God, were capable of receiving divine inspiration. Religious truths do not depend upon miracles, it was held, but neither do they depend upon reason. Nor do they originate only with outside sources; they can arise within us spontaneously. Thus, we are not restricted to ancient prophets and apostles, nor, in the case of our particular interest here, to Jesus Christ himself; but this is not to say that our own reason may not affirm the same truths espoused by Jesus and the others.

In saluting the new concept of religious authority within the individual, some reviewers and critics have tended to minimize Emerson's retention of Jesus as a valid and noble figure. Witness these statements contained in the

Divinity School Address. In the first Emerson cites Jesus as an example of the principle he is declaring, when he refers to expressions of the moral sentiment which dwelt "in the minds of men in the devout and contemplative East; not alone in Palestine, where it reached its purest expression, but in Egypt, in Persia, in India, in China." And he adds, "What these holy bards said, all sane men found agreeable and true." Then he continued, "And the unique impression of Jesus upon mankind, whose name is not so much written as ploughed into the history of this world, is proof of the subtle virtue of this infusion."

Emerson was by no means ignoring or intentionally belittling Jesus. He was clearing his image of superimposed delineations. "Jesus Christ belonged to the true race of prophets," he went on. "He saw with open eye the mystery of the soul. Drawn by its severe harmony, ravished with its beauty, he lived in it, and had his being there. Alone in all history he estimated the greatness of man. One man was true to what is in you and me. He saw that God incarnates himself in man, and evermore goes forth anew to take possession of his World. He said in this jubilee of sublime emotion, 'I am divine. Through me, God acts; through me speaks. Would you see God, see me; or see thee, when thou also thinkest as I now think.' But what a distortion did his doctrine and memory suffer in the same, in the next, and the following ages! There is no doctrine of the Reason which will bear to be taught by the Understanding. The understanding caught this high chant from the poet's lips, and said, in the next age, 'This was Jehovah come down out of heaven. I will kill you, if you say he was a man.' The idioms of his language and the figures of his rhetoric have usurped the place of his truth; and churches are not built on his principles, but on his tropes [i.e., figures of speech]. Christianity became a Mythus, as the poetic teaching of Greece and of Egypt, before. He spoke of miracles; for he felt that man's life was a miracle, and all that man doth, and he knew that this daily miracle shines as the character ascends. But the word Miracle, as pronounced by Christian churches gives a false impression; it is Monster. It is not one with the blowing clover and the falling rain . . ." As for what Christianity has done with Jesus Christ, Emerson said: "It has dwelt, with noxious exaggeration about the *person* of Jesus. The soul knows no persons. It invites every man to expand to the full circle of the universe . . ."

It should be acknowledged, however, that with the widening of the base of Christian religion beyond the limits of the Bible, with Jesus' miracles disposed of as proof of a valid religion, and with Jesus sharing attention with others as an inspired prophet, the Transcendentalists were departing on a tangent which would lead forever farther from even the liberalized sphere of Jesus' religion, as early Unitarianism had known it. Older Unitarians concretized *their* liberalism into a conservatism, when they were confronted with Emerson's views. Their reactions were perhaps, unnecessarily alarmist, when they limited themselves to what Emerson said. Yet, if they were thinking of the implications of such tendencies to displace Jesus and Christianity from the center of their religion, they can be said to have been right, of course, as developments over the next decades showed. They were confronted with the never-dying question of whether to stand or to move on, of whether to abide by the old Mythus or to embark upon a new course which might, in time, lead to a new Mythus.

There was no real choice, however. A new die was in the casting. The process could not be stopped. Seeds of a new role and characterization of Jesus had been sown, and, in due course, though not immediately, Unitarian churches and Sunday-schools would reflect this influence.

Among those who heard Emerson on that notable day at Harvard, when he addressed the graduating seniors in the cozy little chapel of Divinity Hall, was Theodore Parker, a recent graduate of the School, now minister to seventy families in the farming community of West Roxbury. His own response to Emerson's exposition of the new perspective on religion was to assess it as "the noblest and most inspiring strain I ever listened to." But Parker soon went beyond responding. He made his own mark.

In the last months of his life, destined not quite to reach the age of 50, Theodore Parker wrote down recollections of his boyhood. One of them was the charming incident I heard of in my childhood but never related to young Parker, namely the arresting of his arm as it was poised to strike a tortoise with a stick, by a voice within him, which declared, "clear and loud, 'it is wrong!' " His mother explained to him, when he told her later, " 'Some men call it conscience, but I prefer to call it the voice of God and the soul of man.' " After saying a few more excellent words about listening to the conscience, Parker's mother concluded, " 'Your life depends on heeding this little voice.' "[1] Parker heeded it. He had a keen ear for the voice of God, not only in matters of conscience, but in concern for human kindred, to so remarkable and consistent a degree that after Parker's death, Ralph Waldo Emerson wrote that Parker's commanding merit as a reformer was that he insisted more than any of his contemporary preachers that the essence of Christianity is its practical morals.

All of Parker's readers and disciples have marked these words, whether they knew to relate them to Emerson or not, to such an extent that sight is lost of the place of Jesus Christ in Parker's religious thinking. Again, it would seem that even today, taking their cue from the fact of Parker's ostracism even by fellow Unitarian ministers in his own time, let alone by the orthodox, the majority impression is that Parker set a pattern for the rejection or down-grading of Jesus, which was followed in succeeding years.

When one takes a careful look at Parker's writings, however, one finds not only that Jesus was very much in Parker's mind, but that distortions of Jesus' true nature and purpose and intentions were disturbing to Parker. He vigorously opposed them. Jesus' place in Parker's religion is more eminent than many persons are aware.

It is statements such as the following which have molded opinions of Parker's views of Jesus. "I had found no evidence which to me could authorize a belief in the supernatural birth of Jesus of Nazareth. The two-fold biblical testimony was all; that was contradictory and good for nothing; we had not the Affidavit of the MOTHER, the only competent human witness, nor even the Declaration of the SON; there was no circumstantial evidence to confirm the statement in the Gospels of a most improbable event."[3]

And again we find Parker writing, "Many miracles related in the Old and New Testament seemed incredible to me; some were clearly impossible, others ridiculous, and a few were wicked; such, of course, I rejected at once, while I still arbitrarily admitted others. The general question of miracles was one which gave me much uneasiness, for I had not learned carefully to examine evidence for alleged historical events, and had, besides, no clear conception of what is involved in the notion that God ever violates the else constant mode of operation of the universe. Of course I had not then that philosophical idea of God which makes a theological miracle as impossible as a round triangle, or any other self-evident contradiction."[4]

But no one should dismiss Parker's Christology with negatively worded criticisms. His rejection of Jesus' miracles by no means made Jesus an ineffectual figure for him. His eloquence bespeaks not only an intellectual but an emotional response. Consider words such as these found in, of all places, the controversial sermon which brought Parker so much opprobrium, "The Transient and Permanent in Christianity." An anti-Christ could not have written: "Christ says his word shall never pass away [Luke 21:33]. Yet, at first sight, something seems more fleeting than a word. It is an evanescent impulse of the most fickle element. It leaves no track where it went through the air. Yet to this, and only this, did Jesus intrust the truth wherewith he came laden to the earth; truth for the salvation of the world . . . He felt his words were for eternity. So he trusted them to the uncertain air; and for eighteen hundred years that faithful element has held them good — distinct as when first warm from his lips."[5]

For those who think there is a precedent in Parker for the abandonment of Christ, listen to his comments on Jesus' utterances: " 'Now they are translated into every human speech, and murmured in all earth's thousand tongues, from the pine forests of the north to the palm groves of eastern Ind[ia]. They mingle, as it were, with the roar of a prosperous city and join the chime of the desert sea. Of a Sabbath morn they are repeated from church to church, from isle to isle, and land to land, till their music goes round the world. These words have become the breath of the good, the hope of the wise, the joy of the pious, and that for many millions of hearts. They are the prayers of our churches, our better devotions by fireside and fieldside; the enchantment of our hearts. It is these words that still work wonders, to which the first recorded miracles were nothing in grandeur and utility. It is these which built our temples and beautify our homes. They raise our thoughts of sublimity; they purify our ideal of purity; they hallow our prayer for truth and love. They make beauteous and divine the life which plain men lead. They give wings to our aspirations. What charmers they are! Sorrow is lulled at their bidding. They take the sting out of disease, and rob adversity of his power to disappoint. They give health and wings to the pious soul, broken-hearted and shipwrecked in his voyage through life, and encourage him to tempt the perilous way once more. They make all things ours: Christ our brother; time our servant; death our ally, and the witness of our triumph. They reveal to us the presence of God, which else we might not have seen so clearly, in the first windflower of spring, in the falling of a sparrow, in the distress of a nation, in the sorrow or the rapture of the world. Silence the voice of Christianity, and the world is well-nigh dumb, for gone is that sweet music which kept in awe the rulers of the people, which cheers the poor widow in her lonely toil, and comes like light through the windows of morning, to men who sit stooping and feeble, with failing eyes and a hungering heart. It is gone — all gone! only the cold, bleak world left before them.' "[6]

A very little farther along in his sermon, Parker says, " 'The old heavens and the old earth are indeed passed away, but the word stands. Nothing shows clearer than this how fleeting is what a man calls great, how lasting what God pronounces true.

" 'Looking at the word of Jesus, at real Christianity, the pure religion he taught, nothing appears more fixed and certain. Its influence widens as light extends; it deepens as the nations grow more wise.' "

It is not Jesus Christ, but those who have misrepresented him, whom Channing and Emerson and Parker and many other able men have opposed. Persons have mistaken a new idiom for an abandonment of truth. Parker seemed to speak to this point when he said: " 'But looking at the history of what men call Christianity, nothing seems more uncertain and perishable. While true religion is always the same thing, in each century and every land, in each man that feels it, the Christianity of the pulpit, which is the religion taught, the Christianity of the people, which is the religion that is accepted and lived out, has never been the same thing in any two centuries or lands, except only in name. The difference between what is called Christianity by the Unitarians in our times, and that of some ages past, is greater than the difference between Mahomet and the Messiah. The difference at this day between opposing classes of Christians, the difference between the Christianity of some sects, and that of Christ himself, is deeper and more vital than that between Jesus and Plato, pagan as we call him.' "[7]

Parker was the champion of Jesus, but not the champion of the various

Ralph Waldo Emerson

Theodore Parker

notions of him which men have held, at variance with one another, and changing down through the years. He makes a fine distinction many Christians miss, when he points out that " 'the immutable truth of the doctrines themselves, or the authority of God, who sent [Jesus] into the world,' " are sufficient authority unto themselves. " 'It is hard to see why the great truths of Christianity rest on the personal authority of Jesus, more than the axioms of geometry rest on the personal authority of Euclid or Archimedes. The authority of Jesus, as of all teachers, one would naturally think, must rest on the truth of his words, and not their truth on his authority.' "

Parker recognized the different concepts of the nature of Christ and concluded, " 'But, all this time, scarce any two eminent teachers agree on these points, however orthodox they may be called. What a difference between the Christ of John Gerson and John Calvin — yet were both accepted teachers and pious men. What a difference between the Christ of the Unitarians and the Methodists — yet many men of both sects be true Christians and acceptable with God. What a difference between the Christ of Matthew and John — yet both were disciples, and their influence is wide as Christendom and deep as the heart of man. But on this, there is not time to enlarge.' "[8]

I cannot forbear sharing with you a few more sentences of Parker's personal testimony regarding Jesus. " 'So if it could be proved — as it cannot — in opposition to the greatest amount of historical evidence ever collected on any similar point, that the gospels were the fabrication of designing and artful men, that Jesus of Nazareth had never lived, still Christianity would stand firm, and fear no evil. None of the doctrines of that religion would fall to the ground; for, if true, they stand by themselves. But we should lose — oh, irreparable loss! — the example of that character, so beautiful, so divine, that no human genius could have conceived it, as none, after all the progress and refinement of eighteen centuries, seems fully to have comprehended its lustrous life.' " But Parker does not lose sight of his point: " 'If [Christian truth] rest on the personal authority of Jesus alone, then there is no certainty of its truth if he were ever mistaken in the smallest matter, as some Christians have thought he was in predicting his second coming.' "[9]

" 'His life is the perpetual rebuke of all time since. It condemns ancient civilization; it condemns modern civilization . . . This Galilean youth strode before the world whole thousands of years, so much of divinity was in him. His words solve the questions of this present age. In him the godlike and the human met and embraced, and a divine life was born . . .' " " 'But if . . . you take a heathen view, and make him a god, the Son of God in a peculiar and exclusive sense, much of the significance of his character is gone.' "[10]

" 'To turn away from the disputes of the Catholics and the Protestants, of the Unitarian and the Trinitarian, of old school and new school, and come to the plain words of Jesus of Nazareth, Christianity is a simple thing, very simple. It is absolute, pure morality; absolute, pure religion; the love of man;

the love of God acting without let or hindrance. The only creed it lays down is the great truth which springs up spontaneous in the holy heart — there is a God. Its watchword is, Be perfect as your Father in heaven. The only form it demands is a divine life; doing the best thing in the best way, from the highest motives; perfect obedience to the great law of God. Its sanction is the voice of God in your heart; the perpetual presence of him who made us and the stars over our heads; Christ and the Father abiding within us. All this is very simple — a little child can understand it; very beautiful — the loftiest mind can find nothing so lovely. Try it . . .' "[11]

" 'Real Christianity gives men new life. It is the growth and perfect action of the holy spirit God puts into the sons of men. It makes us outgrow any form or any system of doctrines we have devised, and approach still closer to the truth. It would lead us to take what help we can find. It would make the Bible our servant, not our master.[12] It would teach us to profit by the wisdom and piety of David and Solomon, but not to sin their sins nor bow to their idols. It would make us revere the holy words spoken by 'godly men of old,' but revere still more the word of God spoken through conscience, reason, and faith, as the holiest of all. It would not make Christ the despot of the soul, but the brother of all men.' "[13]

With respect to the life, death, and resurrection of Jesus Christ for Theodore Parker, it may be said that what mattered most for him was Jesus' life, just as living this present earthly life was the sole matter of his concern. He appeared to accept the resurrection in others' beliefs found in "the writings of those men who, even after his resurrection, expected him to be a Jewish king."[14] But he left no doubt in anyone's mind that the resurrection which counted most for him was the resurrection of Jesus' spirit in each one's way of living. Herein lay salvation, both for the believer-doer, and for the world. " '[M]ay God send us some new manifestation of the Christian faith, that shall stir men's hearts as they were never stirred; some new word, which shall teach us what we are, and renew us all in the image of God . . .' "[15]

Parker was, then, bound to the words spoken by Jesus, the truths uttered and practised, the spirit manifest in all his living; and these are the aspects of Christ he salutes. He lacked devotion to the person of Christ; he even appeared to shy away from it, in contrast to Channing, who maintained a mystical union with Christ. With Emerson, he withheld sole and final authority from Jesus, but, lacking Emerson's depth of religious and mystical experience and his poetic insights, he gave credit, drew from the wells of Jesus' wisdom, and went on to preach and to live a life of practical doing and unselfish serving, for the glory of God.

While Parker had developed his own simplified Christianity, as we might call it, and in so doing had sowed seeds which would produce a new flower in due course, the young Unitarian Association was trying both to grow in organizational structure and, hopefully, to expand in numbers, and at the same time to arrive at a definitive statement of its characteristics. Concurrently, and not unrelatedly as a sociological proving of Christian principle, the question of the abolition of slavery was receiving much attention from a number of Unitarians, both lay and clerical.

Of especial interest to us is the 28th Annual Report of the American Unitarian Association, in 1853. The old line Unitarians were not ready to go along with the Transcendalists' questioning of the miracles as the only evidence for the validity of Christianity. They expressed their position in the Report just referred to, in these words: "We desire, in a denominational capacity, to assert our profound belief in the Divine origin, the Divine authority, the Divine sanctions, of the religion of Jesus Christ. This is the basis of our associated action. We desire openly to declare our belief as a denomination, so far as it can be officially represented by the American Unitarian Association, that God, moved by his own love, did raise up Jesus to aid in our redemption from sin, did by him pour a fresh flood of purifying life through the withered veins of humanity and along the corrupted channels of the world, and is, by his religion, forever sweeping the nations with regenerating gales from heaven, and visiting the hearts of men with celestial solicitations. We receive the teachings of Christ, separated from all foreign admixtures and later accretions, as infallible truth from God."[16]

In the same meeting at which this statement was adopted, a resolution was also adopted, without dissent, which declared that "the Divine authority of the Gospel, as founded on a special and miraculous interposition of God, is the basis of the action of the Association."[17]

During the same period, in May of 1852, the so-called Western Unitarian Churches, representing societies in western New York State, Ohio, West Virginia, Kentucky, Missouri, Illinois and Michigan, created an organization whose constitution declared its purpose to be " 'the promotion of the Christian spirit . . . and the increase of vital, practical religion; the diffusion of Gospel truth and the accomplishment of such works of Christian benevolence as may be agreed upon . . .' "[18]

Notwithstanding these references to "Christian spirit" and "Christian benevolence," the trend away from both the personal Christ and the human Jesus, which came to characterize this "Western Conference," was already taking shape.

Also in 1853, the Reverend Doctor Henry A. Myles became secretary of the American Unitarian Association, and his book on The Birth of Jesus was evidence of Jesus' continuing place in his Unitarianism. Again in that year, 1853, the missionaries of the new Western Conference were instructed that "in spirit and in aim the Conference would be Christian, not sectarian . . . . All that it requires is, that they should be Christians and do Christian work, that they should believe on the Lord Jesus Christ as one who spake with

authority and whose religion is the divinely appointed means for the regener-
ation of man individually and collectively . . ."[19]

In 1854 a report on the doctrinal basis of the Conference, written by
William G. Eliot, of St. Louis, was published under the title, "Unitarian
Views of Christ." In it Jesus Christ was declared to be the Son of God and the
miracles of the New Testament to be facts upon which the Gospel is based. It
was adopted unanimously, with the assertion, "we have no right to adopt any
statement of beliefs as authoritative or as a declaration of the Unitarian faith,
other than the New Testament."[20]

Four years later, however, the Western Conference delivered itself of the
opinion that "all who wish to take upon themselves the Christian name
should be so recognized."[21] In 1859, the conservatives asked for the old faith
of Channing, while the radicals declared their disbelief in miracles and in the
resurrection of Christ. Then, by 1860, only one year farther on, we find the
Conference willing "to welcome as fellow laborers all who are seeking to learn
and to do the will of the Father and work righteousness . . ."[22]

We have come now to a new chapter in both national and denominational
history, and the year is 1860. The character of Jesus Christ has been freed of
theological restraints, and the translation of his spirit into practical living has
been made more specific. Though not the most significant in history, the next
six decades were to be the busiest ever in terms of political and military
incidents in sequences involving an extraordinarily large proportion of the
countries of the world. We shall begin the next chapter with a brief recital of
events occurring around the world, in a corner of which our tiny group of
liberal Christians was working out its religious destiny.

Chapter 4

James Freeman Clarke and Frederic Henry Hedge, Nineteenth Century Unitarian Christians

To go back just a bit, Protestantism in England suffered a fright when Anglicans under John Henry Newman's influence seceded to the church of Rome, and a papal bull published by Pius IX in 1850 set up a hierarchy of bishops in England, who were to receive their titles from English sees created by the bull. But the government was on the side of the majority of the citizenry, and no significant change in the religious climate occurred. Those Presbyterians who were unitarian in their theology, and called themselves Rational Dissenters, were getting along relatively peacefully with their orthodox brethren. In 1871 Oxford and Cambridge students were granted the right to receive university degrees and to hold lay offices in colleges and universities, without subscribing to religious tests. Ten years later, an atheist was elected to the House of Commons and in subsequent years was instrumental in removing the requirement of a religious oath of office, characterized by the words "So help me God!" A great international exhibit staged in 1851, for which Prince Albert was largely responsible, sounded a note of prosperity and indicated a confidence that the world would continue to be at peace.

Across the sea, however, Napoleon III sought to establish a Catholic Latin empire in Mexico, and in 1861 France, England, and Spain all had troops in that country. Napoleon's aim was not achieved, however, and the Mexican affair was concluded, unsuccessfully for the French, soon after the end of the Civil War in the United States.

A dream of continuing peace was not to be allowed to persist. Beginning in 1870 and extending until 1914, there was an incredible amount of international maneuvering on the part of European and Near Eastern nations. It was an age of giants: Bismarck, Disraeli, and Gladstone.

In the Roman Church, the dogma of the Immaculate Conception had been ennuniciated in 1854. A Vatican Council held from December 1869 to October 1870 produced the dogma of papal infallibility, which marked the final triumph of the papacy over the episcopal and conciliar tendencies of the church. But the attempt to exalt the papacy above all secular states and to extend "faith and morals" to the political domain failed. Such theological dominance, had it been achieved, would have truncated the history of Protestantism.

The next Pope, Leo XIII, 1878-1903, was more liberal and tolerant than his predecessor, but his liberalism did not lead him to condone others' liberalism and was related to practical ways of improving the role of the church and to extending its influence to such areas of concern as the relationship between capital and labor.

Through all this period, informed, thoughtful Americans could not be wholly untouched by the world-wide unrest. At home, everyone was preoccupied by the affairs of their nation, involved in civil war. The conflict had been brewing for many years. It had evoked humanitarian principles and induced humanitarian acts, not only with regard to slavery but also to a multitude of social problems. In this field American Unitarians were in the vanguard, moving forward under the Christian banner, variously conceived.

Unitarian ministers served as chaplains in the Civil War, and several lost their lives while so serving. Others, notably the Reverend Dr. Henry W. Bellows, were active in the Sanitation Commission, which was an outgrowth on the national level of the need to forestall recurring epidemics of smallpox, typhus, typhoid, cholera, scarlet fever, and yellow fever, in Philadelphia, New York, Boston, Baltimore, Washington, Memphis, and New Orleans. The Commission also served in a broad area of humanitarian efforts, including rectifying errors affecting the pay and welfare of soldiers of the Civil War. A state Board of Health was established in Massachusetts as a result of Unitarian practical Christianity.

New territories were opened to mining and homesteading, even during the Civil War, and Americans Indians were simultaneously being gradually herded into areas. Negro suffrage and woman suffrage as social advances shared attention with the development of transportation by railroad across the entire country. The typewriter, the telephone, and barbed wire were invented, and silver was discovered in Nevada. Farmers' parties were organized, and the American Federation of Labor came into being. The Vice President of the United States and a number of members of Congress were involved in corruption, in connection with the construction of the Union Pacific Railroad, and other government officials were guilty of other offenses. All of these activities occurred in the twenty years' period following the Civil War. The next decades, up to the involvement of the United States in the First World War, were marked chiefly by the United States' concern with international policies and agreements involving money and trade, and with labor problems. The hard heart of ownership-management was being increasingly put to the fiery test of a growing labor movement. Labor was given a seat in the Cabinet in 1913. American neutrality in the face of the war in Europe was finally abandoned, largely due to the torpedoing of our American shipping.

The same post-Civil War period was marked by the growth and advance of the individual as well as of the government. Persons on a broadening scale were reading, and they were being provided with a new kind of reading. Novels and the Bible were supplemented with reports of research in both sociological and scientific areas. The people began to see themselves objectively and to learn about themselves. As, earlier, the role of men in shaping national destiny had been discovered, now the importance of man as an entity, a person to be recognized and provided for, began to receive increasing attention.

If the Industrial Revolution and wars and the thoughtless operations of business bosses called for the practice of Christian love and ethics, the role of the individual as a cause unto himself surely recalled the preoccupation of Jesus with the individual person, however inconsequential. Current novels helped the people to see themselves, or to wonder at others whom they did not recognize as themselves. The improvement in postal services aided in the distribution of such enlightening and broadening printed material.

We have reviewed the setting for mid-and latter-nineteenth century Christianity and have been reminded of needs and opportunities for the social, political, and personal application of Jesus' teachings. Let us turn now to Unitarian individuals who were making their respective responses to the world about them in terms of their adaptation of Jesus Christ to the times, with a hoped-for modification of existing social conditions and the salvation of souls. We know that about us at almost any moment are persons whose understanding, insights, and wisdom offer much to their local scene and their own time, yet for lack of accidents of recognition or failure to publish their thoughts, their fame and influence must be better recognized by God than by any sizable number of men. And even for many whose conclusions have reached the printed page, new demands for attention cause them to be laid aside unappreciated, that that which has already come next may have its turn. Thus it is that little remains from generation to generation for the informing of those who come after. And thus it is that the excellent thoughts, sound conclusions, and brilliant foresights of many worthy persons are overlooked here, though not without respect, in our giving attention to a few individuals, who, in their time and later, received more than usual recognition.

The first person to whose work we shall turn for insights into Unitarian Christology in the Civil War-post-Civil War period is James Freeman Clarke. Dr. Clarke was an active figure in denominational affairs. He was a professional contemporary of Theodore Parker and of Frederic Hedge and Henry Whitney Bellows, whom we shall turn to later. A learned man of deep convictions regarding the characteristics of Christianity, Dr. Clarke nonetheless espoused an open relationship with those whose views were liberal but at variance. For example, when most other Boston ministers refused to exchange with Theodore Parker because of his unacceptable views of Christ, Clarke did exchange with him. And if there were to be an association of Unitarian churches, he went so far as to indicate he felt the denomination should include "all who desire to work with us in advancing the kingdom of God." This was, incidentally, a position proposed by him but not accepted at the second session of the National Conference, held in New York City October 7-19th, 1868.

Although Clarke was a member of the early group of Transcendentalists, and although he was tolerant of Theodore Parker's new departures in establishing religion's role, Jesus Christ was central in his religion. He was infinitely nearer to Channing than to Parker. Like Channing, he set forth vigorously and unequivocally the Unitarian estimates of Christ, and in this respect he was more scholarly and more academically specific than was Channing. Where Channing preached his Christianity, Clarke not only preached it but delineated it brilliantly in helpful detail in other writings, as well. He has been described in part as "a typical Unitarian minister, who wrote poetry, was more than once an editor, often appeared on the lecture platform, was a frequent contributor to the leading periodicals, wrote several works of biography and history, gave himself zealously to the advocacy of the noblest reforms, and produced many volumes of sermons that have in an unusual degree the merit of directness, literary grace, suggestiveness, and spiritual warmth and insight. His theological writings have been widely read by Unitarians and those not of that fellowship . . . . He was a maker of many books, and all of them were well made. His theology was all the more humane, and his preaching was all the more effective, because he was interested in many subjects and had a real mastery of them."[1]

Joseph Henry Allen, a lecturer on ecclesiastical history at Harvard University in the 19th century, in a brief personal recollection of Dr. Clarke, concluded, "[H]e has left the impression of one averse to contention and the strife of tongues. No one that we can anywhere recall has led the intellectual life in an atmosphere quite so radiant with the gladness and affection of a great host of friends; no apostle of the Word, whom we can readily name, but sent forth that word so penetrating and so broadly into the hearts of those waiting to be delivered from bondage to error and fear, who received it in the spirit of glad confidence which was so eminently the spirit of his gospel."[2]

Allen quoted from a letter to him from Dr. Clarke. The sentence reveals at once Clarke's modesty and warmth of personality. "We do not care for praise as we grow old, but we always are made happy by sympathy."[3]

Clarke's contribution to Unitarian theology is contained principally in a volume entitled *Orthodoxy, Its Truths and Errors.* First printed in 1866 by the American Unitarian Association, it had reached its 18th edition by 1894. Quotations and references used here are from that edition.

Clarke's Preface is characteristic: "The Protestant Reformation has its Principle and its Method. Its Principle is Salvation by Faith, not by Sacraments. Its method is Private Judgment, not Church Authority. But private judgment generates authority; authority, first legitimate, that of knowledge, grows into the illegitimate authority of prescription, calling itself Orthodoxy. Then Private Judgment comes forth again to criticise and reform. It thus becomes the duty of each individual to judge the Church; and out of innumerable individual judgments the insight of the Church is kept living and progressive. We contribute one such private judgment; not, we trust, in conceit, but in the hope of provoking other minds to further examinations."[4] We can gain a very clear idea of Clarke's Christ from this volume. A brief review of his points may seem long, but one must appreciate that Dr. Clarke was writing in minute detail.

"Let us remember how empty the world was of God at the time of Christ's coming," Clarke wrote. "Then Christ came; and in all he said and did, he spoke from the knowledge of God, he acted from the life of God. Here was one, then, at last, to whom God was not an opinion, but a reality; through whose life flowed the life of God in a steady current . . . . Those, therefore, who could find God nowhere else, found him in Christ."[5]

Was Christ human? "We agree with the Orthodox," wrote Clarke, "in saying that Christ had two natures — a divine nature and a human nature . . . But the question comes, Was that one person divine or human, finite or infinite, dependent or absolute?" Clarke's reply is "[T]he person of Christ is human, but is intimately united and in perfect union with the indwelling God — [thus making] all Scripture intelligible . . . . If Christ is really a man like ourselves, made in all respects like his brethren, and yet is thus at one with God, thus full of God, it shows us that sin and separation from God are accidental things, and not anything necessary." Jesus is our prototype, said Clarke. "What he has been is a type of what all men may be." He is the "new creation of Paul, and the Amen, the faithful and true Witness, the Beginning of the creation of God," in Revelation 3:14.[6]

Christ is "a supernatural creation — a creation of life eternal, which, beginning in Christ, is to embrace the whole of humanity." "[He] was something more than mere man, — something more than Moses and Elijah, — something more than a man of great religious genius. The peculiarity of Christ was, that he was chosen by God's wisdom, and prepared by God's providence, to be the typical man of the race, — the God-man, in whom the divine Spirit and human soul become one in a perfect union. He was, perhaps, placed, by an exceptional birth, where the first Adam stood, —

rescued from inherited depravity, made in the image of God. Then the Spirit was given him without measure. The word of God *dwelt* in him, and did not merely come to him as a transient influence for a special purpose. Add to this a freely chosen aim of life, and a fidelity which was always about his Father's business, and aiming to finish the work which was given him to do, and we have a being in whom we can see either a manifestation of God or a manifestation of man. The Spirit in Christ was one with God; the soul and body were human."[7]

So much for Clarke and the nature of Christ. What does he say of his death and resurrection? "The death of Christ . . . is not merely an *emblem* of God's love, but an *act* of God's love. It draws us to him . . . . The blood of Christ makes those who were afar off nigh." How? "We look at Christ, and see the brightness of God's glory and express image of his person . . . a character infinitely beautiful and lovely . . . and we hear God say, 'This is my beloved Son, in whom I am well pleased' . . . [Matthew 3:17] "[W]e look at the world, and see it 'lying' in wickedness;' we see men . . . cruelly oppressing each other, and boldly defying and mocking at the Almighty. What does he then? . . . [H]e sends his holy child among them . . . to be cruelly and shamefully killed by a death of agony, in order that *we*, sinful and miserable, may be reconciled. We say . . . 'He who spared not his own Son . . . how shall he not *with* him freely give us all things?' . . . . Thus, in the midst of the gloom of that horrible scene on Calvary, when the power of darkness was at its height, . . . the heavens were opened, and a new ray of divine love poured into the world."[8]

"Death, to a Christian, is but a point on the line of advancing being; a door through which we pass; a momentary sleep between two days. In the same sense the Saviour says, 'He that liveth and believeth on me shall never die.' . . . "Certainly Jesus could not have spoken of death this way if he regarded it as the awful and solemn thing which most believers consider it. If it is the moment that decides our eternal destiny, which shuts the gate of probation, which terminates for the sinner all opportunity of repentance and conversion, for the saint all danger of relapse and fall, — then death is surely something, and something of the most immense importance.

"But Christ has really destroyed death both in the Pagan and in the Jewish feeling concerning it. He destroys the Pagan idea of death as a plunge downward from something into nothing, a descent into non-entity or half-entity, a diminution of our being, a passage from the substantial to the shadowy and unreal. "For, according to Christianity, we do not descend in death; we ascend into more of reality, into higher life. Death is a passage onward and upward . . . . "The meaning of the resurrection of Christ is not, as has been often supposed, that after death he came to life *again*, but that at death he rose; that his death was rising up, ascent."[9]

It is in this area of the subject of resurrection, where Clarke has shown the most original and the highest degree of scholarship. He says, "The immense stress laid, in the New Testament, on the resurrection of Jesus, is by no means explained by supposing that after his death he came to life again, and so proved that there is a life after death. What he showed his disciples was, that death was not going down, but going up; not descent into the grave, or Hades, but ascent to a higher world."[10] He takes the Greek word *anastasis*, commonly translated, "resurrection," or "rising again," and declares its proper meaning to be "rising up." It does not mean coming back to life as before. That is not what Christian resurrection is. It is rising up, *ascending*, to a higher state. "What seems death is only change, and a change from a lower to a higher state, therefore rising up, or resurrection. Christ, then, the love of truth of God in the soul, *is* the life and the resurrection. He fills the soul with that life which causes it to rise with every change, to go up and on evermore to a higher state . . . . The only real death is the immersion of the soul in sense and evil, the turning away from truth and God."[11]

"One power of Christ's resurrection was to abolish the *fear of death*. It brought life and immortality to *light*. It showed men their immortality."[12]

I am moved to ask where does one find such idealism and sensibility today? Although it is not commonly expressed, I do find it in the hearts of some persons at rare times, particularly at funerals, when in the retrospect such occasions prompt, one becomes aware of the essence of fineness and of goodness, so to speak, and suddenly enjoys an intuitive understanding of Jesus' words, "I am the resurrection, and the life: he that believeth in me, though he were dead, yet shall he live: And whosoever liveth and believeth in me shall never die." But Dr. Clarke, like Channing, maintained this lofty way of thinking characteristically.

"The Creeds teach that the souls of the good either sleep till a future resurrection, or are absorbed into God until then, while the souls of the impenitent descend to a lower sphere. Christ teaches that at death *all* rise to a higher state — of life and love to the loving, or judgment by the sight of truth to the selfish; but *higher* to all. Paul declares that 'as in Adam All die, even so in Christ shall All be made alive,' making the rise equivalent in extent to the fall."[13]

Here, then, is Clarke's summary of the meaning of Christ's resurrection and of Christian resurrection: "All the proof rests on the historic fact of the resurrection. Was Christ seen in this higher spiritual and bodily state, or was he not?"

If he was, then we have a fact of history and experience to rely upon to show us that the future life involves an ascent both spiritual and bodily. And this is the reason why such stress has been laid on the resurrection. "This raising of man, through the power of Christ's life, to a higher state, is not a mere matter of speculation, then, not an opinion, not something pleasant to think of and hope for, but it is a fundamental fact of Christian faith. Because Christ has arisen and passed up, we must all arise and pass up, too, with him.

He is the first fruits of those who sleep. In proportion as the Spirit of Christ is in us, in that proportion in the power in us which shall carry us upward towards him. He wishes that those who believe in him shall be where he is. We shall belong to him and to his higher world, not arbitrarily, but naturally; not by any positive decree of God, but by the nature of things. "The essential fact in the resurrection is, that Christ rose, through death, to a higher state. The essential doctrine of the resurrection is, that death is the transistion from a lower to a higher condition in all who have the life which makes them capable of it."[14]

Elsewhere Clarke takes up Paul's thought of the natural body and the spiritual body. The fulfillment of the natural body comes hereafter, in the spiritual body. This future spiritual body is, first, "an organization connecting us with the outward universe of space and time; second, "it is identical with the present true body;" and, third, "it is a development and advance of this into a higher organization."[15] We shall not go further into Clarke's discussion of his ingenious view which enables one to refer to the resurrection of the body. It suffices for our purpose to know that he held such a view. His conclusion is, "All the proof rests on the historic fact of the resurrection."[16]

Let us continue, then, to see what Clarke says of the significance and purpose of Christ's coming and of the manner and time of it. In the first place, there is only one "coming" of Christ, and that is the occasion of his advent as the Messiah. His historical ministry, of which the gospels tell us, was not his "coming" as the Messiah. That manifestation would take place "at the end of the age." Thus it is that the disciples asked him, "What shall be the signal for your coming, and the end of the age?" (Matthew 24:3)

Christ's coming would be spiritual, and not wholly future, outward, or local. The disciples expected he would come in time of great spiritual darkness. "It was to be preceded by wars, commotions, and misery in every form; preceded also by the preaching of the truth in many lands. It was to be as difficult to locate Christ at his coming, as to fix the lightning, which comes out of the east and shines to the west .... The sun, and moon, and stars of the moral world were to be darkened, and the powers of the heaven to be shaken; and of ten virgins, all going together to meet the bridegroom, half would be found spiritually asleep when he came. Christ's coming would be especially judgment and punishment. He would part the sheep from the goats. He would consume with the brightness of his coming the man of sin."[17]

But what does Clarke think of the coming? He says, "[A]s the Jewish age did come to an end at the destruction of Jerusalem, and Christianity, as the universal religion, took the place of Judaism in the education of the human race, this really was the coming of the Messiah and the end of the age."[18] "So Christ himself came as King at the taking of Jerusalem, but has come since, again and again, more plainly and fully, in other triumphs of his truths, in other manifestations of his power. We believe that the coming of Christ took place at the destruction of Jerusalem. We believe that it has taken place since, in other historical events. We believe that it is to take place more fully hereafter, in this life and in the other life."[19]

Note especially this point that Christ has already come repeatedly in human history: At the destruction of Jerusalem; as a revealer of divine love and truth, and so as the ruler of men's hearts; into dark ages from which men were rescued by Christian self-discipline and self-culture; to overcome the spirit of AntiChrist in the spiritual despotism of the papacy; in the conversion of barbarous tribes to Christianity, when Christ came again "as the Prince of Peace, breaking down the partition walls, and proclaiming a brotherhood of man." The Lutheran Reformation was yet another instance: "[W]e cannot doubt that this also was a coming of Jesus, the unfolding of a new and higher power in Christianity."[20]

On the sticky question of Jesus' role as a judge, Clarke digs right in, in characteristic, thorough-going fashion. He observes that, "in some places Jesus says that he is made Judge of mankind, and in other places denies that he is to judge any one."[21] Clarke goes on to cite five conflicting passages in the gospel of John and to ask how they are to be explained. If Christ said he did not come to judge any man or the world, how can it be said that he came into the world for judgment or that God committed all judgment to him?

Clarke concludes: "Christ's coming was simply to do good; to make men better; to save them from their sins; to reveal pardons; to offer salvation; to manifest God's love. 'The law was given by Moses, but grace and truth came by Jesus Christ.' It is the law, and not the gospel, which judges and condemns the evil-doer. . . . The whole influence of the gospel is a bountiful and gracious one, intended and adapted to make it easier to do right, to add new motives to virtue. Christ is no strict, severe judge, deciding by the letter of the law, bound by his office to show no favor or compassion, but the sinner's advocate and friend. And hence it may truly be said that he came not to judge the world, but to save the world."[22] In a summarizing statement Clarke says, "Orthodoxy is right in expecting the coming of Christ in this world, but wrong in supposing it wholly future and wholly outward. It is right in making it a *personal* coming, and not merely the coming of his truth apart from him, but wrong in conceiving of this personal coming, as material to the senses, instead of spiritual to the soul. It is right in expecting a judgment, but wrong in placing it only in the other world. It is right in supposing that all mankind, the converted, the unconverted, and the heathen, are to be judged by Christian truth, but wrong in supposing that this judgment must occur in one place or at one time. Finally, in this, as in regard to many other doctrines, Orthodoxy fails by neglecting the great saying of Jesus, 'THE SPIRIT QUICKENETH, THE FLESH PROFITETH NOTHING,' and a similar statement of Paul, 'THE LETTER KILLETH.' "[23]

Before we move on, let us spend just a moment in reconstructing an outline of the pertinence of Christianity for liberal Christians, from Dr. Clarke's point of view, and ask ourselves if there may not well be something there for Unitarians, and all persons of free minds and religions, today. Clarke held that faith is the important fact in religion, not works. He noted that peace was in the minds of the first Christians and asked its source. His conclusion was that their peace found its origin in the simplicity of their faith. "They looked to Jesus and their faces were lightened," wrote Clarke. "They *saw* the love of God in him; they felt it in their hearts; they reposed on it undoubtingly. In quietness and confidence was their strength. O, happy days! in which men's minds had not yet been harrassed by thousands of vain controversies and empty verbal disputes; by questions, and strifes of words; by most profound theologial discussions, ending in nothing but weariness; but were satisfied, that, if men would go to Christ, they would find truth. O, happy time! in which men had not learned to dissect their own hearts, and pry curiously into their feelings, and torture themselves by anxious efforts to *feel* right, and tormenting doubts as to whether their inward experiences were as they ought to be, but believed that all good feelings would come in their own time out of Christian faith. O, happy, golden hour! when love, and joy, and duty were all one; when men did not prescribe for themselves and others a task-work, an outward routine of duties; but had confidence, that, if they lived in the Spirit, they would also walk in the Spirit."[24]

The happy days and golden hours passed away, and the helpful teachings of Christianity were lost to the controlling doctrines of the church. Luther came and called men back to simple faith in the Saviour. "But," observed Clarke, "there is a continual tendency to fall back again from faith upon works. Ever as the life of religion weakens, ever as the strength of holy confidence decays, men betake themselves to some outward forms or efforts. When they cease to lean on the love of God, they begin to lean on sacraments and ceremonies, on opinions and doctrines, on feelings and experiences, on morality and works of duty. Ever, as the cold winter of worldliness and sin causes the stream of holy faith to shrink back into its channel, the ice forms accumulate along its shores; and then, as the inevitable consequence and sign of the decay of faith, we find the Church becoming anxious and troubled, confidence giving way to anxiety, cheerfulness to gloom, hope to fear. Everything terrifies the unbelieving Church; new opinions terrify it; new measures terrify it. It has ashes instead of beauty, mourning for joy, the spirit of heaviness instead of the garment of praise."[25]

Liberal Christians have fallen into a misconception of how they shall be justified. "They seek to be justified, not by opinion nor by feeling, but by action; by works of righteousness, honesty, charity; by the faithful performance of social duties; by an act of obedience to the law of God. Looking at the Scriptures . . . they say that a man is forgiven when he has corrected his fault, and not before; that repentance and reformation are the only means of atonement with God; that, if we wish to be forgiven, we must reform our conduct and change our character. Accordingly, they lay great stress on *DUTY*, and are continually exhorting them to the performance of their duties in order to be forgiven." Men are not enabled to do their duties simply by being admonished, "but the sight of God's love in Jesus Christ *does* create in them new strength."[26]

"[W]ithout [a] feeling of peace with God, the effort to do our duties only harrasses and irritates our conscience: it produces weariness of heart, a constant feeling of unworthiness and failure, a constant sense of obligations and responsibilities which we do not and cannot fulfil. . . . But if we begin right, and come to God first, and lean on his love, and rely on his promise, then we are filled with hope and joyful assurance, and failure does not dismay us, for we say 'God's truth is pledged for our success; and if, while we were enemies, we were reconciled to God by the death of his Son, much more, being reconciled, we shall be saved by his life.' "[27]

True to the implications of his lack of fear of death, as exemplified in that statement quoted earlier, "One power of Christ's resurrection was to abolish the *fear of death*,"[28] because it brought life and immortality to light and showed men their immortality, Clarke says elsewhere "death glorifies life." He goes on to cite the recent instance of President Lincoln's death as an example. Clarke agrees with the point of view of an orthodox opponent: "In his book, lately published, Dr. Bushnell teaches that the vicarious sacrifice of Jesus consists in his sympathy with sinners. He suffers with them and for them, as a friend suffers for a friend, or a mother for a child, — in the same way, and in no exceptional or uncommon way. He did not die officially, but naturally. He did not come here to die, but he died because he was here."[29] "The parable of the prodigal son teaches us plainly that when we repent and return to God, we shall be received, and that without any reference to belief in the atonement."[30]

We come now to Unitarian views of Jesus Christ as represented by another of the exceptionally able figures who were at their prime in the middle and third quarter of the nineteenth century, Frederic Henry Hedge. If there were nothing else to note about Dr. Hedge, his early years of education would be of more than ordinary interest in themselves. He was born in December of 1805. His father, the son of a Loyalist minister in the time of the Revolution, was a professor of logic and metaphysics at Harvard. His maternal grandmother was the daughter of President Edward Holyoke of Harvard. It is interesting to note that the same Edward Holyoke had been the first minister of the Second Congregational Church in Marblehead, a church which came into existence because of the more liberal and more intellectual outlook of some of the members of the First Church, who could not agree to the lower standards observed by the majority of the members in choosing a new minister. It was

Frederic Henry Hedge

James Freeman Clarke

not surprising that the Second Church became Unitarian, when the time for that option arrived.

Hedge was an intellectual and a scholar from his earliest years. He reported in later life that "he never had a purer delight in letters than in committing to memory, at seven, the Eclogues of Virgil in the original, and at ten he knew by heart long passages of Homer in Greek."[20] At thirteen young Hedge was sent, with the future eminent historian George Bancroft as his tutor, to study the classics in Germany, for four years. This is not the occasion to review all of his own brief recollections of those years written late in life, but a simple paragraph will afford a charming insight. "At the age of thirteen, having first been duly instituted in the mysteries of the German language at a private *pension,* I was put to a school at a gymnasium in north Germany, situated in a romantic valley among the southward-stretching spurs of the Harz, permeated by a small stream fordable in summer, swelled to a roaring torrent by the melting snows of winter, and washing the base of the Herzberg, a mountain somewhat less than a thousand feet in height." He goes on to describe the ancient buildings, once a monastery, where he studied and roomed, with their stone floors and identical rooms about ten feet square, formerly the monks' cells, with little bedrooms attached. "Underneath the portion of the building inhabited by the officers and scholars was the crypt, lined with perpendicular tombstones, each faced with an effigy in relief of the sainted brother who slumbered beneath."

To this bit of eerie information, one oddment may be added: "The official intercourse between pupils and teachers, outside of the lecture-room or social communion, was conducted in Latin." It is interesting to note, also, that at the second of the two principal schools where Hedge boarded in Germany, his roommate was young Baron von Münchhausen, nephew of him whom Hedge termed "the veritable but unveracious story-teller of that name." And one more digression from our main subject lies in the report that when young Hedge would take long walks in the country with his tutor, the latter would keep up young Hedge's spirits by plying him with a glass of undiluted gin.[32]

Hedge returned to America in 1822 to attend Harvard. He was graduated in 1825 with classmates Charles Francis Adams and Horatio Greenough, in a period of literary brilliance at the college. An insight into the type of minds which produced the Christian ideas and concepts we are about to sample is afforded by the following observation of his friend Joseph Henry Allen. "Dr. Hedge," wrote Allen, "felt a certain impatience and disdain of that intellectual method which affects logical completeness, and tries to formulate all modes of being in a coherent system. From his own mind he seems distinctly to have excluded anything that could be called a theory of the universe . . . What was not in the Divine order of Ideas touched neither his philosophy nor his religion. If he tended more and more, in later life, to a way of thinking that refused to regard the Eternal God as the Creator of material things, and set up an illogical Dualism over against our traditional Theism, it was, I think, more from a moral than from an intellectual motive: he would not make the Holy One responsible for the woe and wickedness we see; he would at least reserve a sanctuary of worship for the soul, undisturbed by the jarring and painful argument that ever seeks and ever fails to reconcile the facts of daily life with the conception the mind loves to frame of a purely benevolent Creator."[33]

Hedge eschewed "the optimism which consoles the average religious mind . . . In the constant mood of his inward life he was a reverent, submissive, and humble worshipper of the Living God; while he refused to lift with daring hand the veil that hides the mystery of the Eternal, and repudiated the pious logic by which many have thought to bolster up their faith."[34]

"A mind so individual, and so far apart from the conventional beliefs of Christendom, was slow in finding wide popular recognition, and long failed of its proper weight among those of its generation [Ralph Waldo Emerson, for example, was only two years his senior] . . . . His word was always 'weighty and powerful,' — the more, because much of what he said, and often the best of what he said, had to do not with matters of speculation, but with every-day ethics, the personal experience of religion, and the successive crises of our public life."[35] But recognition finally came to Hedge after he was fifty, and for the next thirty years he was "fully recognized as without a peer in the communion to which he loyally belonged from first to last, certainly without a superior among the intellectual leaders of our country."[36]

Now let us taste Hedge's Christology.

At the outset, it is important to know how Hedge treats myth in relation to the evangelists' narrations. It was simply that he recognizes as myth much of what was said and, what is more important, he feels that the acknowledgment of myth does not detract at all from the value and significance of the subject material. He says, "[T]he Holy Spirit may and does instruct by fiction as well as fact. If I am asked to draw the line which separates fact from fiction, or to fix the criterion by which to discriminate the one from the other, I answer that I do not pretend to decide this point for myself, much less should I presume to attempt to settle it for others. I am not disposed to dogmatize on the subject. It is a matter in which each must judge for himself. I will only say that for myself I do not place the line of demarcation between miracle and the unmiraculous, for the reason that it seems to me, as I said before, unphilosophical to make our every day experience of the limits of human power and the capabilities of Nature an absolute standard by which to measure the possible scope of the one or the other."

So with the story of the annunciation of Christ's birth. "The angel Gabriel is sent to a virgin named Mary, and surprises her with the tidings, 'Thou shalt conceive in thy womb, and shalt bring forth a son, and shalt call his name

Jesus. He shall be great, and shall be called the Son of the Highest. And the Lord God shall give unto him the throne of his father David. And he shall reign over the house of Jacob forever, and of his kingdom there shall be no end.' This beautiful legend, the most beautiful, I think, of all the legends connected with the birth of Christ, the favorite theme of Christian art, so lovingly handled by Fra Angelico, by Correggio, Raphael, Titian, Andrea del Sarto, and a host of others, is best understood as a Jewish-Christian conception, taking an historic form and 'shaped into a fact.' The legend represents the humility and faith of a pious maiden communing with the heavenly Presence, drawing to herself divine revelations of grace and promise, and thus sanctioning the hopes so dear to every Jewish maiden, — that of becoming the mother of the Messiah. The sudden inspiration of that hope is the angel of the Annunciation."[37]

"Recount to a little child a fable of Pilpay or Aesop, and his questions betray his inability to apprehend it otherwise than as literal fact. He has no doubt of the truth of the story. 'What did the lion say then?' he asks; and 'what did the fox do next?' The maturer mind has also no doubt of the truth of the story, but sees that its truth is the moral it embodies. Of many of the Gospel stories the moral contained in them is the real truth. In the height of our late civil war, there appeared in a popular journal a story entitled 'A Man without a Country,' related with such artistic verisimilitude, such minuteness of detail, such grave official references, that many who read it not once suspected the clever invention, and felt themselves somewhat aggrieved when apprised that fiction, not fact, had conveyed the moral intended by the genial author. But those who saw from the first through the veil of fiction the needful truth and the patriotic intent, were not less edified than if they had believed the characters real, and every incident vouched by contemporary record."[38]

"I only contend that historic truth is not the only truth; that a fact, — if I may use that term in this connection for want of a better, — that a fact which is not historically true may yet be true on a higher plane than that of history; true to reason, to moral and religious sentiment and human need. The story of Christ's temptation is none the less true, but a great deal more so when the narrative which embodies the interior psychological fact is conceived as myth, than when it is interpreted as veritable history."[39]

What does Hedge say of Christ's character? "The mythical interpretation of certain portions of the Gospel has no appreciable bearing on the Character of Christ. The impartial reader of the record must see that the evangelists did not invent that character; they did not make the Jesus of their story; on the contrary it was he that made them. It is a true saying that only a Christ could invent a Christ. The Christ of history is a true reflection of the image which Jesus of Nazareth imprinted on the mind of his contemporaries. In that image the spiritual greatness, the moral perfection, are not more conspicious than the well-defined individuality which permeates the story, and which no genius could invent."[40]

The living Jesus of Nazareth is the basis of the idealized Christ of the Church. Hedge goes on to apply this principle of idealization, he might well have said deification, to American heroes. He asserts, "History strips off the indignities of earth when she dresses her heroes for immortality." Thus we see "Washington without his fiery choler, Lincoln without his coarseness."[41]

It is surprising to observe Hedge's familiarity with and understanding of the concepts and terminology of orthodoxy. Perhaps we see here the results of his early and repeated association with religious thought on the continent of Europe. Let us first examine his thoughts on Incarnation.

Hedge makes a matter-of-fact statement about the early years of Christianity, which has great appeal. He says, "The Christians of the first century were strict monotheists, — Unitarians. They speculated very little, if at all, about the person of Christ. The facts of his history were too near to allow of such speculation . . . . Here was the story of a man who had lived and died like other men, distinguished only by his moral elevation, his wonder-working power, and his martyr-death. Jewish converts still looked upon him, through the medium of their Messianic idea, as the national Messiah who would reappear as earthly potentate and establish his throne in Jerusalem. Gentile Christians were content to see in him a teacher of saving truths, a deliverer from the errors of polytheism, from the bondage of superstition and sin, — the authoritative witness of the doctrine of one God and of the resurrection."[42]

We see here a scholar who can accept myth, who can live with it, as the manner of speaking has it today, and yet who is quite capable of bringing to bear the searchlight of scholarship, and able to live with what scholarship, and good reasoning, produce at variance with myth. Hedge faces up to the evidence and states candidly the conclusion indicated. "When the historical Christ had receded into the distance of a by-gone age; when his image, as an actual person, had grown dim, and the tendencies of the Gentile mind, especially the tendency to deify illustrious and extraordinary men, had begun to react on the simplicity of the gospel, — Christian faith, no longer satisfied with bare historic fact, idealized the person of Christ, exalted him above earthly limitations into something superhuman and divine; and here and there went so far as to make him pure spirit, assuming the likeness of man but divested of all natural belongings, without flesh and blood, a divine apparition."[43]

It may be commented that "the Gentile mind" is broadly inclusive, when one stops to consider the presence of legends and myths revolving around ancient historic figures in probably every literature and culture. The mythologizing of Christ can provide a most effective stimulation to the emulation of the virtuous characteristics of the historical Christ. It results in teaching through the appeal of example rather than through command.

After the tendency to deify Jesus came his identification, by some, with personified Wisdom, "in Jewish phrase, 'the first begotten Son of God.' " Figuratively, wisdom is God's first creation, but the idolizing Christian must seize this identity literally for Jesus, thus uniting Jesus and God and constituting "the true Christ."

There followed upon this development, the elaboration of the redemption of man, his reconciliation with God, through the mediation of Jesus Christ. In this concept, then, we see how the human Jesus has been left behind, and how Jesus, as the incarnation, the embodiment of the Word, of God's wisdom, becomes a very part of the nature or substance of God himself, born of God from eternity, uncreated, "without beginning of existence."[44]

At this point some of us, like many other persons of a questioning mind and rational bent, with liberal inclinations, unafraid of departing from traditional theological guidelines, may turn away in impatience and disgust. Hedge speaks to those who so react: "The superficial mind is apt to regard these questions, which then agitated the Church and the world, as empty abstractions, senseless quibbles." But, he says, "the union of God with man is no quibble; it is a truth of profound significance; and the Council of Nicaea which declared it is one of the most important assemblies that was ever convened on this earth: it dates a new era in the history of human thought. God in actual contact with man — God in man and man in God — is the underlying idea of the Athanasian dogma which asserts that the Son is consubstantial with the Father."[45]

The shortcoming of Athanasius' doctrine of two natures in Christ, human and divine, was that its purpose was not clear. "Of what avail to mankind at large," asks Hedge, "that a single individual, of the countless millions who in all the ages of human history have walked the earth, was substantially united to God, if all the rest are substantially separated from him?" Hedge concludes, "If Christ was really man, he differed from other men only in degree. What he by nature possessed without measure, all men in a measure must also possess."[46] "The fault of the Trinitarian doctrine, so far as this point is concerned, is not what it teaches, but what it omits to teach. It is not the assertion of divinity in Christ, but the limitation of divine humanity to him, the implied exclusion of the rest of mankind from any part or lot in this matter." And Hedge reminds us of Jesus' own words " 'that they all may be one; as Thou, Father, art in me and I in Thee, that they may be one in us.' "[47]

To remedy this defect, Hedge says, was the purpose of the doctrine of transubstantiation. In the doctrine of transubstantiation, those who partake of the bread, after its consecration by the priest, in the rite of the Eucharist, or Last Supper, are partaking of the body of Christ, and so are united to Christ and God.

The doctrines of incarnation and transubstantiation are repudiated by many Christians, as incompatible with reason and common sense. Included in this rejecting category are, of course, the Unitarians. But hear what Hedge says on this point, and note, probably with surprise, the relationship, after all, between the Unitarians and the doctrine of Athanasius, the same whose name is used to identify the most involved of the Christian creeds. Hedge finds in both doctrines "an element of truth which, stripped of its doctrinal embodiment, is worth considering, and which most of us, I think, will heartily accept. To say that God incarnated himself in a single individual of all the multitude of the human family; that once, and once only, in all the ages of time he manifested himself in a human person, — is a proposition which cannot satisfy, if it does not shock, the unprejudiced mind. But expand the proposition; say that God is manifest (and that is the only logical sense in which we can speak of incarnation), — that God is manifest in every inspired teacher and prophet of truth and righteousness, in every holy, self-sacrificing life, in every martyr who, living or dying, devotes himself to any great and worthy cause, — manifest in all in whom love of truth or love of God and man is the ruling motive and principle of action; say, with Paul, that all 'who are led by the Spirit of God are sons of God' in precisely the sense, if not in the degree, in which Jesus was the Son of God; that the real distinction and peculiarity of Christ was not an exceptional, but a sublimely typical, nature and life; not that he was the only God-man, but the type of the God-man, in all generations, — say this, and you assert what no unprejudiced thinker and no philosophic student of religion will deny. And this I believe to be the real interior truth of the Athanasian doctrine, albeit Athanasius himself may not have seized it in its fulness, as certainly he did not unfold it in his teachings."[48]

Hedge here demonstrates the kind of thinking, which has been helpful to many Christians and has been largely lost to younger, present-day liberals. It merits the closest attention. "The doctrine of transubstantiation, in its gross and literal sense the most monstrous that was ever propounded by any religion, has yet its true side. Strip it of the technicalities and sensuous imagery with which it has been associated by the Church of Rome, and it means that the consecrating action of faith transmutes the material into the spiritual; discerns a spiritual presence and finds spiritual nourishment in material things. It means the participation and assimilation of the spirit of Christ, symbolized by the eating of the bread which he called his body. Christ told his people, 'Except ye eat of the flesh of the Son of Man ye have no life abiding in you.' It was a daring figure which the Church understood in a coarse and literal way, and of which the doctrine in question was the practical interpretation. Let us understand by it the application of Christian truth to the present earthly life. Christianity requires the flesh of the Son of Man; that is a visible world, in which the spirit of the Son of Man, a divine spirit shall embody itself. And this idea, amid all the superstitions and monstrous perversions which gathered around it, is dimly shadowed forth in the Roman Church dogma of transubstantiation. Bread, which forms so important a part of this 'flesh' or visible world, may be regarded as symbolizing the whole. The consecrated wafer, which Romish superstition conceives to be bread converted into Deity by the word of a priest, may be taken to represent the looked-for universal transformation of this human world by the communication of a higher and divine life."[49] And, continuing, "The thing embodied, divine humanity, across all the mists of theology is struggling into light, is struggling into practical self-demonstration across all the atrocities and woes of time. Side by side with the horrors of carnage and the desolations of war, it bids the eternal charities bloom. It accompanies the march of devastating hosts with the sacred band of self-elected comforters, whose service no softness shuns and no danger dismays. It summons the civilized world to minister to the wants and woes of countries laid waste by famine or fire. It challenges science to show how ancient wrongs may be abated, and the life of man in society be made more beautiful and safe.' 'Thus, practical Christianity fulfills the truth that was hidden in the obsolete dogmas of the Church; and thus, where 'the letter killeth, the spirit maketh alive.' "[50]

Lest one conclude that Hedge, like so many Unitarians, is more concerned with the letter of Christianity than with its spirit, a few miscellaneous paragraphs, which constitute a modified Sermon on the Mount, that is, a collection of sound principles and suggestions, will induce the opposite view. "I rejoice in all topographical adjustments and illustrations; in all that local researches, following in the steps of 'those blessed feet,' have gleaned from the soil of Palestine. But all this is important only as it draws its inspiration from and leads my aspiration to the ideal Christ, 'the same yesterday, to-day, and forever.' Dissociated from this idea, the acres of Palestine are as barren as any which the ebbing of a nation's life has left desolate."[51]

In very different places, Hedge decries the inadequacy of the historical record. He does not minimize its value, but he sees that to tell the history is not to catch the spirit. He writes, "Had we no other data from which to judge of the future of humanity than what is chronicled in the books, one might almost despair of the gospel and of man .... So many centuries has Christianity builded its churches and administered its sacraments and published its scriptures, and so little as yet has been seen and felt of Christ! The written chronicle seems rather to conceal [Christ] than to reveal him."[52]

History tells us the external life of the Church, but not the essential growth of the spirit, says Hedge. He sees man farther along than the written evidences indicate. "It would not be difficult to trace through all these centuries of revolution and misrule, of strife and oppression, of theological hatred and priestly persecution, the secret windings and subtle ramifications of a sacred artery, a spiritual aorta, connecting the heart of Christendom with its uttermost fibres, and filled with the blood of Christ. It would not be difficult to show that each century in turn has eaten of the flesh of the Son of Man and had his life, however latent, abiding in it. And in this our day, amid all the indifference and supineness, the skepticism and the scorn, the madness and the crime, which meet and appall us on every hand, it would not be difficult to discover unmistakable signs of deeper earnestness and truer devotion, of a more thorough penetration and occupation of this age by the spirit of Christ, than any past time has known."[53]

And Hedge saw the need of optimism. His contemporary, James Freeman Clarke, was the author of the five points long and widely accepted as a statement of Unitarian faith. They were:

I believe in the Fatherhood of God.
I believe in the Brotherhood of Man.
I believe in the leadership of Jesus.
I believe in salvation by character.
I believe in the progress of mankind onward and upward forever.

This last point, if I may digress for a moment, has been seized upon in this cynical age and been ridiculed to death. Admittedly the record of these latest generations can show that they have carried a burden of disillusionment in man, not to say of despair of him. But it is my conviction that unless a person believes he can progress, he is unlikely to do so; and unless he is convinced he can climb to a higher place, he will remain in his present valley, or crevasse. One may recall Dr. Clarke's particular belief in an ascent after death "to a higher state — of life and love to the loving, or judgment by the sight of truth to the selfish; but *higher* to all."[54] This thought may well be reflected in the last of the five assertions: "I believe in the progress of mankind onward and upward forever." Man's progress will not end with the death of the earthly body.

Whether Hedge influenced Clarke or Clarke influenced Hedge, and both of these alternatives are possible, or whether the idea occurred to each independently, one sees the same hope expressed by Hedge, when he says, "The only philosophy of history which satisfies mind and heart is optimism, — the belief that all things tend to good and produce good in the final result . . . . Christian history, especially, is studied to little purpose unless we learn from it the Christian lessons of patience and hope. It reveals not only an unlooked-for power of self-recovery in man through the agency of the Holy Spirit, and shows how impossible it is for God to withdraw or man to drive that Spirit from the world . . . but it also discloses to careful observation a steady progression in good hitherto, which points to a future better than this present and better than all the past, — a height and breadth of social development, a spiritual maturity of human kind, which secular philosophy concurs with divine revelation in predicting, and to which both have assigned the august title, 'City of God.' "[55]

Here we come to the end of really active and thorough pursuit of the subject of Jesus Christ in American Unitarianism. This is not to say that the life of Jesus is over at this point in Unitarianism, but merely that its expressions from here on are involved with Jesus Christ in one or another more limited context, ranging from loyalty to his name to emphasis upon his spirit as an influence in one's life. We have not yet come to the time of his virtual dismissal from many Unitarian churches. We shall reach that point after our review of the latter nineteenth and early twentieth centuries. It may be observed, incidentally, that the political, economic, industrial, and social history in the making, beginning with the Civil War and extending through World War I, is roughly paralleled or reflected, so far as its earthiness and its crudities are concerned, in the diminishing involvement of an ever increasing number of individuals with the person of Christ and the presence of the Holy Spirit.

Chapter 5

Henry Whitney Bellows, Preacher of Jesus Christ; Francis Greenwood Peabody's Humane Jesus

Let us turn now to an individual who was mighty in organizational work, able in the ministry, a late contemporary of Clarke and Hedge, and, in a sense, a harbinger of the modified role which was to be assigned Jesus by many Unitarians. This was not a deliberate, studied development, I would suggest, but, rather, the result of preoccupation with other concerns, concerns which, obviously, seemed of more importance than the rescue of Jesus Christ from the trammels and trappings of orthodoxy. The individual here referred to is Henry Whitney Bellows.

It is surprising to note that the most available references to Henry W. Bellows speak of his organizing activities, his apparent but not paraded conservatism in Christology, and his conciliatory inclination in dealing with the advocates of varying theological points of view. A reading of Bellows' sermons, however, quickly reveals a preacher of the old school, who bears down hard in making his point and overwhelming his listener with an express train of examples and similies, which follow one after another in rapid succession.

As should be expected, one finds in Bellows' writings the preacher's illuminated presentation of Christian doctrine, as opposed to the theologian's systematic presentation. Jesus Christ is central in his thinking, but it is not the miracle-performing Christ of Channing, nor is it the Jesus among-other-religious figures of Emerson and Theodore Parker. Rather, Bellows' Jesus Christ is a model and figure to emulate, whose efficacy does not reside in him by mandate, but in the disciple by practice.

Bellows asserts that God "planted Christianity in the moral world, just as he planted wheat in the natural, to grow with or against the consent of man; to be a great and unspeakable blessing to those accepting it."[1] "It sprang up a living fountain, by the Word of God, out of the heart of Christ .... The man who could say it was a matter of absolute indifference to him whether Christ were an impostor or a prophet, whether the Gospel were true or false, would be a man not to be believed, or, at any rate, not to be trusted with such an inquiry."[2]

Bellows combined practicality, idealism, and humanitarianism in his living and working. During the Civil War, to meet the personal needs of the Union's soldiers and members of their families, he organized the Sanitary Commission, something of a forerunner to the present American Red Cross, and thereby gained nation-wide repute. In 1865 he organized the National Conference of Unitarian Churches, to give life and movement to the administrative core which had been established in 1825. Each church would be represented in an annual meeting by three delegates. Such a means of communication would be helpful in working out the differences and relieving the serious tensions which existed between the conservatives and the "radicals." Professor Conrad Wright sums up their differences: "The more conservative wing was insistent that Christianity was of divine origin and sanction and that Jesus Christ, though not a person of the Trinity, was divinely authorized to proclaim the way of salvation to erring men. At the other extreme the 'radicals' — as they were coming to call themselves — were moving toward a wholly naturalistic interpretation of religion, which allowed no specially privileged place for Jesus. Emerson had referred to the tendency of historic Christianity to dwell 'with noxious exaggeration' on the person of Jesus. By way of reaction against traditional Christian piety quite as much as against orthodox Christian doctrine, some radicals had developed an extremely negative response to even the most liberal interpretation of the personality of Jesus. But to the extent that Unitarianism was becoming polarized this way, it was also becoming paralyzed, and support for the Unitarian Association was diminished."[3]

Bellows disliked extremes and preferred to be grouped with "Broad Church men," such as Clarke and Hedge, rather than to be considered either a conservative or a radical. In fact, he was a conservative in his personal views of Christ, but preferred not to appear to be at variance with those who took the radical position. In an 1865 letter to Edward Everett Hale, Bellows indicated his desire for " 'a creed that should show the continuity of the Christian consciousness . . . , & form the bridge *over*" for those seeking to leave orthodoxy. He decided, however, that members were not prepared for such and concluded, in his letter to Hale, "I think in place of a Christian symbol our people *are prepared for a practical statement* of our fundamental & distinctive ideas.' "[4] Although he was not disturbed by the Transcendentalist view that God is everywhere and all persons are capable of religious perception, he was convinced that the church was a necessary instrument to keep man's relation with God and Christ a steady and forceful influence.[5]

Bellows' church would not be exclusive, however. He expressed this view in an unintentionally macabre figure, when writing to James Freeman Clarke in 1865: "We want to describe a large eno' circle to take in all who really belong with us — and provided one, & the *fixed* leg of the compasses is in the heart of Jesus Christ I care very little how wide & far the other wanders."[6] An article published in the Christian Register for April 15, 1865 observed of Bellows' position, "He desired the sympathy and affection of both sides, but if he had to choose between the two he frankly avowed that he would go rather with Orthodoxy in any form in which it could be stated than with those who would put Jesus Christ into comparative contempt."[7]

Let us look at Bellows' own words as found in his colorful and oratorical sermons. He straightens out in careful exposition the confusion which has developed in persons' minds about what constitutes "the Word of God." The Word of God for Christ and the Apostles was not what is found written in the Bible, but rather *the mind and will and spirit* of God. It is not the words of God, but the thing to be done, not his command, but his wisdom. Bellows makes a curious, and a liberal, observation about the Christ of the orthodox Christian church: "The New Testament is the criticism and correction of the Old, and the life and character of Christ is the criticism and correction of what his disciples have said about him."[8]

Bellows declares there were evidences of messianic expectation in the classical writings of Greece and Rome, traceable to the influence of Jewish superstition; but he said "It is hardly necessary to look to supernatural prophecy, or even to the predictions of sensitive and prescient genius, for the origin of the hopes finally gratified in Christ's birth. Humanity contains in its very constitution a prediction of the Messiah."[9] Adam foreshadows the Lord from heaven. This view that man is essentially hopeful and basically optimistic, that deliverance to better times will ultimately be offered him, is highly appealing and speaks effectively to those overcome by the cynicism and disillusionment of today.

"Human nature is everywhere the same — a boundless, half-blind, half-seeing capacity, in pursuit of an ideal. It contains within itself a longing to rise above itself; an impatience of the material limits of its prison-house; a consciousness of powers which here have no adequate field; a sense of justice which is perpetually outraged by the actual condition of affairs; a love of consistency, of order, of beginning, middle and end, which is violated by this chaotic and defeated life of man." Christ's religion has emancipated the human heart "from its permanent alliance with the doomed flesh, from its short date of mortal life, and from its ignorance of its destiny."[10] If this is so, why was man kept waiting? The withholding of Christ, Bellows answers, "was the moral education of the world. Christ's *promise* did for the Israelites what Christ, *given*, has done for us."[11] "Christ's Gospel was welcomed in its newness of spirit and wonderful works, with astonishing rapidity. But in a few centuries it exhausted the latent longing, the secret expectation and desire which had slowly accumulated in the world."[12]

The people of the world who have known Christianity have tended to rely on some outside force from Christ to serve them, and therefore Christ's birth in a spiritual sense has been hindered. Christ has not yet wholly come, because he has been born only in the flesh, not in the spirit. In the heart of Christendom, it is yet as though Christ were hid 1800 years deep in the future. The condition of our seeing Christ is our strong desire for him and the manner of our living. Christ's efficacy has not been lost, however. Rather, how it is to be enjoyed has been misunderstood. "Christ born!" exclaims Bellows, "and the world neither glad or pious? Christ is not born then! The salvation of the world awaits his spiritual coming."[13]

Bellows' portrait of the Christian Christ as opposed to Christ immanent in the individual person is eloquent. "Now he is hid, not indeed in his mother's heart, but in the womb of superstition and worldly misconception; in the indifference and apathy of society. Is it Christ whom the Catholic world expects to-day, upon its tapestried altars, and in its purfumed temples? Is the bedizened doll, the sacred bambino, who in Rome walks in stately procession, with all the homage that silken robes and mitred bishops and the triple-crowned pope can bestow, the symbol of that Jesus, who is, or ought to be, the desire of all nations? Is it Christ whom the Protestant world expects to-day in its theological assemblies; the second person in the Trinity, God, the fulfill-ment of Mosaic prophecies, the antitype of Adam? Is it Christ whom the liberal school of thinkers expects to-day in its rational and intelligent congre-gations — the model man, the excellent example, the exalted Saviour? Alas! neither ecclesiastical mummeries nor theological formulas, nor sensible opin-ions, can bring Jesus Christ to the birth. He seeks some other Bethlehem than these to be born in. The pious Romanist, the conscientious Puritan, the pure but cold worshiper of reason, have each and all seen him in their private vigils, though he comes not to any class, and knows no sect or order. But he is born wherever love unfeigned is found; born into every heart that sincerely and tenderly suffers and labors for humanity; born in every peacemaker's spirits; born in every soul that rises above the power of selfishness and worldly greed, and uses its means and powers to promote the good of mankind; born where humility, gentleness, purity of body and soul, trust and submission, faith, hope and charity are seen to dwell."[14]

"What God wills," writes Bellows, "is, that our hearts and minds shall be conformed to Christ's; that is the salvation he offers and promises."[15] There are those who may object. "But we are such powerless agents in our own life! If our salvation depends upon our achieving the likeness of Christ, our cause is hopeless." Bellows' reply to this contention of weakness, characteristically full of imagery, runs for several printed pages. His own succinct summary is,

"There is nothing so remarkable about man as his improvableness."[16] He continues: "Shall not he, who improves everything else, improve himself? Shall not he, who out of rude logs can frame a graceful ship, or from rough stones erect a shapely temple; or from the coarse ore of the mine melt out the iron, the silver and the gold, which he forges, shapes and polishes into the art and beauty of the world; — shall he have no power to fashion himself as he will, to purge out his own dross, to hew away his own knots and splinters, to build up his own being? Shall man be the miner of the earth, and not explore his own soul; the subduer of the forest and sea, and not subjugate himself; the sculptor of adamant, and the liquefier of iron, and not the shaper of his own will; the architect of pyramid and cathedral, and not the designer and builder of his own character?"[17] One is reminded of that tenet of James Freeman Clarke's statement of faith, "We believe in salvation by character," when Bellows declares that God has not pledged himself "to make us holy and happy, like Christ and himself, whether we will or no, and by instrumentalities aside from our own exertions."[18]

If the reality of Christ and the efficacy of Christ depend upon our desire for him and our own emulation of him, what of the suffering Christ and the law of vicariousness? These last words are the title of one of Bellows' sermons. In it he first treats of Christ's physical sufferings as though they were a natural and expected concomitant of one who would serve others: "Christ's sufferings followed the law of all sufferings borne in the cause of humanity." "[His] immediate sufferings upon the cross, the agonies of his death, are not properly separable from his other afflictions. His life was one long martyrdom for humanity. He died daily. Every hour had its cross for him." We do "a thankless wrong" to Christ's other "perhaps more patient and costly afflictions," if we concentrate on the agony of the cross, but it is a natural reaction for us to do so. "It is because the cross was Christ's life-long posture; because his death was one with his life — always suffering, self-sacrificing, and devoted — always afflicted with wrong, violence, and persecution — that we are led to sum up all our memory of his sorrows in the last fatal agony of his death. But let us not superstitiously allow this natural and becoming sensibility to harden into dogma, until we end in attaching to the death of Christ a mysterious efficacy which did not belong to his life, and separate the anguish of his cross from the afflictions of his ministry. [Paul is quoted, Romans 5:10:] 'For if, when we were enemies, we were reconciled to God by the *death* of his Son, much more being reconciled, we shall be saved by his *life*.' " And Bellows adds: "[T]here can be no greater or more blinding heresy than that which would teach that Christ's sufferings, or any sufferings in behalf of virtue and human sins and sorrows, are strictly substitutional or literally vicarious."[19]

The truth is, literal substitution of moral penalties is a thing absolutely impossible! Vicarious punishment, in its technical and theological sense, is forbidden by the very laws of our nature and moral constitution!"[20] After all, the effectiveness of Christ's sufferings on our behalf is to be measured by the quality of a man's life. "The real substitution and vicariousness . . . which is honored and illustrated so splendidly by Christ's cross [is] the transmutation of the sufferings of sin into the sufferings of innocency; . . . the removal of guilt by the labors and sacrifices of goodness."[21]

"The real change which Christianity is gradually effecting," concludes Bellows, "[is not that it has] *diminished* the suffering in the world — but it has altered its expression, and is transmuting its character." "In this great substitutional and sacrificial work, of putting innocent suffering and self-sacrifice in the place of guilty suffering and *soul*-sacrifice — all the genuine followers of Christ are engaged, and are thus made partakers of his sufferings and death, and 'fill out what is behind of the afflictions of Christ.' "[22] "*Our* Calvary," says Bellows, "is the mountain on which our moral intelligence and gracious privileges have lifted us, in the midst of this spiritual wickedness and destitution!"[23]

In the paragraph which concludes his sermon on the Suffering Christ, Bellows presents a statement of the kernel of Christ's religious purpose, as seen in Parker's thought and expressed in the many and great acts of humanitarianism which characterized the Unitarians who were active in social reform in the 19th century, to their everlasting credit and the glory of God: "Welcome the sufferings of innocency, the sacrifice of love! Welcome a state of society, a world, all whose griefs shall be those of sympathy, all its wounds those of charity, all its afflictions those of submission! For the end of such a world must be the end of Christ's sufferings, a perfect redemption from moral evil, and a quick ascension into the perfect joy and undimmed glory of the city of God in heaven."[24]

What fate can we sophisticated people expect in our worldly world? We are endowed with the knowledge of good and evil; we are both tempted and inspired; and we have spirits of evil for enemies, as well as spirits of good for allies. What are the chances for our moral survival? God will never permit the powers of evil to equal the powers of good. And Bellows quotes Paul again: "For I am persuaded, that neither death, nor life, nor angels, nor principalities, nor powers, nor things present, nor things to come, nor height, nor depth, nor any other creature, shall be able to separate us from the love of God which is in Christ Jesus, our Lord." (Romans 8:38-39)

Christ was no mere prophet or wise man. To minimize him by setting him in an historical perspective is to ignore the fact that: "In Jesus Christ there broke into the world a mighty and shaping influence, a holy will, a spiritual sovereignty, an illuminating, warming, inspiring principle of mingled thought, affection, and volition, which was, among the other moral and spiritual influences at work upon the will of feeling and opinion, what the mighty gulf-stream is among the other currents of the ocean — changing the temperature of the most distant seas, ameliorating the climates of far-off boreal shores, and modifying the navigation and the commerce of the globe."[25] "Christ's influence, called the Church, has poured a pure and purifying stream into a polluted and polluting channel, and it has not been easy to distinguish between the feculence of the channel and the filth of the stream, except by observing that wherever Christianity has poured, it has, sooner or later, made civilization, however turbid at the start, run clear in the end." Is there some help here for us in our time? Bellows anticipates our question: "My brethren, amid the evil principalities and powers that are still influencing the world and above them all — amid the good principalities and powers that are helping us on, and above them all — is the head of all principality and power, Christ and Christianity, a principality and power, the immeasureable significant and value of which cannot be exaggerated, and which it becomes us most gratefully and humbly to adore and glorify."[26]

There were radical thinkers in those times, too, even as now, and persons who advocated the new departure, or rather I should say here, the complete departure and separation from the past, the break with what is old and the embracing of what seemed to be new. Bellows said of this inclination, "[I]f there be one folly greater than another, it is in our day, the attempt to pronounce the Gospel outworn; Christ a mere name among other great names; Christianity a superstition, and the Church a prison for the intellect, and a strait-jacket for the world."[27]

Bellows had a ready answer for those who feel no need for a church with its God and its Christ. "Those who deny the Church its place, because they see so fine a place of worship in outward nature, have yet to learn that the love and the worship of nature is itself the fruit of that sensibility which Christianity has communicated."[28] " 'Beware, lest any man spoil you through philosophy and vain deceit, after the tradition of men, after the rudiments of the world, and not after Christ. For in him dwelleth all the fullness of the God-head, bodily.' "[29] (Colossians 2:8, 9)

Bellows' remarkable apostrophe to Jesus Christ is quoted here in part. " 'Whom do men say that I am?' We reply, the Church Universal, all Christendom, unite in saying that you are the all-sufficient Saviour; the light of the moral world; the pattern of all graces and perfections; the only perfect humanity the race has seen. They say truly that about you have crystalized the affections of all the purest saints and the reverence of all the devoutest hearts. They say that you are nearest to God, and that you stand, and will stand, the blessed mediator between your brethren and your Father and theirs. They say that your words remain true in all ages, and that your example never grows antiquated or needless.

―――――――――――――――

"And *we* say, that, doubting and denying the titles and deific ascriptions that the Church still offers you, *we* say that you are to us inexpressibly dear and venerable; that we will yield to none in the affectionate homage we pay you in our hearts and homes and churches;

"You have taught us two inexpressibly glorious things, and taught them by illustrating them in your life, — the *humanity* of God, the *divinity* of man."[30]

We move on now from Bellows, with the observation that the subtle tendencies and influences which can be detected in the thoughts and words of these extraordinary liberal Christian thinkers of the mid-19th century had a long and widely expanding effect upon the Christology of Unitarianism for many years afterward. Indeed, their influence has been unending because, though many persons have moved farther away from Jesus Christ, none has gone quite so far back behind these men as the position of Channing and yet remained in the camp of the liberals. Reversions to orthodoxy, indeed, to extreme orthodoxy, there have been; but they are scarce and isolated instances. And it may be fairly said that such reversions, while serving the needs of the individuals involved, have brought to bear a significant influence, even though not intended or hoped for, upon both the continuing body of orthodox Christianity in America and upon such liberals as the Unitarians. Travelers between the two worlds have introduced their souvenirs.

As the Unitarian movement grew, so did contention. Orthodox opposition could be disregarded in the face of internal differences. They were inevitable. When a liberal approach to any given subject is espoused, unforeseen freedoms will be taken, until the original position may be lost sight of, and a new characteristic developed. We have seen the relaxing of the stand of the Christo-centric Unitarians, in the desire that varying points of view might be happily accommodated. It was but the beginning. The Western Conference, which had declared a broader religious stand from the beginning, became the center of a new kind of undogmatic, universal religion of brotherly love and good works, although there were similar influences in the East as well. It should be made clear that it was not that most of the very liberal Unitarians had any intention of leaving their own positions in camp with God and Christ, so to speak, but that they wanted those who differed with them in religious beliefs to feel at home and to remain a part of the company, that all might work together for the achievement of the good life, the moral life, the Kingdom of God on earth, by whatever name it might be called.

In 1867 those who wanted to be free of the restrictions implied by being called Christian formed the Free Religious Association. Francis Ellingwood Abbot, its chief organizer, compiled "Fifty Affirmations" of Free Religion. Jesus Christ was mentioned in the following ways: "The completion of the religious protests against authority must be the extinction of faith in the Christian Confession" [i.e., the belief that Jesus was the Messiah]. "The corner-stone of Christianity is faith in the Christ. The corner-stone of Free

Religion is faith in Human Nature." "The great institution of Christianity is the Christian Church, the will of Christ being its supreme law. The great institution of Free Religion is the coming Republic of the World, the universal conscience and reason of mankind being its supreme organic law or constitution." "The fellowship of Christianity is limited by the Christian Confession; its brotherhood includes all subjects of the Christ and excludes all others. The fellowship of Free Religion is universal and free; it proclaims the great brotherhood of man without limit or bound."

"The practical work of Christianity is to Christianize the world, — to convert all souls to Christ, and insure their salvation from the wrath of God. The practical work of Free Religion is to humanize the world, — to make the individual nobler here and now, and to convert the human race into a vast Co-operative Union devoted to universal ends." "The spiritual ideal of Christianity is the suppression of self and the perfect imitation of Jesus the Christ. The spiritual ideal of Free Religion is the free development of self, and the harmonious education of all its powers to the highest possible degree."

"The essential spirit of Christianity is that of self-humiliation at the feet of Jesus, and passionate devotion to his person. The essential spirit of Free Religion is that of self-respect and free self-devotion to great ideas. Christianity is prostrate on its face; Free Religion is erect on its feet."

"The noblest fruit of Christianity is a self-sacrificing love of man for Jesus' sake. — The noblest fruit of Free Religion is a self-sacrificing love of man for man's own sake."

"Christianity is the faith of the soul's childhood; Free Religion is the faith of the soul's manhood. In the gradual growth of mankind out of Christianity into Free Religion, lies the only hope of the spiritual perfection of the individual and the spiritual unity of the race."[31]

Of a very different point of view were a conservative element within the denomination who, in 1870, considered creating an Evangelical Unitarian Association, with its own creed. The National Conference in the fall of that year endeavored to meet those so inclined at least part way, by adopting a statement of position which read in part: "Re-affirming our allegiance to the Gospel of Jesus Christ, . . . we invite to our fellowship all who wish to be followers of Christ."[32]

On the national level, the liberal spirit (meaning here, a willingness to accede to the wishes of those who eschewed the limitations of Christian terminology) began more noticeably to prevail, and in 1882, the National Conference issued this statement: "The Preamble and Articles of our Constitution . . . are no authoritative test of Unitarianism, and are not intended to exclude from our fellowship any who, while differing from us in belief, are in general sympathy with our purposes and practical aims."[33]

The un-Christian, universal religion emphasis persisted, until in the early 1880's, it had become a trying subject in the Western Conference. In 1886,

Jabez T. Sunderland made a strong stand against further diminution of the Christian character of Unitarianism in that sector. He opposed such positions as: "Unitarianism must stand for ethical beliefs and beliefs in certain so-called 'principles,' but not for belief in anything that will commit it to theism or Christianity." In contrast, he wrote: "We have always stood, and it is a very new and strange condition of things if we do not still stand, in a large way, in a fluent, elastic way, in an undogmatic and non-creedal way, . . . for the great, simple, primal, self-evidencing faiths of religion — God, worship, the immortal life, the supremacy of character, the spiritual leadership of Jesus."[34]

In the same year, the National Conference, meeting in Cincinnati, revealed a conciliatory attitude and recognized that the differences lay partly in the "question whether the Conference should insist first upon the beliefs it stood for, or upon the work it aimed to do; and whether it was willing to shut out any one from joining in that work simply because he did not profess certain beliefs."[35] In an attempt to reconcile the different factions in the Western Conference, William Channing Gannett introduced a statement of "Things Commonly Believed Among Us." He said, for example, "Whoever loves Truth and lives the Good is, in a broad sense, of our religious fellowship." He continued, "The general faith is hinted well in words which several of our churches have adopted for their covenant: 'In the freedom of the Truth and in the spirit of Jesus Christ, we unite for the worship of God and the service of man.' " He included such other statements as these: "We believe that to love the Good and to live the Good is the supreme thing in religion." and "We revere Jesus, and all holy souls that have taught men truth and righteousness and love, as prophets of religion."[36] A reconciliation in the Western Conference was achieved by 1894, but one can readily see that the price of such a reconciliation was a steady diminution of the role of Jesus Christ in religion and the steady trend toward reference to "all holy souls" and to the lights of the individual. The type of statement found generally acceptable was one in which belief in striving for goodness was the principal tenet, without a key role reserved for Jesus Christ.

The end of the tendency to become more inclusive and less specific in terms of God and Christ was arrived at in the creation of a statement called a "Humanist Manifesto," in 1933. Presumably this tendency in liberal religion to widen its inclusiveness reflected a much broader development in American culture. Whereas in Channing's time, religious thought, like political thought, worked from existing known bases and premises, the latter 19th century saw the beginning of an era when government and universities undertook to get beneath superficial appearances to basic truths and inherent causes. This mood of questioning and searching extended to individuals, as well, who by now could enjoy the facilities of public libraries. In addition, the concern for slaves grew steadily to concern for human welfare in society in general. It may easily be forgotten today that appalling conditions of hardship, destitution, and mistreatment existed for millions of persons, whites as well as negroes, in these new United States. The abolition of slavery had demonstrated that socially corrective action could be taken: bad conditions need not be resignedly accepted forever. If research revealed deeper levels of truth than what one could see on the surface, then existing institutions and concepts could be challenged, perhaps even abolished. Darwin startled the world with his theory of evolution (a theory not subscribed, surprisingly, by some Boston liberals); while socially concerned writers like Thorstein Veblen daringly threw suspicion on financiers and capitalists, as though they were not above attack, let alone reproach.

So it was in religion. The many faults of the social order had grown in a new country which was ostensibly "under God," in fact, nominally, under a Christian God. Perhaps there was a better religion, a religion born in the hearts of sincere and earnest persons, free of the creeds and bounds of the Christian religion. Whether those who chose to say, "I will retain Jesus Christ in my religious thinking, but I do not want that fact to exclude you from religious fellowship with me, if you differ from me," were right or wrong in the long run, it is easy to see how those who differed happened to do so, and how those who opened the doors of the church to these differing souls, may well have done so, partly because they desired to be at one with the others, but partly, too, because they were not sure that all religious truth was on their side. Had not faults in Christian institutions revealed themselves?

The open-door policy was not as effective as it was hoped that it would be, because there was confusion as to basic factors. The important point, in the light of hindsight, was not after all, a brotherhood of all who were motivated to rectify the evils which afflicted others. I say this because a primary concern for the common welfare and societal values — factors involving "others", was not matched, in this era, with an equivalent concern for the spiritual welfare and values of the socially conscious individual himself. Care for the material, physical welfare of others could be pre-eminent at the same moment that the spiritual, value-conscious welfare of the very individual concerned about others was neglected, or even deliberately put out of mind. It was in this atmosphere that persons whose principles were questionable could justify themselves with the good works of benefactions bestowed upon "worthy causes" and "needy cases." A concern for social improvements was regarded as a desirable common ground in liberal religious thinking. Thus, we see a great emphasis upon the good samaritan kind of behavior, as represented in statements coming out of the Unitarian groups such as the American Unitarian Association National Conference resolution of 1875, "[We welcome] all . . . who desire to work . . . in advancing the Kingdom of God"[37] and the statement quoted above, "We believe that to love the Good and to live the Good is the supreme thing in religion."[38] But it would appear in our world today that humanitarian concerns are not an adequate motivation and guide in themselves after all. Indeed, institutions and devices to implement our good intentions and lofty social welfare motivations, though sound in principle, have gone awry in many instances, to varying degrees, as witnessed in some labor union activities and public welfare transgressions. We shall return to the subject of the need for personal religious concern in our last lecture. In the meantime, there were those who maintained their loyalty to Jesus Christ and Christian concepts. Let us see how the thinking was going along these lines.

In 1904, Professor Francis Greenwood Peabody of Harvard delivered the Lyman Beecher Lectures at Yale University. The over-all title was *Jesus Christ and the Christian Character*. Eight subjects were covered, which appeared as eight chapters in the printed lectures.[39] These were: "The Modern World and the Christian Character," "The Character of Jesus Christ," "The Roots of the Christian Character," "The Growth of the Christian Character," "The Personal Consequences of the Christian Character," "The Social Consequences of the Christian Character," "The Ascent of Ethics," and "The Descent of Faith."

What Professor Peabody believed about Jesus Christ is expressed throughout these chapters. Although he was not a parish minister, many of his students became the ministers of Unitarian churches, and his influence on the characterization and casting of Jesus Christ among Unitarians must have been very extensive. He himself was the product of Boston Unitarian culture, and it is reasonable to believe that his thoughts on Jesus which influenced others also reflected, to some extent, the thoughts on Jesus maintained in his native environment.

The initial impression Jesus created was not by his teaching but by his demeanor and personality as a teacher. " 'He taught as one having authority,' is the first comment of the narrator," says Peabody. "There was a calmness and mastery, a force and restraint, an originality and reverence, which dominated the scenes. . . . To a soldier he seemed like a commander who was born to be obeyed; to many a hearer he had but to say, 'Follow me,' and busy men left all and followed; to minds possessed by devils he had but to speak and they grew self-controlled and calm; to those who would seize him at the last his very presence seemed to strike a blow, so that, as the fourth Gospel says, 'They went backward, and fell to the ground.' [John 18:6] Little children, on the other hand, came when he called, and nestled in his arms; women followed him and ministered unto him gladly. Command and sympathy, power and charm, must have been singularly blended in a person who drew to himself these varied types of loyalty. Authority and affection, playfulness and gravity, the light of love and the shadow of rebuke, must have touched in quick succession the face of Jesus. He smiles at the sport of children; he perceives with sympathetic imagination the symbolism of the woman's costly gift; he stands before the representative of Caesar and asserts himself a king; and all these moods, childlike, poetic, kingly, are genuine and consistent expressions of his many-sided character."[40]

At this remove in time, one is tempted to poke a little gentle but irreverent fun at Peabody's delineations of Jesus' person and personality: Jesus was the wholly acceptable person, who lived and thought just as proper Bostonians are supposed to live and think. In the terminology of William James' *The Varieties of Religious Experience*, Peabody writes: "[Jesus] is no example of the 'twice-born' conception of piety, which has been of late presented to us with such vigor and charm. His 'Religion of Healthy-mindedness' is not a psychopathic emotionalism, but a normal, rational, ethical growth. His method is not that of ecstasy, vision, nervous agitation, issuing in neurological saintliness; it is educative, sane, consistent with wise service of the world, capable of being likened in an infinite variety of ways to the decisions and obligations which every honest man must meet."[41] Yes, Jesus would have fitted very well into the community on Beacon Hill.

At the same time, for all the varying enthusiasm developed by Unitarian ministers for Jesus Christ during the preceding century, none of them ever showed in any comparable degree, the intimate, detailed familiarity with the Gospel accounts of Jesus and his teachings, with which to support their enthusiasm. Peabody's Jesus may be desirably cool and calculating, but Peabody shows with admirable specificity how Jesus' example and teachings fitted the early 20th Century scene. Indeed, any attribute of Jesus which Peabody chooses to mention is documented with chapter and verse references.

Peabody's admiration has many bases. Aside from his charming manner and forceful personality, Jesus' mind was incomparably suited to his role. He was not an untutored peasant, as many have assumed. He may not have attended Rabinical schools, but it is evident he knew well whereof he spoke. Jesus was brilliant in using against his enemies their own weapons of dialectic. Yet he was a seer, not a critic. He possessed the eye and sensitivity of a poet, as witnessed in his references to nature, although he was not a naturalist. He employed irony and a lightness of touch verging on humor, when engaged in controversy. "His enemies attack him with bludgeons, and he defends himself with a rapier," says Peabody.[42] He was not a "recluse or peasant or passive saint."[43]

In giving of himself to others, Jesus yet reserved "a sphere of isolation and reserve" for himself. Note this example of Peabody's analysis of Jesus. "The reserve of Jesus is the background and the support of his sympathy. The throng that presses about him seems to drain his strength, and he seeks the solitude of the hills or of the lake to recover poise and peace. Here is the meaning of those passive virtues which appear to give the note of asceticism to the Gospels. Meekness, patience, forbearance, silence, — these are not the

Henry Whitney Bellows

Francis Greenwood Peabody

signs of mere self-mortification, they are the signs of power in reserve. They are the marks of one who can afford to wait, who expects to suffer, who need not contend; and all this, not because he is simply meek and lowly, but because he is also strong and calm."[44] "It was in this detachment of nature, this isolation of the inner life, that Jesus found his communion with the life of God. At this point his ethics melt into his religion."[45]

Jesus' character and characteristics are but the jumping-off place for Peabody, however. His principle concern is the application of Jesus' teachings and influence, particularly his ethics, to the contemporary scene, both in terms of the individual and of society. "The social teaching of Jesus was the corollary from his religious faith," writes Peabody, "a by-product of his religious mission."[46] Jesus was not a social agitator and reformer, but a teacher and Revealer.

"Practical morality, the conduct of life, the traits of the Christian character, have seemed too elementary and obvious subjects of inquiry to command the attention of scholars," says Peabody. "What they have sought is a background for morality, a metaphysics of religion, the satisfaction of the thirst of the mind for the living God. To define the place of Jesus in God's plan for humanity, and the place of humanity in God's plan for eternity, has been the absorbing passion of the theological habit of mind. From this habit of mind has issued what may be called a dramatic rather than an ethical conception of the Christian religion."[47]

The practical morality of Jesus and the ethics of the New Testament deserve our consideration. Peabody was prescient in speculating that the faith of the future may grow out of the application of Christian ethics in social service. When we speak of ethics, however, we tend to think in terms of codes of rules. Peabody warns that a loving spirit, not these, was Jesus' concern. It is not a question of memorizing aphorisms of Jesus, but of discerning the underlying principles on which his mind operates.

If there is one characteristic of our contemporary thinking which has been dominant and obvious, it is the by-passing of unpleasant facts for the immediate realization of ideals. Many of our well-intentioned citizens have ignored as individual personalities the very people they would help, or have written them off as undesirable. But there they are, nonetheless, in the flesh, and despised of the Pharisees. There are three great words in Jesus' teaching which together express the moral ideal of the Christian character for Peabody: Righteousness, Love, Life. "The words seemed to represent distinct moral types," says Peabody. "One suggests a character which is upright but severe; another a character which is gentle but soft; the third a character which is large but vague; . . . each in turn contributes to the growth and is essential to the completeness of the Christian character."[48] One cannot read Peabody's chapters in which he discusses Christianity with respect to its potential for the society of the early 1900's, without recognizing characteristics which seem to hold a remarkable resemblance to the early 1970's. A significantly illustrative passage is quoted in Appendix E of this chapter, on page 97.

What is the total effect of Jesus' influence upon the person? Peabody finds it to be represented by Poise, Simplicity, and Peace. The person who has Poise is balanced, sound, and neither excited nor temporizing. One characterized by Simplicity shows a singleness of mind, not divided aims. And the man of Peace is free from inward conflict. Together these attributes add up to Grace. Surely today's world can use persons who have thus benefited from Jesus' influence! The final consequence of the Christian character is a person perfectly balanced in all respects, but not too much so, for "Precisely the reverse of [admirable but unlovable] saintliness is the type which reproduces the character of Jesus," says Peabody. The proper Christian is gracious, considerate, patient with defects, and capable of discovering the excellent in uninteresting lives. Persons in this category "have received the final benediction of the Christian character, the grace of the Lord Jesus Christ."[49]

In his chapter, The Social Consequences of the Christian Character, Peabody points out with his usual keen discernment, that Jesus' attention was to the individual person, but his purpose involved the world. He notes three social principles from Jesus' teachings. Each is a worthwhile end matched with an inherent fault or weakness. These paradoxical social principles are:

Sacrifice: Self-realization through self-surrender.[50]

Service: Who would be great, let him be the servant.[51]

Idealism: Idealism may be visionary, but its opposite, realism, "instead of offering a satisfying creed, often presents a pathetically meager and colorless picture of life."[52]

"The social paradoxes of Jesus are not propositions of the Christian reason; they are consequences of the Christian character."[53]

Along this line, when Jesus said he came not to destroy the Law, but to fulfill it, his thought was not in terms of specific laws as they existed, but of law in its ideal expression. "The reason one is sure that to lose life is to find it, and that to serve is to command, is because he is antecedently sure that the world is not what it seems to be, — a world of material gains and glory; but that the real is the ideal, and that the unseen things are eternal. Here is the explanation of the curious mingling of conservatism and radicalism in the teaching of Jesus which has perplexed many an observer."[54]

We cannot stop with the ethical teachings of Jesus, says Peabody. There is something more represented, something beyond: "Jesus . . . is fundamentally not a teacher of morals, but a witness of religion. The supreme motive of his conduct is his relation to the Father."[55] Ethics is but a sign-post on the way to religion. To change the figure of speech, "[Jesus'] ethics speak, not of stones to be moved, but of seeds to be planted."[56]

The practice of virtue should be seen as the emergence of idealism, as "the translation of duty-doing into faith." "The Christian life trudges through the valleys," says Peabody, "but its face is set to the hills."[57] "This, if there be any way to a revival of religion, is the way now open; — not by the assent to opinions, but by the asent of ethics."[58]

The practice of good, then, is an upward progress, which ends in religious faith. Peabody continues this theme in his final chapter by completing the parabola. He says, "[T]he straight path of Christian discipleship, leads from duty-doing to faith . . . from the plain of ethics to the heights of religion."[59] Again, he describes this evolvement concept, which obviously has much attraction for him: "A slow ascent of duty to the horizon of God, a quick glance, a long breath, a far-away look, and then the descent of faith to the plains of human need — such is the picture of the life of Jesus."[60]

Peabody introduces the element of moral obligation. "The whole duty of man," he says, "is not to enjoy God forever, but to descend with the grace of God to the help of man."[61] He uses the image of angels ascending and descending on Jacob's Ladder to heaven and declares, "Ethics fulfils itself in its ascent [to religious faith]; religion is perfected in its descent [to good works]; and life keeps time to this rhythmic movement, from tasks to visions, and from visions back to tasks."[62]

Surely no one can fail to recognize the central place of Jesus in Peabody's ethical and religious thinking. He may have created his own Christ and have systematized Jesus' life, teachings, and influence, in keeping with his own pre-conceived notions, but two appreciative observations may be made. First, he has provided us with detailed documentation from the Gospels in support of a humanitarian Christ; and second, he has provided extraordinarily helpful guidelines for anyone who would expose himself to Jesus' influence and avail himself of Jesus' practical leadership, to the present age.

There is one question we may raise, and that is whether this intellectualization of Jesus' usefulness for us provides an implementing force of motivation. Peabody expects that to come from the inspiration we gain on the heights, which we have reached by way of ethical works. I suggest, however, that he may have missed an important assist in this desirable development, in leaving out the idea of personal devotion to Jesus, a religious enthusiasm centered in the Christ. But, of course, this sort of relationship with Jesus Christ would not be in keeping with Peabody's preference for freedom from emotional involvement and for the maintenance of a decent restraint, measured by the intellect and the guidelines of his own social milieu.

We must say, nevertheless, that Jesus would be very much alive in American Unitarianism if he occupied the place Peabody gives him in the scheme of social and personal life. Not all Unitarians in America were so minded, however. The element among them which espoused liberalism in religion to the extent that it not only omitted Christianity from its religious references but also thoroughly removed doctrinal boundary lines, until there was no identity, either Christian or any other, remaining, persisted in their influence. Perhaps the events surrounding and following World War I induced disillusionment to so great a degree that a renunciation of Jesus Christ and his religion seemed reasonable and justifiable to many persons.

Not all idealism was dead, however, for it would be presumptuous to say that social idealism can spring only from a Christian environment. Besides, the un-Christian stance of a too liberal Unitarian did not characterize the country as a whole. A vigorous and hefty idealism was demonstrated by an earnest Presbyterian Christian named Woodrow Wilson, for example. He was striving to help nations of peoples to live together peaceably. And one can say that, in America, such attempted reforms for the good of society as the implementation of the Volstead Act, showed a commendable, though vain, aspiration on the part of a segment of the people and of their lawmakers.

In both of these instances, however, the ultimate breakdown came from the foibles and moral weaknesses of individual persons — the persons who made up the whole body of citizenry, which included the generally law-abiding members of society, as well as the law-makers and the law-breakers. Peabody says, "Social morality is a corollary of personal morality,"[63] and the strength of personal morality does not come from law but from a spiritual revival. Jesus Christ provides both the inspiration and the norm for such a revival, but his services were widely ignored, if not rejected, then as now.

It would be my conclusion, therefore, that World War I and the domestic moral confusion which led to the War, and the ugliness of its aftermath, should not be considered an excuse for abandoning Christ, but, to the contrary, the reason for reaching out for him and drawing closer to him.

Appendix A

"It [the Word of God] wants a warm strong soil for a vigorous and aspiring seed; and until we learn to read the Bible and study religion, in the great exercise of all our powers, in the fullest light of all our experience, in the most rigorous application of common sense, God's Word, and God's truth, and Christ's cause will be in the eclipse they now suffer — will be not the light, and help, and glory of the strong, the resolute, the thoughtful, and the free, but the refuge of the superstitious and ignorant; the policy of the prudent, the machinery of a priesthood; the useless and decaying heirlooms of a venerable past; the source of convenient prejudices for governing the weak-hearted and the feeble-minded. The seed is the Word of God."[64]

Appendix B

"Doubtless, as you look about you and see in men the unpromising materials from which God seeks to make these likenesses of Christ — you tremble with doubts of his success! Perhaps you feel in yourselves the hardness and reluctance of the substance that he would fashion after the holy and lovely model of Jesus Christ. But surely we have seen the most rude and ungracious, the most awkward and unpromising children, trained into accomplished, gentle and noble men and women. What fruits of discipline, study, self-denial, patience, perseverance, have not fallen under our notice, in our general observations of society? There is nothing so remarkable about man as his improvableness. Shall not he, who improves everything else, improve himself? Shall not he, who out of rude logs can frame a graceful ship, or from rough stones erect a shapely temple; or from the coarse ore of the mine melt out the iron, the silver and the gold, which he forges, shapes and polishes into the art and beauty of the world; — shall he have no power to fashion himself as he will, to purge out his own dross, to hew away his own knots and splinters, to build up his own being? Shall man be the miner of the earth, and not explore his own soul; the subduer of the forest and sea, and not subjugate himself; the sculptor of adamant, and the liquefier of iron, and not the shaper of his own will; the architect of pyramid and cathedral, and not the designer and builder of his own character? We ought, my brethren, to gather faith from our observations of nature, commerce and art. Your own daily pursuits should teach you to believe in the possibilities of conforming yourself to any model you really love and reverence, and desire to resemble. Does distance or difficulty obstruct any genuine passion of your hearts? You will go round the world for the guano that warms your soil, the quicksilver that separates your gold, the spices that flavor your food, the seeds and gums that are your medicines. You bring your teas from China, your dye-woods from New Holland, your oil from the poles, your sugar from the equator. Distance and difficulty, deserts and depths, cannot deter nor defeat your designs. Nor can any unseemliness and roughness of Nature's products withstand the transforming power of your mills and crucibles, your furnaces and cisterns, your saws and hammers. You put the cumbrous yellow cane of Louisiana into the cauldron, and take out the glistening crystals of snow that sweeten your daily drink; you shear the shaggy sheep of the Green Mountains, and weave the delicate and various clothes you wear. You tap the trees of Para, and from their gums you fashion the defenses of your feet — the impenetrable garments that defy the storms of sea in winter; and presently you mimic the woods and the metals, and give the softest pliancy or toughest rigidity, as you will, to the curious substance you have gathered. What transformations do you not effect in the substances you choose to work in? Is there any quality you wish to communicate to any substance, that you despair of finally effecting it? Will you have wood that will not burn, or water that will; iron that will float, or electricity that will talk, do you not attain these wishes? And is it only humanity that does not reward zeal, and labor, and thought? Is it only the soul's qualities that cannot be enriched, improved and refined? Can you transform the metals and the gases, melt the ores and solidify the airs, handle the lightning and fix the sunbeams — and can you not transform yourselves into the image of Christ; transplant his graces into your souls; import from Palestine the fragrance of his virtues, exhume his ashes and enrich your sterile clay; reliquify his spilled and precious blood to re-animate your hearts, weave his precepts into the fabric of your souls; catch his spirit, and fix it in the substance of your lives? Cannot you, who reform and transform every thing else, be transformed in the spirit of your minds, and conform to the image of God's Son?

"Do not doubt your ability, my brethren. Nothing is so ductile, transformable, improvable, as the soul. The powers of Nature are dull scholars beside the powers of humanity. You can, if you will, do any thing, every thing, good and right, noble and glorious, with your nature and character. And, believe me, God will not let you do any thing else without solemn and painful remonstrance! You are quarreling with his predestination, his sacred will and purpose, in every hour's neglect, disobedience or delay."[65]

Appendix C

" 'Whom do men say that I am?' We reply, the Church Universal, all Christendom, unite in saying that you are the all-sufficient Saviour; the light of the moral world; the pattern of all graces and perfections; the only perfect humanity the race has seen. They say truly that about you have crystalized the affections of all the purest saints and the reverence of all the devoutest hearts. They say that you are nearest to God, and that you stand, and will stand, the blessed mediator between your brethren and your Father and theirs. They say that your words remain true in all ages, and that your example never grows antiquated or needless. They say that in your life and character and spirit God has revealed all that can be considered necessary or useful for men to know concerning his moral purposes and spiritual affections. They say that your insight into your Father's will verifies itself by all that trust it; that your guidance never misleads a faithful follower; and that ages on ages only add to its significance and value. They say that every superstition and old theory which sought to make you great according to mere human standards, when it falls away, only discloses higher claims, until your authority is independent of doubtful testimony and of supports that are adventitious or questionable, and stands, in its own self-evident weight and worth, more immovable than the mountains.

"And *we* say that, doubting and denying the titles and deific ascriptions that the Church still offers you, *we* say that you are to us inexpressibly dear and venerable; that we will yield to none in the affectionate homage we pay you in our hearts and homes and churches; that the songs of angels did not and could not exaggerate the importance and blessedness of your advent, or overstate the claim you have established in nearly nineteen centuries, during which your religion has been the chief light and consolation and guidance of humanity. You have taught us two inexpressibly glorious things, and taught them by illustrating them in your life, — the *humanity* of God, the *divinity* of man. You have authorized us to see in what was a dim, distant, dreadful, unapproachable Being, called God, a Father whose greatness and power do not render him inhuman, do not make him incapable of caring for and listening to, of pitying, pardoning, loving, and saving, his children on the earth. You have proclaimed the humanity of God and banished the dreadful feeling that God was too great, too distant, too mysterious to be known, approached, loved, and trusted. This alone made a religion of love and mercy possible among men; this alone has made God intelligible as the loving Friend and Father of his lowly but his veritable human off-spring. And you have made man conscious of his divinity by revealing in your spirit and human life, and on the earth and among its temptations and sufferings, a faith, capacity, and holiness, a singleness and a superiority to all evil and all trials, that has not only glorified you, but us. In calling us to follow and resemble you, you have owned our divine capacity, you have brought God down to man, you have lifted man up to God. You are thus the Mediator indeed, — the true Messiah, the son of man and son of God! And we hail your name and influence with inexpressible joy, and with songs of triumph and gratitude, throughout the Church and the Christian world!"[66]

Appendix D

"Practical morality, the conduct of life, the traits of the Christian character, have seemed too elementary and obvious subjects of inquiry to command the attention of scholars. What they have sought is a background for morality, a metaphysics of religion, the satisfaction of the thirst of the mind for the living God. To define the place of Jesus in God's plan for humanity, and the place of humanity in God's plan for eternity, has been the absorbing passion of the theological habit of mind. From this habit of mind has issued what may be called a dramatic rather than an ethical conception of the Christian religion. A vast world-drama appears to unfold its plan, from the first act of creation to the climax of redemption, and when the spectator of this scheme of universal love is called to consider the details of personal character, it may well seem a trifling, if not a sacrilegious interruption. It is that sense of deprivation and regret which the disciples felt when they were bidden to go down from the mount of transfiguration; a descent to the valley of commonplace, when one has seen the vision on the heights. The theology of the New Testament invites us to the large horizon of God; the ethics of the New Testament calls us down to the common people and the demoniac boy."[67]

Appendix E

"Here is the final consequence of the Christian character. Much goodness, though it compels respect, repels affection. It is severe, restless, strained, uncomfortable. We admire, but we do not love. We wish there were more persons so excellent, but we do not wish them near to ourselves. Much which has been mistaken for the Christian character has had this repelling and exasperating quality. The saints have not been the pleasantest of neighbors. Precisely the reverse of such saintliness is the type which reproduces the character of Jesus. Beyond the poise, simplicity, and peace of these rare lives, there is the abiding sense of their charm. They are not incapable of severity, of indignation, of rebuke; but their characteristic quality is graciousness, considerateness, patience with defeats, insight for the excellent in uninteresting lives. They do not strive or cry for leadership; they go their way and speak their word, and men are drawn to them by the natural law of attraction, which draws small bodies to greater. The sheep hear their voice and follow. They do not drive, they draw. When one thinks of them, he recalls not so much their greatness as their grace. They have received the final benediction of the Christian character, the grace of the Lord Jesus Christ."[68]

Appendix F

"How shall one act who finds duty real, but faith, a receding vision? There is but one path to the rediscovery of faith, and it runs straight through the duty which is real. 'It is an awful moment,' said Frederick Robertson, 'when the soul begins to find that the props on which it has blindly rested so long are, many of them, rotten, and begins to suspect them all. . . . In that fearful loneliness of spirit . . . . I know but one way in which a man may come forth from his agony scatheless; it is by holding fast to those things which are certain still — the grand, simple landmarks of morality. . . . If there be no God and no future state, yet even then it is better to be generous than selfish, better to be chaste than licentious, better to be true than false, better to be brave than to be a coward. . . . Thrice blessed is he who — when all is drear and cheerless — has obstinately clung to moral good. Thrice blessed, because his nights shall pass into clear, bright day.' "[69]

Chapter 6

Two Twentieth Century Unitarian Teachers:
Francis A. Christie, Clayton R. Bowen

It is easily understandable that among institutions of learning Harvard should receive most of the attention in reviewing the history of unitarian thought in America: it was located at the center of activity and produced the leaders. In 1844, however, the Unitarians founded their own theological school in Meadville, Pennsylvania. From that time on the percentage of Unitarian ministers trained at Harvard declined, while the Meadville percentage steadily increased. By 1975, of the Unitarian Universalist ministers in fellowship, seventeen percent had received their first theological degree from Meadville and fifteen percent from Harvard.[1]

In 1927 the School was moved to Chicago, in the immediate environment of the University of Chicago, with varying degrees of affiliation with that University's Divinity School enjoyed over the ensuing years.

Two of the outstanding teachers at Meadville, both in the first half of the twentieth century, were Francis A. Christie and Clayton R. Bowen. Francis A. Christie was born in 1858 and died, in his eightieth year, on 3 August 1938. A graduate of Amherst College, in the class of 1881, he taught at Roxbury Latin School, Johns Hopkins University, Lawrenceville School, and Harvard Divinity School, before joining the Meadville faculty in 1893, where he remained for thirty-three years. He was a modest, sensitive, gentle soul, and his teaching reflected the highest caliber of scholarship. The late Reverend Dr. John Howland Lathrop has reported "[O]n one occasion when lecturing on John Calvin [Christie] closed his notebook when only half way through and stalked out of the room with a flush upon his face [declaring], 'the theology of an inhuman man.' "[2] This intrusion of his own opinions was not, however, a characteristic of Dr. Christie.

One may obtain an insight into Christie's thinking on the subject of Jesus Christ in his address to the 24th Meeting of the General Conference of

Unitarian and Other Christian Churches, delivered in Washington, D.C. in October, 1911. The title of his address was, "The Historical Element in Christianity as a Spiritual Religion." He said on that occasion, in part: "According to [Andrews] Norton we hold convictions about God and duty and immortality because these truths were uttered in the past by one or more persons whose supernatural miracles accredited them as divinely authorized to convey truth. We are rationally convinced by this historical demonstration." "The view of Norton is now thoroughly antiquated. In America, Parker and Ripley and Emerson emancipated us both from the argument and from its cold, bare intellectualism."

He said further: "Calvin spoke of God as unconditioned power, but we revert to the speech of Jesus knowing that only a Fatherhood of God can be a gospel for us, can be the character possessed of unconditioned power over moral persons. . . . We heed Christianity's affirmation of redemptive healing and invigoration in a communing with the Father since our response of spiritual experience reaffirms the truth. . . . We may not retain all the imagery of ancient Messianic hopes for earth and heaven; but we are responsive still to that which begat all Messianic hopes for earth and heaven."

"Our critical history shows us a man holding many beliefs of his place and time, which we have replaced by truer beliefs. But it shows us a man who became Jesus of Nazareth because he yielded his whole being to the faiths which are above all science of the world of sense, because he was wholly possessed by a sense of the illimitable beneficence of God, the illimitable duty of human love, the invincible, redemptive friendship of the holiness that condemns us, the absolute authority and certainty of that perfect life which is the vision of duty and the satisfaction of purest yearnings. We see a man who, without guarantee of miracle to protect him, to empower him, to give him bread, accepted all the responsibilities of such a faith, unfolded its meaning in simple and universal terms, accepted the peril of conflict with instituted teaching, interpreted the danger and the death and defeat as within the providence of God's good will, and communicated his own trust in victory over defeat and death, in exaltation to higher service for the will of God. Such a man obtained personal being in the faith which united him with God, the faith which can unite us spiritually with God. Such a man is man's spiritual experience writ large. He is a symbol, a sacramental power. In his presence or in his memory we find the means of grace, the provocation of our apprehension of the divine. . . . Still to-day we men discover that Jesus performs this office of a holy friend: he wakens the soul's response to the eternal and divine object of faith. He himself asked but one office from God. He came, he said, 'to minister.' So long as he continues to minister to many for their highest good, the great memory of our religious inheritance will centre in the memory of him."[3]

Andrews Norton and his contemporaries of like mind had "cleansed" traditional Christian beliefs regarding Jesus Christ, while retaining the centrality of the miracles. Christie moved away from the miracles and emphasized Jesus' spiritual qualities. In an article entitled "One Body in Christ, Rom. xii, I Cor. xii,"[4] Christie wrote: "*The risen Lord is a pneumatic being.*" "The risen Christ . . . has a wholly spiritual form, and the Christian's consummation is to be conformed to it, so as to wear the image and the Glory of God. In that heavenly future there is no mention of the *ekklesia,* no mention of the Holy Spirit as distinct from Christ's own personal nature. The final picture is only complete, personal identification of individual men with the Lord by conformity to his holy body." In other words, the Church is not the body of Christ.

As for the Holy Spirit, "We have come to a notion of the Holy Spirit as almost identical with Christ and quite free from the pantheistic nuance."

"*The eucharist is a reception of Christ's body of spirit.* . . . There is a consubstantiation of bread and Christ, and of the Christian and Christ. . . . A real fellowship with Christ is proven by the parallel case of eating meats known to be consecrated to demons. [I Cor. 10:20] The eater becomes a partner of the demonic being." As all are assimilated to Christ, so, "by becoming Christ, [all] are directly and perfectly the image of God, 'that God may be all in all.' " [I Cor. 15:28]

It may be observed, in conclusion, that, notwithstanding Christie's updating of Norton's Christology, Jesus Christ is still central for this American teacher of unitarianism.

We turn now to Clayton R. Bowen, who produced one of the most useful handbooks of this century on the realistic interpretation of gospel records. It is, at the same time, probably one of the least known works of important biblical scholarship. This unfortunate fact may possibly be attributed to its Unitarian auspices on the one hand, and its liberal-rational interpretation of the life of Jesus, on the other hand. The book was entitled, simply, *The Gospel of Jesus.*[5]

Clayton Raymond Bowen was born in Wellsboro, Pennsylvania, on November 25, 1877. He was graduated from Franklin College, in New Athens, Ohio, in 1891 and from Meadville Theological School in 1901. He took the degree of B.D. at Meadville in 1903 and received his ThD. there in 1920. His career as a teacher at Meadville began in 1905, after two years of pastoral ministry. He was made Assistant Professor of New Testament interpretation in 1907 and Professor in 1911. The move of Meadville to Chicago in 1927 provided at once a wider contact for Professor Bowen and a much broader benefit to New Testament scholars and students. On the eve of receiving an appointment as a Professor in the New Testament Department of the University of Chicago, he died unexpectedly, in London, on October 17, 1934.

In spite of the fact that Dr. Bowen published few books, there is, nevertheless, a sufficient quantity of his writings available to afford an important and helpful view of his early twentieth century Unitarian Christology. Unquestionably his thinking on Jesus guided many Unitarian ministers. It will be noted that he was a contemporary of Peabody and Fenn and could well have included Charles E. Parke among the Christocentric ministers whom he influenced. Bowen frankly admitted to the influence of contemporary German biblical scholars upon his views of Jesus, among whom he found much in common with Paul Wernle.

In discovering Bowen's views with regard to Jesus Christ, we can begin with his characteristically succinct statement regarding Jesus' birth. He has no doubt that there was a person named Jesus, and he concludes he was probably born in Nazareth. The idea of the virgin birth was not originally found in Luke, however. Bowen finds verses thirty-four and thirty-five in chapter one "clearly interpolations." "Mary's child is to be the child of Joseph to whom she is betrothed, and whom she is supposed to marry before the action of chapter two begins. The child is to inherit the 'throne of his father David'; it is Joseph who is of the house of David, Mary being a kinswoman of Elisabeth, who is of 'the daughters of Aaron,' i.e., she is of the tribe of Levi, whereas David's tribe is Judah. The child Jesus is to 'be called the Son of the Most High' in the Jewish ethical or spiritual sense, as Messiah, not in the pagan physical sense, as begotten by a divine being as father upon a human mother. This idea is common enough in pagan myths and it appears in Matthew's gospel, but it was not originally in Luke's."[6] Further, "The earliest text of the allusion to Mary here calls her Joseph's wife, though our familiar text reads, 'his betrothed.' Notice how in this whole section Joseph is called the father of Jesus. We have phrases like 'his parents', 'his father and his mother'; Mary even says, 'Thy father and I.' "[7] "The legend of Bethlehem birth is due only to the Jewish belief that Messiah would be born as a descendant of David in David's town."[8]

We move now to the end of Jesus' life to consider Bowen's views of the Eucharist. These were contained in a lecture given at the Meadville Summer Institute on June 29, 1914, entitled "The Last Supper and The Lord's Supper." The Lord's Supper is the most prominent and most notable function of the Christian church. It is commonly called eucharist, "a very early Greek name which means simply thanksgiving, taken from the thanksgiving prayer or grace at the beginning of the Supper. It is called the Last Supper, from the occasion in which it took its rise, or the Lord's Supper, from him who was, and is, its central figure." Bowen points out a curious distinction between the observance of the Lord's Supper in the Roman Catholic Church and in the Protestant Church. The Lord's Supper is the central feature of the mass, and mass means dismissal. In the Protestant church by contrast, the Lord's Supper, or communion, represents fellowship, gathering together, with Jesus and with other believers. "Perhaps this . . . word [communion] comes nearer than any of the others to describing what the service essentially means. It does

Francis A. Christie

Clayton Raymond Bowen

mean, to all, communion with Jesus; that is, I suppose, the fundamental idea behind all views of the service and all fashions of observing it."

The body and blood references in the communion service are symbolic. "It is my body," Jesus said. Mark added, "Take ye." Matthew added, "Eat." Bowen feels that the expressions "This is my body, this is my blood" quite certainly were added by the evangelist Mark, or by church usage. Although Jesus may have thought of establishing a covenant when he said, "My blood," this concept probably reflects later theological development. Bowen believes that Jesus was convinced this was to be his last supper on earth, but there was "nothing calculated or premeditated, nothing didactic or theological, no 'establishing' of a sacrament or observance of any kind," says Bowen. Incidentally, in his distress, Jesus may not have taken anything himself, at this last meal with his disciples.

Reenactment of the Lord's Supper today holds high values for participants. It connects them directly with Jesus as few tenets and practices in our church life do and sums up the meaning of Jesus' heroic life and his sublime death. "I believe that rightly understood, reverently and thoughtfully administered, with the material and sacramental aspects eliminated and the ceremonial and fellowship aspects emphasized, rationally and devoutly received, it may still be an invaluable means of quickening the religious lives of the people in our churches," says Bowen. As for the performance of the communion service, Bowen feels that the truest reenactment is to leave the elements on the table as symbols, which are not partaken of. "This is historically true; it may be religiously sincere. The important thing is that Jesus be remembered, that the unswerving faith, the sure hope, the boundless love, that made him our supreme Master and our supreme Servant, may somehow be kindled in us also, through this simple act that we do in remembrance of him."[9]

On the subject of Jesus' resurrection, Bowen says: "The resurrection stories in our Gospels . . . are one and all legendary. The earliest faith in his resurrection, which is amply attested for us in the Letters of Paul, conceived his spirit or personality to have escaped from the under-world of the dead on the third day (which soon came to be taken quite literally), and to have risen into the heavenly life with God. This did not involve any reanimation of the dead body, and had no concern whatever with the grave.[10] There is no doubt that Jesus' followers, including Peter and Paul, experienced actual ecstatic visions of their resurrected Master. "They were absolutely assured that Jesus was not in the under-world with the rest of those who had died, but alive in glorious power with God in the heavenly world. . . . Their communion was with a living Presence, not with the memory of a dead man."[11] Paul combatted the beginnings of the *physical* resurrection concept, but lost. "[Physical resurrection] is wholly foreign to the thought and promise of Jesus himself, and to the faith of his disciples and earliest followers, those to whom the visions came."[12] If Jesus had never been buried, as most crucified persons were not, "nothing that Paul says of the resurrection would have to be altered, and our faith in Jesus' risen life would be the stronger and purer."[13]

With respect to the resurrected Jesus' admonition to baptize new disciples in the name of the Father, Son, and Holy Spirit, (Matthew 28:19),[14] Bowen believes this formula "replaces in our manuscripts an original baptism 'in my name.' "[15]

Who was Jesus? What was Jesus? Bowen observes that Jesus was a poet. This observation provides a limited criterion for deciding authenticity. Surely he possessed some of the characteristics of a poet. There are those who may see an antithesis between the sacred and the secular, but, says Bowen, subject matter is what makes a work of art sacred. Thus, men and women in the New Testament "are holy if they are holy in life and heart; they are not holy ex officio, because their names are written there."[16]

Jesus is not thought of as a poet or as a holy man primarily, however, although he was both of these persons. Jesus was a Jewish prophet. He was not an expounder of Christian dogma. As a prophet he was concerned with the end of the world and times that were to come. He talked of a kingdom of God, an "eschatalogical term, meaning a new world-order about to come down miraculously upon a hopeless creation, bringing new heavens and a new earth, new conditions, of life social and individual."[17] As a prophet, Jesus looked forward to a future Messiahship as well as a future kingdom which should be "miraculously realized through his supernaturally assisted agency, in his own generation."[18]

In addition to being a poet, a holy man and a prophet, Jesus was, also, a Messiah. The term Messiah (a Greek word meaning Christ) "meant the establisher, under God, of this new world-order."[19] The familiar terminology of Jewish eschatalogy was applied to Jesus by the writers of the Gospels. It has been commonly regarded that John the Baptist was prophesying of Jesus, but Bowen has this to say on that subject: "[B]y his great Coming One [John] meant not the Messiah, and in particular not Jesus, but rather the great prophet, the second Elijah, who was expected to appear before 'the day of the Lord'. (Mal. 3:1-3, 4:5-6)"[20] Bowen felt that the dual roles of Prophet and Messiah did not overlap. Jesus had intended his Messiahship to remain a secret until his advent as Messiah, "when the angels and the opening clouds of heaven should tell the world." "For [Jesus] alone, who expected to assume the role, the word ["Messiah"] meant not exultation, but service, not *Gabe*, but *Aufgabe*, as the Germans say. It was a tremendous *task*, which he accepted with trembling hands only because he believed his Father laid it upon him." "Not only did Jesus certainly and literally expect the realization of his people's hope in his own generation, but he did believe, at least during the later months of his mission, that to him would be committed the task of carrying out for his God and Father, that realization."[21] He admitted the same to his Jewish judges: hence the placard raised above his head at his crucifixion: "King of the Jews."

Again, "He expected to be Messiah, Son of Man, expected the Parousia with the holy angels, the catastrophe and the new world-order. All of this he expected in *simple literalness.* Yet the idea of service that really drew him and dominated him and made it a solemn joy for him to drink its cup and accept its baptism was a service at once more humble and immediate, and more grandly heroic. It was the task of kindling in men the religious experience he knew, bringing them to the consciousness of the divine Fatherhood and the human brotherhood as he was conscious of them. — That was not establishing the kingdom, but getting men ready to share in its blessed life when it should come."[22]

Jesus accepted the fact he must die, that "Messiah must enter into his glory by the Passion." "Strip off, then, from the Gospels this Messianic color; set it over, as Jesus did in his own thought, into the period subsequent to Good Friday, and you have the Jesus who re-made the world .... His shall be, not theologically or mystically, but literally and historically, the name that is above every name, the seat — not on the throne of the world — but at the right hand of that God whose is the Kingdom and the power and glory, for ever and ever. Amen."[23]

If Jesus was poet, holy man, prophet, and Messiah, "[He] was not in any sense a theologian," declares Bowen. "What theology he consciously possessed and gave expression to was the common theology of the Pharisaic type of Judaism of his time. . . . [H]e was, in his theological ideas, essentially a Pharisee. . . . No single specifically Christian proposition will be found among [his sayings], above all, no one of the familiar evangelical dogmas. If we ask him for his view of God, he replies with the one simple word 'Father,' a divine name in their sense specifically Jewish."[24]

What has Bowen to say of Jesus' experience and of his personality? "The religious experience of Jesus was the unique act of his own spiritual nature; it was an expression of religious genius. He drew directly from the divine sources, communed at first hand with God. For him there was no Master to whom he was disciple, no Messiah, no Saviour, Mediator, Redeemer." And Bowen concludes that Jesus' religious experience was apparently more serene and calm than that of Paul.[25]

With respect to the personality of Jesus and its attraction for his disciples, Bowen was influenced by the early twentieth century observations of Wernle and Foakes-Jackson. Jesus drew men to himself so powerfully that, "despite his shameful death, they were ready to live and die for him," and herein lies the genius of Christianity. From the beginning, the unique characteristic of Christianity has been "the personal note, the relation to a living personality, a human experience." Jesus is not God, or a god, or the ideal principle of humanity, or the framer of the perfect law, "he is a man engaged in a simple business of human living, and doing it divinely. To him was committed, as to each of us, 'the swift and solemn trust of life.' He discharged this trust as God gave him light and leading, and his manliness, his human excellence, has made the greatest dynamic that other men's lives have known in all history."[26]

When Jesus thought of Messiahship, "It was for him a duty laid on by God, an opportunity to serve supremely, which he gladly embraced in all humility and courage." "[I]t is utterly untrue that Jesus in taking this title [Messiah] was an egotist, a megalomaniac, or a fanatic."[27] "Here was a stream of spiritual dynamic, which rose in the breast of the young man of Galilee, which flowed from life to life transforming the centuries, which is sweeping full flood through our complex life today, beating at every closed door, inundating every withered and distorted life. In many different aspects Christianity is the most astounding phenomenon of the ages; in none more so than as an inexhaustible force. It is Truth, it is Worship, it is Holiness, it is Brotherhood. But behind all and in all and through all, it is a Power of God."[28]

Thus, Bowen demonstrates in his own feeling and words, that "Christianity is in essence adherence to the Person of Jesus Christ." This emphasis Bowen carried to his students well into the twentieth century.

Chapter 7

William Wallace Fenn's Conventional Christ; Charles E. Park, Christ's Disciple

It is reported that William Ellery Channing revealed traits of the preacher at a very early age, about five, as I recall it. We find a match for the precocious Channing in young William Wallace Fenn. A memorandum recalling incidents from Dean Fenn's life, written by his friend and admirer Walter F. Greenman, contains this incident: "His summers were passed at Weston, Vt. Never missing an episode of any importance, his five year old legs took him to the riverside to witness a genuinely evangelical baptism. Duly impressed, a couple of days later his mother saw him standing on an old hollowed out log used for a drinking trough in the barn yard. In an instant standing back to the water filled trough, she heard him say in tones imitating those of the local preacher, — 'I baptize thee William Wallace Fenn in the name of the Father, the Son and over she goes,' with that he gallantly threw himself over backward into the water."

Mr. Greenman's narration continues: "Perhaps a year later, when corrected for some naughtiness by his mother, with finality in his tones as if to close the matter, he asked in words from the catechism, 'What can you expect of a child of wrath, conceived in sin and born in iniquity?' 'I told him,' said his mother, 'that he was nothing of the kind and that he was going to be my good obedient little boy.' She also confessed that as she dared to make that assertion, she felt her orthodoxy weakening. About this time, or a little later, she told of his delight of standing up in a wooden bottom chair, and with the local evangelist as a pattern warned sinners of their doom and called them to repentance."[1]

The following incident, which occurred many years later, has been reported to me by Dean Fenn's grandson from Milton, Massachusetts, Mr. Donald C. Duncan. "My mother told the following story about her father, W.W. Fenn. He was going over a sermon with a young divinity student who asked if sermons were always going to be as difficult to prepare as this first one had been. He replied, 'Into every sermon a certain amount of pain must always go; it is your choice whether it will be yours or your congregation's.' "

In an address upon the occasion of the dedication of a tablet in memory of Dean Fenn, Dr. Charles Edwards Park spoke of Dean Fenn's splendid qualities, which included a forceful personality, a great mind, and a self-integrated unity of these two attributes, which reflected a man who had found himself. Dr. Park said further, toward the end of his address: "[H]e impressed us as an advocate, as one speaking for something greater than himself. All his life he appeared as one standing forth in front of a vast, dim Reality, and proclaiming that Reality, proclaiming it boldly and confidently, and with tremendous force and vigor."[2]

William Wallace Fenn was a Unitarian minister. He served as Bussey Professor of Theology at Harvard from 1901 to 1932 and as Dean of the Divinity School, from 1906 to 1922. In 1905 he gave a series of lectures at the Summer School of Theology at Harvard, entitled, "The Theological Method of Jesus." It was just one year after Francis Greenwood Peabody, also a professor at Harvard, had given his lectures at Yale, "Jesus Christ and the Christian Character." Fenn's lectures were considerably briefer, but they reflected more of the same interest in retaining Jesus. (Fenn never calls him Jesus Christ in his own references.) His proposition is to defend Jesus as a theologian, against detractors,[3] but he does more than that, as we shall see in reviewing these lectures and also in referring briefly to a separate and later lecture. Fenn early states categorically that Jesus was "the most influential person in all human history" and, he continues confidently, his influence is not only not abating, but "bids fair to increase."[4]

Jesus had a theology, because he thought about God and man, and their relationships. "The fact that [Jesus] was a thinking man, who believed that God was to be loved with the mind as well as with the heart and who sought to communicate truth to men, constitutes him a theologian in the truest and most just use of the term and warrants us in seeking for his theological method."[5] Jesus was a religious genius who perceived truths independent of the process of ratiocination, but that does not preclude considering his manner of perception an implicit intellectual process.

As the Jewish Scribes derived their theology from Scripture, so it has been with Christian theologians. Jesus, however, was not a Scribe, nor did he work within the Scribes' Scripture-basis pattern. Although he affirmed the Law, even to every jot and tittle, we need not look for consistency, nor should we overlook the fact that "Jesus consciously and explicitly rejected the contemporary idea of the authoritative Law." Jesus did revere the Scripture, however, and he may not have been aware that at times his teaching was contradictory. Wilhelm Bousset neatly resolved these apparent inconsistencies by saying, " 'the Scriptures spoke to him with an authoritative voice, but he heard only that to which his ear was attuned.' "[6] One may react: How human a trait!

But the Scriptures were not the principal source of Jesus' religious thought. Rather, "his thought rested ultimately upon his experience in the world of nature and of human life."[7] This is Fenn's main thesis. Jesus' authority was derived from personal experience; the Scribes' was derived from tradition. Jesus' emphasis was upon the inner, personal life, whereas the religion of his contemporary Scribes and Pharisees was upon external things. Jesus regarded the achieving of purity within as primary. Fenn refers to a point made by the eminent English Unitarian theologian of the 19th Century, James Martineau, that "the fundamental idea of Christianity is ascent through conscience into communion with God,"[8] and declares, "this, at all events, seems to have been the thought of Jesus. 'Blessed are the pure in heart, for they shall see God.' "[9]

Jesus' words and deeds came from his communion with God, then, but whence did his thought come? Not from "moments of rapture," says Fenn, but from his seeing "deeper meanings in the ordinary circumstances and events of life."[10] He found God, not by closing his eyes to the world about him, but by looking at it more sharply and penetratingly. His teachings were in terms of common life, not of the un-earthly. They were based on his own experiences with nature and man. Jesus' parables abound with references and comparisons to nature, and Jesus taught like "the sower [who] casts his seed broadcast, not trying sedulously to choose his soil." "His thought was one with the blowing clover and the falling rain, because through these and through all the processes of nature God was teaching him of His truth."[11]

While John the Baptist was ascetic and kept to the wilderness, Jesus liked to be where the people were. "Sham, pretense, and mere conventionality were odious to him."[12] He was even called "a gluttonous man and a winebibber." Fenn quotes Zangwill's reference to Jesus " 'as a joyous comrade, seeking to uplift and guide the life of his fellows from within.' "[13] His religion was a layman's religion, for, after all, he was himself a layman.[14]

Fenn goes on to make a point which may be original with him, when he observes that while Jesus knew well the ways of "ordinary human life,"[15] and "the cruelty of weakness and inferiority invested with temporary power,"[16] he was "off his own ground,"[17] in speaking of rich men and stewards and business transactions. But when it comes to the Prodigal Son, "the greatest and best of all the parables of Jesus," "Jesus is dealing with domestic life, . . . [and] is plainly on familiar ground and at his best."[18]

What of Jesus and the Messiahship? Fenn does not think Jesus considered himself to be the Messiah at the time of his baptism, when he heard God's voice say, "This is my beloved Son, in whom I am well pleased." (Matthew 3:17. The wording in the new English bible for this passage is: "This is my Son, my Beloved, on whom my favour rests.") Jesus was merely called "Son" here, nothing else. Jesus spoke of the near coming of the King: that would be the advent of the Messiah. Jesus' thought of himself as Messiah came only with his growing experiences. He was pressed from without by the hopeful people and his eager disciples, all of whom were impatient for the coming of the Messiah. And certain experiences, such as instances of his power over demoniacs, caused the question to arise in his own mind: "But if I cast out devils by the Spirit of God, then the kingdom of God is come unto you." (Matthew 12:28) Jesus was conscious of "peculiar nearness to God." Was this evidence of God's choice of him to be the Messiah? By the time of the incident at Caesarea Philippi, when Jesus asked his disciples, "Who do men say that the Son of Man is?", and Peter blurted out his "impetuous confession," as Fenn calls it, "that [Jesus] was actually the Messiah," Jesus himself had come to that conclusion.[19] What was Jesus' attitude toward "the outside world?" With acceptance of the conviction that he was the Messiah, his foreordained suffering and death, "in some way not clearly formed, [meant that] the blessings of the Kingdom of God were then to be opened to the Gentiles as well as the Jews."[20]

On the subject of Jesus' death and resurrection, Fenn wrote elsewhere: "[W]hat happened to the body of Jesus after death is not nearly as important as what went on in the soul of Jesus before death.

"It is not the conquered grave in the soul of Palestine, but the conquered fear of pain in the soul of Jesus which should engage our attention now.

"We shall enter into the real gladness of Easter only as we turn from an outward event to the study of an inward experience."[3]

How, then, did Jesus deal with his experiential materials in developing his theology? Jesus applied *a fortiori* reasoning, in the manner of the first Hillel's seven rules, "the role of Qal-ve-Chomer or Light and Heavy." For example, "If God so clothe the grass of the field which today is and tomorrow is cast into the oven, shall he not much more clothe you, O ye of little faith?" Or in the case of Jesus' examples which begin with, "What man of you?", the argument is: ". . . if man ought to deal thus with man, much more will God deal thus with man."[22] "This, then, is the principal logical method of Jesus. As God deals with man in nature, so He deals with the soul of man."[23] The ethical aspect of this principle amounts to this: "Treat men as God treats them, that ye may be the sons of your Father who is in heaven." Fenn concluded that "from both nature and man came just, though insufficient, revelations of the nature and operation of God."[24]

What sort of man was Jesus; was he in some way abnormal, aberrant? Fenn says that he has "spoken of [Jesus'] experiences in the world of nature and of man first, in order to show that it was while he was so living, and not in the least in an ecstatic state, that the marvelous inner experiences of communion with God were his. . . . The realism of Jesus is the best surety for his idealism. The normality of his experience when it lies within our ken inspires confidence in its equal normality when it goes beyond our vision into the secret place of the soul, where man and God come together. Jesus argued from the deepest feelings of his own soul by the same method up to God from whom they proceeded and of whom they bore witness."[25] Jesus' teaching of the simple essence of religion as love to God and love to man was the secret of his power, and it came of his own experience. Its genuineness stood against any conditions set up by others, who presumed to control a person's communion with God. "Thus he taught and thus he lived, with an authority personal, not derived, which has carried through the ages, and which today makes the experience of Jesus of Nazareth the supremely significant fact of human history."[26]

"The simplest and most natural idea is that Jesus believed in the Kingdom of God as both present and growing in the world and to be consummated in the near future by a catastrophic coming of the Kingdom of God in power and glory." "It is probably also true that Jesus expected his own return as the Messiah of glory, and the establishment of the Kingdom within the generation of men then living. In these two particulars, as well as in the notion of the catastrophic setting up of the Kingdom, the thought of Jesus may have become meaningless to us. But, whatever may be said on these points or in general about his thought as to the way in which the Kingdom was to be realized, there can be no doubt that he confidently believed that the time was coming in which men should live together upon the earth as members of one family in mutual love and trust, children of the one Father. This he designated as the Kingdom of God."[27]

Fenn's own summary of his view of Jesus' method, characteristics and purpose were: "Jesus' thought did not rest upon Scripture or traditions, but upon personal experience. That experience was not in ecstatic moments, but in the normal ways of nature and the ordinary paths of men. By a most simple, logical method he argued from the facts of his experience up to the will of God, with perfect belief in truth and good will as the supreme forces of the world, whose supremacy was to become visible in the Kingdom of God.[28]

"Whether there be a God or not," Fenn says to doubters, ". . . we know that we ought to work for the coming of a social order in which all men shall be governed by the family feeling, for a social state in which justice prevails and good will governs . . . every true heart answers to the call and the challenge of this ideal, which is precisely the ideal which we have denominated the Kingdom of God . . . whether the theistic view of the world be true or not, every man ought to live as if it were true, giving his life to the ideal which it presents and encourages. Thus and only thus, as I firmly believe, one comes to believe profoundly in the theistic view of the world. To live the life of Jesus is the way to make ours the faith and hope of Jesus. To live by the method of Jesus is to come to full personal conviction, through an experience which is for us finally authoritative, that the God in whom he believed and trusted is our God; that we are in truth His children, living and working in His growing world, and that our determinations are His purposes, our ideals are disclosures of His will, our hopes His promises, our aspirations, His aspirations."[29]

These lectures of Dean Fenn were delivered in 1905. Before taking our leave of him, let us jump ahead to 1924, when he delivered the Essex Hall lecture, in London. It was entitled, "The Christian Way of Life," with explanatory sub-title, "As Illustrated In The History of Religion In New England."

Most of this lecture is not pertinent to our subject, but a few brief references are appropriate. He says, for example, that up to the middle of the 19th century, there is an almost complete lack of any reference to the character of Christ. "His name indeed everywhere appears, but the figure is that of the Pauline Christ instead of the historical Jesus. To the incidents of his earthly life, exemplifying his loving kindness and tender mercy, there is hardly an allusion."[30]

"Channing's exalted tribute to the character of Christ struck a note which has now swelled into a triumphant chorus. The person of Jesus has emerged from the glorymists of tradition and over-passed the bounds of officialdom. In the light of his personality, men see the Christian way of life differently. What indeed can it be but the way Christ himself lived? What a simple observation! Or, rather, how simple men have been never to have made it before! He went about doing good, he loved his fellowmen and was ready to lay down his life for them. Can a man venture to call himself a follower of Jesus, a Christian, if he is indifferent to the sufferings of others, if he is not doing everything in his power to relieve them?"[31]

"The human Jesus became the inspiration to a humanitarian Christianity."[32] "[B]ut to make Christianity coterminous with social service . . . is to lose sight of the deepest significance of Jesus himself, and to miss the very heart of Christianity. And this, for the very simple reason that Christianity is a form of religion."[33]

"[T]he first service of Jesus to mankind lies in the fact that he taught and exemplified a singularly pure and lofty form of religion. It is written of him indeed, that he went about doing good, but it is written again that he was in the habit of spending solitary hours in meditation and prayer. If we would follow him truly and fully must it not be both in prayer and in service, in thoughtful communion with God as well as in unsparing service of man?"[34]

Fenn suggests that men may come to find a stronger appeal in Christ as the exemplar of the Christian way of life, which consists of humble devotion to God as well as the sympathetic service of man, than in Christ as the incarnate God, the Messiah, the Saviour. With "a vision splendid," he was in company with God.

Fenn was determined that good works should be balanced with prayer and communion with God. Nevertheless, the vast preponderance of Fenn's words

William Wallace Fenn

are devoted to subjects other than this personal religion. It is a right emphasis in point, if not in volume, and it is good that this balance was maintained and advocated. Fenn was in this respect, as in all others, the product of his culture and of a disciplined temperament. Others might venture more extensively into the subject of the characteristics and practices of the inward personal religious life, in terms of the discipleship of Jesus Christ, but he intuitively understood the fullest implication of Jesus for his disciples in any age.

Bearing in mind that in reading these last sentiments we have jumped into the mid 1920's, let us go back a bit and pick up the story of Jesus Christ in American Unitarianism in its other, or negative, aspects for the interim period.

Within American Unitarianism there was a lively growth of what was called humanism. It was not the classical recognition of the potential and social and moral and cultural worth of the individual, which tended toward humanitarianism, but a simple, bold, setting of man as the primary, principal agent of the universe, with God assigned to a secondary inactive role, if any, and Jesus Christ a discarded appendage. I would not disparage, however, the sincerity, nor underrate the vigor, of those who adopted the humanist position. They were earnest men, dismayed by the weakness and distortions of Christianity, who knew what was right in life, and what man needed physically and ideologically, if not spiritually. The question arises with respect to their understanding of how to achieve the desired end. Our aim at this juncture is not to debate the merits of theocentric, Christo-centric thinking *versus* those of humanism, but to note the blow dealt indirectly to the place of Jesus Christ in many Unitarian churches, through the preachings of humanism.

Although he does not so state specifically, the humanist says by implication that an individual's loyalty cannot be to Jesus Christ. Curtis Reese in an address at the Harvard Summer School of Theology in 1920 said: "If liberalism can be reduced to a single statement, I think this is it: Conscious committal and loyalty to worthwhile causes and goals in order that free and positive personality may be developed, intelligently associated, and cosmically related."[35] Evidently one unaccountably arrives at a sociological, moral, or ethical position, and goals are either recognized and accepted, or they are declined, without outside reference or source. In any case, one's loyalty is to "worthwhile causes", not to Jesus Christ, who, in some way, would interfere with the development of a "free and positive personality."

Reese, himself, said: "For a long time prophets, poets and statesmen have proclaimed the ambition of the race to be linked together for mutual service; and now biology and social science agree that there is and can be no complete self-realization aside from co-operation with other selves.

"Ideally this is the heart of Christianity. The organic unity of the race is found in the teachings of Christianity. Jesus, at his best, thought and spoke in world-terms. Human solidarity is the heart of the labor movement. This finds expression in the motto: 'An injury to one is an injury to all.' The red flag is meant to be symbolic of the blood of the race. The latest and best type of statesmanship thinks in world terms. We are now becoming accustomed to world issues, programs and achievements."[36]

It may be concluded from this statement that reference is made to Jesus and to Christianity only as they may be said to tie in with the point Reese is making at the moment, namely, "co-operation with other selves." He went on to declare, "Liberalism is building a religion that would not be shaken even if the thought of God were out-grown."[37] In terms of the struggle of the human mind with the problems and challenges of life, and of finding grounds for idealism and hope in the face of cynicism and anti-social acts, this cold espousal of "worthwhile causes" displays incredible naiveté!

In 1933 a statement of humanism was compiled and published as the Humanist Manifesto. It contains no mention whatsoever of Jesus Christ, Christianity, or God. Fifteen affirmations were presented. The first one of these was: "Religious humanists regard the universe as self-existing and not created." The last one was: "We assert that humanism will: (a) affirm life rather than deny it; (b) seek to elicit the possibilities of life, not flee from it; and (c) endeavor to establish the conditions of a satisfactory life for all, not merely for a few. By this positive morale and intention humanism will be guided, and from this perspective and alignment the techniques and efforts of humanism will flow."[38] Here, obviously, are a sheer intellectualism, a complete lack of accounting or providing for motivation and loyalty to principle, and a pathetic failure of distinction between socio-economic proposals and religious thinking growing out of fundamental causes and aims. We can make this sort of criticism, but that is not enough. It must be recognized that for a significant percentage of American Unitarians this was the death knell of Jesus Christ, indeed, of God, his Father, and our Father. This active increment of American Unitarianism did not have the only say, however. Let us turn now to another American Unitarian, who still had a place for Jesus Christ in his religious thinking, and who represented and led other Unitarians in maintaining a vestige of life in the historic Jesus and the theological Christ, Charles Edwards Park.

Charles Edwards Park was born March 14, 1873, in Mahabaleshwar, India, the son and grandson of Congregational ministers who served as missionaries in India, covering together, the period 1835 to 1881. He was graduated from Phillips Academy, in Andover, and from Yale in the class of 1896. He was called to be the minister of First Church in Boston, in 1906, at the age of 33, and remained as minister there for 40 years, until his retirement in 1946. Even after that, he appeared often in the pulpit of that church and, on various occasions, elsewhere, almost until his death in 1962, at the age of 89.

During his ministry, the humanist movement was born and rose to its peak within American Unitarianism. The emphasis upon good works for the benefit of society flourished, until the social gospel all but replaced, and did indeed replace in some churches, the gospel of Jesus Christ. Dr. Park never changed. To him religion was a highly personal thing, and church was a place where one went to worship, not to be lectured on the proper course to take in any given social issue. He refused to announce his sermon topics in advance, to ensure that those who came to the Sunday morning services were there to praise God and not to appraise his position on some current problem of the city's or the nation's people. He personally set the type and printed the weekly calendar of the church. And he made the cross which hung above the communion table. He was proud of its perfect proportions, and it is a blessing he was not alive at the time it was lost in the fire which destroyed the church he had hallowed with the name of God, the person of Jesus, and his own quiet, scholarly, disciplined life. The perpetual hint of a smile on his face permeated the church even after he had left it forever.

On the first Sunday in June of 1946, the year of his retirement, the next to the last Sunday before the discontinuance of services for the summer season, he wrote his customary little piece for the weekly bulletin. It was, characteristically, about Jesus, and he concluded it with these sentences: "The only factor that rescues our religion from the blight of our own indifference and gives it a potent appeal to our personal interest and vivid sympathy is the presence of the man Jesus of Nazareth. The only portion of our religion which we care to accept as authentic and viable is the portion we may consider as his own spiritual biography. Even great ideas can leave us cold until they are brought to life by their obvious point for us. The single power that brings Christianity to life is Jesus himself."[39]

This was Dr. Park's thesis, and one repeatedly encountered it in his sermons, prayers, and writings. We shall look especially at his book, *The Way of Jesus*, but also, briefly, at his shorter volume, *Christianity: How It Came To Us; What It Is; What It Might Be*, which consists of the Minns Lectures for 1947.

It is interesting to note that *The Way of Jesus*, is dedicated to "W.W.F." These are the initials of William Wallace Fenn, whose own appreciation of Jesus we have surveyed. Reminders of Fenn's views can be found in this book of Dr. Park, and it may also be noted that Dr. Park's living, human Jesus also reflects Professor Francis Greenwood Peabody's conception of Jesus. There is every reason to believe that both Fenn and Peabody had a noticeable influence upon the young, new minister of First Church and were respected guides throughout his developing years. All three of these men made of Jesus a companion in life's experiences, as opposed to the impersonal, doctrinal figure in the religion of the latter-day disciples of orthodox Christianity.

Charles Edwards Park

Those who were Jesus' actual companions found in their eighteen to twenty months with him "a new and infinitely happier way to live," says Dr. Park. It was the way of Jesus. Even before the cognomen "Christian" had been introduced, the early associates of Jesus were known as "Those of the Way."[40] Jesus' views were new and revolutionary, and whereas the intellectual and educated classes could not tolerate them, the humble people were completely captivated by the novelty and charm of Jesus' religion. The course of action which followed Jesus' advent in the religious scene of his native land was perhaps more neatly defined for Dr. Park than it was for Jesus' contemporaries, but as Dr. Park reviews the situation, it appears like this: "There was but one accommodation possible [for the people]: adopt Jesus as their titular head: promote him to the status of divinity; and thus make him, so to speak, sponsor for a theology that bore his name but had not the slightest regard for his teachings. This theological fabric was also known as Christianity, and passed for such for the next ten or twelve centuries."[41]

Then the common people of Europe who could read began to discover from the newly printed Bible that there was a different religion and a different Jesus from what they had learned theretofore. They were able to discover that "Jesus starts with the postulate that man is the child of God who loves him, forgives him with inexhaustible patience, and seeks his co-operation; and goes on to urge his hearers to cultivate a truer opinion of themselves, discover their own powers, rouse themselves to intelligent activity, and by their heartfelt service to God earn their own salvation."[42]

Dr. Park sees the time as ripe for the Messiah at Jesus' advent. When John the Baptist asked, "Are you ready?" Jesus felt impelled, after his baptism, to prepare the people of his native Galilee, for the coming kingdom. Dr. Park states the situation in his inimitable manner: "That [his baptism] was a moment of great importance to himself is evident from the little experience of inward exaltation which came to him as he was leaving the water. He had found his real work in life; and an inner voice told him that he had decided rightly; he had God's approval; God's own gift of pure motive and right spirit was sent down to him. He was now another voice crying: Prepare ye in the wilderness a highway for our God. It was the beginning of a career destined to change the course of human history."[43]

What were some of Jesus' outstanding traits? Dr. Park finds them in the Synoptic Gospels.[44]

1. He was intensely religious.
2. He hated oppression.
3. He possessed faith which was "the secret of his self-organization; for he had a conspicuously powerful nature, balanced and organized, that gave an irresistible authority to his words."
4. "His human interest was deep and quick."

5. "Pity was about the only thing that could break down his self-possession and make him act impulsively."[45]

6. His social status was "humble but perfectly respectable."

7. He was remarkably well educated for his status.

8. There is no information on his physical appearance, but "We may conjecture that his temperament was quiet and equable, that he had an air of tranquil confidence and modest self-sufficiency, that he preferred to keep his private problems to himself and find their solution by himself, that he was neither conspicuously grave nor gay. He was by no means a sombre man. He had a full share of the sense of humor, howbeit of a somewhat gentler type than that which passed for humor among his countrymen."

9. He was not an ascetic recluse like John the Baptist, but while the people rejected John, Jesus observed he fared no better: "You seize upon my conventionality as an excuse to ignore me. 'A gluttonous man, and a wine-bibber,' you say, 'just like all the rest of us. There is nothing extraordinary about him. Why should we listen to him?' You are just as hard to please as the sulky children in the marketplace."

10. He used irony, and he used exaggeration, to make his points, but he could lay aside petulance and impatience to reveal a genuine solicitude: " 'Come unto me, all ye that labor and are heavy laden; I can give what you want. Learn of me; yet shall find rest unto your souls.' "

To summarize this human Jesus, Dr. Park says, and again we find the result not only a wholly commendable and admirable person, but one, we can hardly fail to think, who would fit well in Dr. Park's church at the corner of Berkeley and Marlborough Streets: "We should find him a strong, clean, reverent, generous nature, a great heart, a singularly keen and active mind, a boundless sympathy and a practical solicitude, and exceedingly sensitive to spiritual values. He lived his life just as near to the heart of God as a human creature can get. His foremost aim was to do the will of his Father in Heaven. To that aim he devoted himself with a consecration that only death could defeat."[46]

In his religious thought, it is evident that Jesus understood the Scriptures better than most people. He sought the spirit and reason behind the arbitrary statement, and his aim was to make the Scriptures live in the hearts of the people, as they did in his.

Unlike the characteristic of the Jewish religion, which was national, Jesus' religion was personal. Dr. Park suggests a plausible thesis regarding how Jesus came to think of God as Father. It may be inferred from gospel accounts that Jesus had four older brothers and some sisters. Actually these were half-brothers and half-sisters, the children of Jesus' father by an earlier wife. Jesus was the first-born of Joseph and Mary. As the younger son, Jesus was much in the company of his father, who taught him his craft, and listened sympathetically to the young Jesus' ideas and questions. But the father died when Jesus was young, and Jesus missed him sorely. He had been the most precious thing in his life. That is what the word "father" represented to Jesus.[47] This Father, God, was "the Eternal Oneness, Beginning and End, from whom all things come, to whom all things return . . . the sum-total of all the good, virtue, grace, excellence, righteousness, power, and beauty to be found in his creation; and how much more than that no man can say."[48]

Though not placed in a physical frame, Jesus' God is nevertheless a personality, so that Jesus may address him, "Our Father in Heaven." God was never an afterthought with Jesus, as he is with us. God was constant and foremost in his thought. His teaching that God was "an intimate presence in the heart was something fresh and striking, and in sharp contrast to the teaching of the scribes and Pharisees."[49]

A religion of escape and redemption served early Christians, but Modern Man can find his best religion in the faith and spirit of Jesus' religion, Jesus' Way. This kind of Christianity "would occasionally break the monotony of disapproval and allow him the respite of a gratified God, who loves him and is proud of him, [and] it would make all the difference in the world."[50] Duty and compulsion would be placed by a spontaneous desire to do the Heavenly Father's will. Each one must act for himself, however. "All Jesus can do is to help us find a way."[51]

For Jesus, loving God meant loving one's fellow men, with all their imperfections; and loving one's neighbor meant brotherhood. Jesus himself was to everybody "far more than the theory of human brotherhood; he was the fact."[52]

The Law of the Pharisees lacked an adequate motivation. Jesus' righteousness, in contrast, gained its motivation from his love for his Heavenly Father. Jesus "might very probably say: If you could love your Heavenly Father as I love him, and if you could feel as I do that his intimate and momentary companionship is the richest possession that life has brought you, your righteousness would present no problem whatever. The simple thought that you could please and gratify your Heavenly Father by thinking, and wishing, and speaking, and living as he wants you to, would be your abundant incentive to righteousness."[53]

Jesus knew no dichotomy of the individual person and the divine. God "incarnated himself in his creation, and most abundantly in his human creatures." Dr. Park says that, in Jesus' concept, a man's individuality "was God's thought concerning that man, for that man to discover and actualize. His own individuality was God's pencil sketch of the nature he was to be, the talents he was to possess, the service he was to render, all waiting for him to ink in."[54] Jesus, himself, found both life and individuality in carrying out what he believed God's expectations of him to be.

Jesus' thought of God and man was revolutionary. His conviction was that "Man is God's Son, Junior Partner, Instrument, Executive Vice President."[55] And "righteousness is no mere innocence, but the exceeding righteousness of one who knows himself, and has discovered his own power, and can recognize his function, and give himself, an eager volunteer rejoicing in the opportunity"[56] to work in God's vineyard.

Jesus' Way provides an answer to the question, Why was man created? Jesus led men away from the conviction that they were of no avail: "An inspired rebel named Jesus of Nazareth appeared . . . with an idea so revolutionary that the moment he grasped it this aimless well-behaved spectator leaped to his feet with a shout of relief. Man is no puzzling anomaly but the Son of God; an earthly incarnation of the Holy Spirit; gifted with the talents of thoughts and conscience and idealism which qualified him to be God's instrument and partner in a holy design. He has an indispensable function in this world; to serve as the outlet of that Holy Spirit which resides in him, thinks through his mind, hopes through his vision, builds through his hands. He is no unnecessary spectator whose single task is to keep out of God's way. He is God's Executive Arm, to whom the Father says: Son, I need you. Go work today in my vineyard. His ideal of righteousness is no mere innocence, but the exceeding righteousness of one who knows himself, and has discovered his own power, and can recognize his function, and give himself, an eager volunter rejoicing in the opportunity."[57]

It is well to remind ourselves, Dr. Park admonishes us, that a Christianity that offers only an escape to heaven from the prison-house of earthly life "could not have been derived from the teachings of Jesus, except by laying a false emphasis on some of his sayings, and wholly ignoring the rest." Jesus seems to have thought of heaven as a geographical location in the skies and a place where only God's will is done. Earth would be a part of heaven when God's reign was extended to earth. Earth is not a hopeless place, forever doomed to be outside God's Union of Heavenly States. It is God's purpose to fit earth for that Union, and man can help. Finally, "Those who co-operate with God cannot help sharing God's triumph."[58]

Christian theology has distracted man. Jesus "taught that God is, among other things, a Unity of Purpose. . . . He is a toiling God, with a holy end in view. Jesus never presumes to say what that end is; he never defines or specifies. His favorite term for that end is as general as a term can be: the Kingdom of Heaven on earth. He seems to mean by this: that condition in which man's faith in God's benevolent wisdom shall be so compelling, and man's loyalty to God shall be so urgent that in each occasion of life the will of God shall take priority over every vagrant impulse or desire, and 'be done on earth' as promptly and effectively as 'it is done in heaven.' " It was apparent to Jesus "that there is something wrong with this world, too much wilfulness, greed, cruelty, and hard-hearted indifference. It can be put right, and man himself can and must put it right."[59]

The secret of Jesus, says Dr. Park, is that "he had found his predicates. This is why he still towers head and shoulders above a halting, aimless humanity. He had found a Heavenly Father to love, a divine purpose to share, an eternal truth to obey, a loving confidence to vindicate, and a holy pride to justify."[60] Some of Jesus' teachings were valid for his time and place, but some are valid "for all times, places, and degrees of culture." "The Way of Jesus bears an unmistakably adverbial flavor. It is not a WHAT, it is a HOW. He cares nothing that a man is a Romanist, Anglican, Methodist, Baptist or Presbyterian. His only care is: How can I help him to be a good one."[61]

The last section of Dr. Park's Minns lectures *Christianity: How It Came To Us; What It Is; What It Might Be,* has pertinence for our concluding lecture, but not here, except for one or two references to Jesus. Remember that these lectures were written just after the conclusion of World War II. Dr. Park says, "It is no flattery to us that we need a war to show us our purpose and give us an aim in life." It was not so with Jesus. "That is the difference between him and us. Jesus was always at war on God's side, against God's enemies. To him God's victory was just as urgent, just as much jeopardized in the piping times of peace as amid the clash of arms. His ardor for God's Holy Purpose was always of that high voltage we register only when we have before us the rocket's red glare, the bombs bursting in air. There is an aim for us just as soon as we care enough about it to recognize it. If we were more faithful to it every day we would not have to protect it with such desperation when 'the ugly bullets come a-pecking' through the dust.' "[62]

Back in 1902, when Peabody and Fenn were personalizing Jesus and finding him to be a model for both individual living and social improvement, and to that extent were keeping Jesus Christ alive in American Unitarianism, George Willis Cooke, in his admirable *Unitarianism in America,* to which references have been made previously in these chapters, wrote a chapter entitled, "The Future of Unitarianism." It is quite worth recalling, and a small portion of that chapter is offered in the Appendix to this chapter. I quote from it briefly here. "Free inquiry cannot mean liberty to think as one pleases, but only to think the truth, and to recognize with submissive spirit the absolute conditions and the limitations of the truth. Though religion is life and not a creed, it none the less compels the individual to loyalty of social action; and that means nothing more and nothing less than faithfulness to what will make for the common good, and not primarily what will minister to one's own personal development, intellectually and spiritually . . . [The advantage of Unitariansim] cannot be found in the abandonment of Christianity, which has been the source and sustaining power of its life, but in the development of the Christian tradition by the processes of modern thought."[63]

In his book *The Problem of Boston,* which has been earlier referred to in these chapters, Martin Green discusses an apparent process in vital literature which consists of the writer's moral obligation on behalf of culture to express himself in opposition to characteristics of his civilization, such as mechanization, scientism, mass-entertainments, mass-democracy, cultural fragmentation. He says that such concern is evidence of moral and social responsibility and was characteristic of Boston writers in the 19th century. What Green wrote a little farther on is pertinent: "In modern times, it is the work of the critic . . . to build a bridge between the work of art and the social structure — to give it its cultural meaning — however laborious and paradoxical the effort. This bridge-building is central to modern humanism — more central than the creative work itself, which must be allowed a freedom that includes anti-humanist initiatives."[64] By humanism the writer here means the intellectual life characterized by the mind's being caught up in an idealistic enthusiasm: independent, curious, eager, skeptical. The plea is for rising above the standards of one's own time and society, if that is what seems to be called for, and not trying only and always to work within the existing norms.

This kind of bold exploration and reaching-out has characterized much Unitarian thought, and it was in Cooke's mind when he wrote apprehensively, "The real promise of Unitarianism is in identifying itself with the altruistic spirit of the age, and in becoming the spiritual interpreter of the social aspirations of mankind. In order to [achieve] this result it must not only withdraw from its extreme individualism, but bring its liberty into organic relations with its spirit of social fidelity. It will then welcome the fact that freedom and authority was identical in their deeper meanings."[65] Characteristically, Unitarians in thinking religiously have not observed a fidelity to inherited religious norms. At the same time, they have consistently tried to build bridges between the religious intent, or concept, and the social structure, not only to give it cultural meaning, as Green desires, but practical man-in-the-street usefulness.

In 1934 a Commission of Appraisal was appointed to study the health of the American Unitarian Association and to suggest ways of improving its work and condition. The Commission's report was published two years later. It promptly states: "What Channing, Emerson, Parker, Henry W. Bellows, and Thomas Starr King did for their generations must be done anew for ours, but their formulas will not serve to meet our needs,"[66] and it avers that the genius of Unitarianism has been to adapt the vocabulary and practices of past religion to new situations. The new liberal churches "will have none of the arrogance of the older missionary spirit, that sought to convert the rest of the world to its own peculiar dogmas or ecclesiastical forms. They will not desire to 'Christianize the world,' because they believe that religion is deeper and more significant than any of its historic forms — even the Christian. They will affirm the equality of all men in the sight of God — not merely all Christians, and assuredly not merely all liberal Christians, though they will find in their common liberalism a strong bond of fellowship that gives dignity and support to their smaller units of religious organization."[67] Presumably this kind of thinking would please Mr. Green. It would make Mr. Cooke very nervous, indeed.

Our concern, of course, is what does this Unitarian genius for search and change do to the place of Jesus Christ in American Unitarianism, in the post-World War II era? We have examined the Christology of Charles Edwards Park, in books written ten and twenty years later than this report of the Commission. We found Park's Jesus remarkably similar to that of Peabody's and Fenn's at the opening of the twentieth century, and at exactly the time when Cooke felt Unitarian individualists should stay in line. It is obvious that many did not. If Dr. Park was not an exception, he was one of a number growing ever smaller. In its 1936 report, the Commission of Appraisal produced revealing statistics based on its inquiries of 336 Unitarian individuals. In nonstatistical references, presumably the Commission used a wider form of reference. In any case, in its chapter on Doctrine, after listing six points on which Unitarians agree (none of which contained religious terminology), it listed five points on which they disagree. The first two are of particular interest to us: Unitarians disagree: "1. — as to the expediency of using the traditional vocabulary of religion, within a fellowship which includes many who have rejected the ideas commonly associated with such words as 'God,' 'prayer,' 'communion,' 'salvation,' 'immortality.'

"2. — as to the wisdom of maintaining the definitely Christian tradition, and the traditional forms of Christian worship."[68] The Commission allows a statement (in the section written by Commission member James Bissett Pratt, the late eminent Professor of Philosophy at Williams College), which reveals at least an appreciative cognizance of Christianity: "On the whole, no better expression of the Unitarian view of religion is to be found than the 'Two Great Commandments' of the Founder of Christianity." But, "There have been times within the Unitarian communion, as there have been times within Christianity at large, when . . . Humanists and Theists found themselves opposed."[69]

Another member of the Commission, Eduard C. Lindeman, of the New York School of Social Work, indirectly, and perhaps unintentionally, leaves an opening for Jesus' example, when he writes that "the 'spiritual meaning of life' " cannot be "transferred from one person to another either by means of exhortation or logical, reasonable persuasion. It seems to me," he says, "that the spiritual meaning of life will remain a thin and hollow possession unless it is discovered through action."[70] Presumably we are entitled to infer that Jesus did communicate the spiritual meaning of life to his followers, at least in part, or perhaps Mr. Lindeman would say altogether, through the "action" of his living example. Perhaps it may be projected that such a transfer is still a possibility for twentieth century disciples.

As a matter of fact, Lindeman himself chooses to speak of the relatedness of human beings in terms not unfamiliar in Christian thought, and with specific reference to Jesus. He writes: "[W]e may be related to each other in a manner which may be named *super-organic* in the sense that no objective goals are involved in such relationships. This type-form of super-organic relation is love, affection, or pure fellowship. Here, the relation is eternal, cosmic. . . . [O]nly those who are related to each other in a non-exploitive manner can enjoy fellowship. . . . [T]hose who participate in true fellowship are the active and the sensitive. Jesus was such a man. His experiment in fellowship was founded upon faith in men but it was sustained by faith in that cosmic source of rationality which he was pleased to call in utter simplicity 'Our Father.' "[71]

In 340 printed pages the foregoing and perhaps one or two others are the only references or inferences involving Jesus, except for the following statistical reports which are repeated under various headings. Of the 336 Unitarians interrogated, 93% professed adherence to and support of the Christian church; 72% a conscious effort to follow Jesus [the term Jesus Christ was not used]; 68% an effort to realize the Kingdom of God; and 40% participation in the celebration of the Lord's Supper. Curiously a smaller number stated they believed in God, 87%, than professed adherence to support of the Christian church, 93%![72] (Such is likely to be the inconsistency of statistical analyses.)

In a chapter on "Personal Religious Values of Unitarians," an intriguing thought is introduced, prompted by discrepancies revealed in replies to questions. Are Unitarians as "completely emancipated in their ultimate thinking as they are in their private behavior? The values of 'Belief in God,' of 'Conscious effort to follow Jesus,' get a much higher place in the ideal scale than in actuality." In other words, we do not practice what we preach. The question is asked, "Can it be that it is the power of traditionalism still exerting itself, which inclines Unitarians to believe that these ideas ought to have a higher place than they actually do?" If so, then "the way to overcome the discrepancy between the ideal scale and the actual practice would be to degrade these values, bringing them down more nearly to the level of their current place in Unitarian experience."![73] In other words, you would not affirm an ideal which was any higher than the score of your actual practice. Further discussion leads to the suggestion that perhaps Unitarians should be more loyal and devoted to their religious ideas and to their beliefs in God and to making a conscious effort to follow Jesus than they are. Deep within most persons, I feel, even Unitarians, there are basic loyalties early and irradicably related to God and to Jesus Christ.

On the subject of further diversity on the part of the "non-static" Unitarians, the question is raised as to whether Unitarianism is "Christian" or whether it will remain so. An unidentified source is quoted: " 'There are those among us who feel that no fixed pattern, even the religion of Jesus, is sufficiently comprehensive to meet the demands of an expanding life in an expanding universe.' "[74] This is no mean problem. In the expansiveness of theological liberalism, the question is bound to be, How far can we expand and still have a position left? In the case of Christianity, can we afford to let Jesus Christ go?

Finally, in the first revised By-Law suggested by the Commission for the American Unitarian Association, we find this statement of purpose: "To diffuse the knowledge and promote the interests of pure religion which, in accordance with the teachings of Jesus, is summed up in love to God and love to man."[75]

In the present constitutional By-Laws of the Unitarian Universalist Association, the corresponding wording is: "The Association, dedicated to principles of a free faith shall . . . cherish and spread the universal truths taught by the great prophets and teachers of humanity in every age and tradition, immemorially summarized in the Judeo-Christian heritage as love to God and love to man."[76] Here specific reference to Jesus has been dropped.

In something of a rebuttal, a group of Unitarian ministers and laymen formed the "Unitarian Christian Committee," later called the Unitarian Christian Fellowship. The following wording was included in an undated statement circulated while the late Paul Harmon Chapman was secretary of the Committee, and its address was 27 Marlborough Street, Boston: "The genius of our group lies specifically in the cause for which the American Unitarian Asociation was founded: to 'diffuse the knowledge of and promote the interests of pure Christianity.' Our basis of unity is the Unitarian bond which many of our churches have written into their charters: 'In the love of truth and in the spirit of Jesus Christ, we unite for the worship of God and the service of man.' . . . We seek ways of living our simple covenant completely. . . . We believe in God, Jesus Christ, man and the church. . . . In our opinion . . . these goals [of Unitarian Advance], worthy in themselves . . . are not enough to provide the Gospel for which this age (and every age) cries out. Within the framework of our Unitarian fellowship and in accordance with all that is best in our Unitarian faith, we believe, in addition:

"That God, the Father of all men, is to be worshipped with all our hearts and proclaimed to the people as the living God.

"That Jesus of Nazareth exemplified the mind of God in a manner so full and sufficient that his life is our surest guide and most enduring inspiration.

"That we are part of the total Christian Church, which, diverse and manysided, in a multitude of ways has developed the religious movement sprung from the life and teachings of Jesus."

This statement was signed by fourteen persons.

In 1944, the Reverend Doctor Maxwell Savage, minister of what is commonly known as the First Unitarian Church of Worcester, but which is technically named the "Second Parish in the Town of Worcester," published a series of assertions in his weekly bulletin for October 8, which included the following: "Unitarianism is not another one of the too many Protestant sects or denominations of Christendom. It is not milk and water orthodoxy claiming 'liberalism'. . . . It is one branch of Christianity — the other two being Roman Catholicism and Protestantism. . . . It eagerly accepts the essential ethical and religious teachings of Jesus, out flowering from his profound belief in the inherent divinity of Human Nature, potential of limitless fruit. . . . It has profoundest respect for the Bible, from which it takes the pure gold of its spiritual poetry and prose. . . . It sees Sunday as Jesus saw it as 'made for man' and therefore deplores its abuse and neglect by modern society."

About the same time that these mild assertions relative to Jesus were being made, other statements were being made by Unitarians which were notable for their lack of, or casual, reference to Jesus. An example is the statement of the Reverend Lon Ray Call in 1946, relative to the expansion of Unitarian influence through the establishment of small lay groups known as fellowships: "A Unitarian lay group is not a forum. It is not a discussion club. It is not a Sunday School. It is not a prayer meeting. It is not a social club and it is not a church. . . .

"Of course the primary function of a Unitarian lay group is to provide spiritually satisfying meetings for religious liberals in lieu of a church in towns where in all probability religious liberalism is practically unknown. . . .

"Whatever we do must be as modern and interesting and challenging as is necessary to meet the competing interest of present day people with their radios, movies and bridge games."[77]

One may observe that Mr. Call had not yet encountered television. Jesus' life in American Unitarianism was ebbing fast. The attempt to make religion relevant was overlooking the most essential element, namely, the provision of an opportunity for personal identification: the individual with Jesus Christ.

In his collection of significant Unitarian writings, called *The Epic of Unitarianism*, from which we have drawn in several instances, David Parke begins his last section, devoted to excerpts from Professor James Luther Adams' essay, "A Faith For Free Men," with these observations in part: "Paralleling the new frontiers of Unitarian organization, there has emerged in addition a new frontier of faith. It has no name; it is not a party; it desires not controversy but the truth. In seeking an adequate religious faith in the present age, it seeks first of all to understand the realities of the present age. Therefore it is conceived not in optimism but in the chaos, suffering, and anxiety of the modern world. Believing that the traditional liberal answer of Man's primary and ultimate dependence on his own powers to solve his problems has proved inadequate, it is willing to explore new sources of power and truth, most notably Christian theology, Existentialist philosophy and the social and personality sciences."[78]

If Professor Adams, also, felt persons were seeking "to understand the realities of the present age" and would welcome "a new frontier of faith . . . conceived not in optimism but in the chaos, suffering, and anxiety of the modern world," his offer of help to others in his *A Faith for Free Men* seems to lack both emotional appeal and Christian reference, except for such an uninvolved reference to Jesus as, "Jesus uses the figure of the seed to describe this power. The power of God is like a seed that grows of itself if man will use his freedom to meet the conditions for its growth."[79]

One is reminded of Jesus' despair: "O Jerusalem, Jerusalem, the city that murders the prophets and stones the messengers sent to her! How often have I longed to gather your children, as a hen gathers her brood under her wings; but you would not let me. Look, look! there is your temple, forsaken by God." [Matthew 23:37, 38] And one is moved to echo, O Adams and Call and Reese and you unregenerate liberals of the present moment, do you not see that frightened, stumbling human beings — we, who are waiting here — need something more to warm, stimulate, and strengthen them? "There can be no reliable faith for free men unless there are faithful men and women who form the faith into beliefs, who test and criticize the beliefs, and who then transform and transmit the beliefs,"[80] writes Adams. "Test and criticize," "free men": these terms reflect a wrong preoccupation. Of course one should be discriminating, but testing and criticizing, when singled out as the way of "free men," becomes an end in itself. Such a preoccupation of "free men," leaves them no freer than their orthodox brethren. It is merely a substitution of one obsession for another.

" 'Return to religion' as usually understood," says Adams, "restores only the ashes and not the fires of faith."[81] It is well said; but how much new fire is there? Adams pleads for an abstraction: "The Lord of history [who] will not fail nor faint till he have set justice in the earth." "Would any other Lord . . . be lovable? . . . What else could [men of a free faith] or should [men of a free faith] have faith in?"[82] To these questions one may respond, Have you thought of that other Lord, Jesus of Nazareth, Jesus the Christ, the one who effectively links us to this abstract God? An obvious danger of "rational" religion is over-intellectualization and a consequent loss of appeal to the emotions. Mind and heart cannot properly be kept separate in religion. The deep feelings and passionate commitments which intellectual religious liberals may have — and each one of them is a warm, dependent person underneath an apparently cold, independent exterior — are not revealed in their formal utterances. The cause of conveying spiritual nourishment through their religious conclusions goes unserved.

In 1963 a handy little booklet entitled "The Unitarian Universalist Pocket Guide" was published by the Unitarian Universalist Association. It received its third printing in 1967. In it several of our ministers endeavor to convey to the stranger the essence and tone of Unitarian Universalism. The title page carries an extract from the Constitution and By-Laws of the Unitarian Universalist Association, which includes the sentence we have already quoted: "We unite . . . to cherish and spread the universal truths taught by the great prophets and teachers of humanity in every age and tradition, immemorially summarized in the Judeo-Christian heritage as love to God and love to man." Dr. Jack Mendelsohn writes, "We have no ultimate authority [such as a "creed or interpretation of the Bible to which all must give their assent as a condition of church membership"] . . . because religion for us is not something that can be packed into *official* pronouncements on God, Jesus, divine judgment, immortality, prayer, worship, or any of the other theological mysteries covered by creedal statements."[83] It is true that American Unitarians have no *official* stand on Jesus: there is no quarrel with this independence. It simply raises the question as to whether Jesus is taken into the picture to any significant extent. For example, to say nothing more of Jesus than that we have no official pronouncement on him, which is the case here with Mendelsohn, is not to suggest that Jesus is central, or even peripheral, in the Unitarianism Mendelsohn is describing to inquirers.

Some years ago the Department of Religious Education of the American Unitarian Association, when Mrs. Sophia Fahs was head of the Department, published a book for Sunday School use called, *Jesus, The Carpenter's Son.* It has not been featured in our religious education program in recent years, although it may still be available. The course featured currently is "About Your Sexuality." The most recent head of that department, Mrs. Dorothy Spoerl, in this Pocket Guide devotes one paragraph in her article of seven pages to the Bible and Jesus: "What part do the traditional sources of authority play in our religious education program? This question is often asked with reference to the Bible and the place of Jesus of Nazareth. The Bible is an intrinsic and unique part of our heritage. We study it in our church schools and in our adult education programs, but it is not given the central place in our educational framework. The central place is reserved for the living experience of the individual. [In this context, the individual is a child.] What is the place of Jesus? The knowledge of Jesus and his teachings is of great importance, but the 'acceptance' of Jesus is not the yardstick by which we measure success. Our manner of self-acceptance is more important than our acceptance of Jesus. The primary question is not who we think Jesus was, but who we think we are."[84]

In writing on "Our Concern with Social Justice," the Reverend Doctor Homer Jack makes his sole reference to Jesus in his opening paragraph: "The roots of both Unitarianism and Universalism run deep into the Judeo-Christian tradition. Few elements in our heritage have been more precious to us than those teachings of the ancient prophets which place a concern with social justice and righteousness at the center of religion. We would honor by deeds the words of Amos: 'Let justice roll down as the waters and righteousness as a mighty stream.' And the words of Jesus: 'Blessed are the peacemakers for they shall be called the children of God.' We are concerned not with conditions of salvation in the hereafter but with doing some saving in the here-and-now."[85]

And in the final piece in the booklet, the Reverend Doctor Dana McLean Greeley, former president of the American Unitarian Association and the Unitarian Universalist Association, writes on "Our Future," in a chapter of six pages entitled "Pioneers in Mind-Stretching." He fills the mind of the reader with references to commissions and his thoughts on "progress," but nowhere is there a single reference to Christianity or to Jesus Christ. The nearest he comes is this sentence: "It is indeed true that one of the greatest assets which we have as a religious movement is implicit in the fact that the image we have presented to other denominations within the Judeo-Christian tradition, as well as to other world faiths, is an open-minded, inclusive, broadspirited image."[86]

I would not detract from the excellent motives and the genuine aspirations for good of all those American Unitarians who skirt the issue of the Christian religion and its central figure, Jesus Christ, but I would raise again and again the question as to whether they have not left out an essential factor, in Jesus Christ, and deprived themselves of a body of tradition which, for all its distortions, is yet a powerful and helpful tradition, Christianity. As it stands, however, if one is to take a clue from official Unitarian Universalist publications today, it can only be concluded that for American Unitarians, Jesus Christ is indeed dead. Unofficially, the Unitarian Universalist Christian Fellowship and certain individuals strive to keep him alive for themselves; and truly they succeed in doing so, those few, within their narrow framework. In the next chapter we shall consider briefly the possibilities of the "resurrection" of Jesus Christ in American Unitarianism.

Appendix A

Excerpts from a sermon of Dr. Fenn

on the death

and resurrection of Jesus Christ[1]

There was a strain of victory, a note of triumph in the life of Jesus, and one who has found the clew [sic] to a right understanding of his career traces with thrilling interest the passage from the simple, naive joyousness of his early ministry to the struggle-won joy and peace of the closing scenes.

Christendom rarely escapes the danger of forcing the note during Holy week. There is apt to be something of a falsetto character in the church's services. The tone is thin almost to breaking. Similarly on Easter one craves that joy which is the product of deep thoughtfulness and finds too often a sort of emotional hilarity, which goes its ecstatic way unmindful. Hence to me there is always a disagreeable hollowness about the Easter mirth, as there is to every feeling which is not resonant with thought. And the reason for this is clear. Christendom rejoices over an exterior and material event, rather than over a spiritual experience.

The body of Jesus rose from the grave — this is the burden of song and of sermon. But what happened to the body of Jesus after death is not nearly as important as what went on in the soul of Jesus before death.

It is not the conquered grave in the soul of Palestine, but the conquered fear of pain in the soul of Jesus which should engage our attention now.

We shall enter into the real gladness of Easter only as we turn from an outward event to the study of an inward experience.

Without being clear as to how, Jesus nevertheless attained to the belief that somehow his death was to be for the furtherance of the kingdom of God, by breaking down the barriers which had been erected to fence out all but Jews from the Lord's heritage, and by extending the scope of his own activity.

All through the last days of Jesus swells the strain of exultation: Death, yes, but a death which was to be significant for the world, a ransom by which the many would be redeemed from the slavery of sin, and which was to introduce him to a sphere of more abundant life and usefulness.

Not the death of Jesus alone, but all death in its very nature is for the growth of the kingdom of God in humanity. So Jesus divined. So it is in truth. So much as this, then, we can show satisfactorily — that death is not an enemy to humanity, but its friend. We can not prove that for the individual, as for the race, death is gain, but 'what is good for the swarm is good also for the bee.'

The fool wishes his book or plan to end well; the intelligent mind would see that even in the deepest tragedy all still is well because the spirit asserts its supremacy. That vision Jesus won and we always may share it. This is his note of triumph, rising out of the heart of life's tragedy, deep, clear, prevailing.

There is no despair comparable with that which opens to us the lowest hell when the suspicion seizes us that our hardships and troubles are all in vain, that nothing is to come of them after all. But all these are already mastered in the Eternal Mind, whose peace is the very conquest over them.

Many exceedingly good and high-minded persons in these days affirm that evil can not be real since God is perfect goodness, and there is not evil in perfect goodness. To me the philosophy is almost pitiably shallow, though it sounds very profound. There is a divine tragedy. In this the mind of Jesus was a true revelation of the mind of God — he knew suffering and pain, yet held it within the compass of his resolute will, binding his whole being into perfect peace. It was not a peace from which sorrow and pain were absent, but a peace in which they were present, though conquered by the higher power of his pure spirit.

Must God, then, be the saddest of all if all the sadness of all the earth enters into his consciousness? Nay, for over all and comprehending all is the mighty purpose working itself out in humanity whereby all have significance and all fit into the perfect plan.

Appendix B

"Whatever may be said about his thought as to the way in which the Kingdom was to be realized, there can be no doubt that he confidently believed that the time was coming in which men should live together upon the earth as members of one family in mutual love and trust, children of the one Father. This he designated as the Kingdom of God. This was but the old prophetic hope of a day in which the law of God should be universally obeyed, and God Himself should be acknowledged as Lord through all the earth. As might be expected, the attention of Jesus is concentrated upon the ethical characteristics of this Kingdom, rather than upon its outward glory. Its citizens are to be the childlike in spirit, not the proud and arrogant, but the meek, the peacemakers, the pure in heart, the poor in spirit. That is, the Kingdom of God meant for him a state in which the ethical qualities were to prevail everywhere in the world. These were the winning things in the world, they were to grow and spread as the influence of his teaching extended. At God's own appointed time He was to cast out and destroy all else, so that these might survive alone. This was Jesus' great hope and expectation, and as such it was plainly one of the ruling ideas of his life with reference to which all other ideas were judged, and all values established."[88]

Appendix C

"I cannot refrain from a single observation upon the general subject [the duty of the Christian with respect to social reform]. . . . It is not peculiar to New England. It exists everywhere in the English-speaking world. Its leading characteristic is an interpretation of the Christian life in terms of social service, with Christ as the great exemplar to whom the sufferings of human kind made convincing appeal; and, therefore, it is urged, whoever would call himself Christian must be similarly sensible of human need and responsive to it. Mutual helpfulness is an imperative human obligation, recognized and enforced by the teaching of Jesus that all men are members of the one family of God and brothers one of another; but to make Christianity coterminous with social service, and to define a Christian as one who feeds the hungry and clothes the naked, or (to speak more after the mode of scientific charity) who works in settlements and clubs, is active in social reforms and the like, is to lose sight of the deepest significance of Jesus himself, and to miss the very heart of Christianity. And this, for the very simple reason that Christianity is a form of religion, and Jesus was first and foremost a deeply religious man. Now, religion is one of the most exquisite values of life; but it is neither the only nor an all-inclusive value, nor is it the one most important, perhaps, for social welfare; yet life would be sadly impoverished should it lose the precious quality which religion alone supplies, through a heedless sacrifice of its distinctive character in the supposed interests of a wider utility. Whether religion be defined as poetry believed in, or described as the music to which the work of life goes on, is immaterial, provided it be clearly seen that it possesses intrinsic value, in the sense that it is not a means to an end, even to so worthy an end as social service, or one so desirable as the soul's salvation, but is an end in itself, a savour of life lifting it above sordid routine, relieving its sorrows, hallowing its joys, and lightening its burdens by revealing the eternal meaning of our swiftly passing days.

"A man may be an excellent public-spirited citizen and withal thoroughly upright and lovable — no better friend and neighbor than he in all the country round — and still not be religious; precisely as with all these splendid traits he may be without appreciation of literature, art or music. In the interests of religion and its distinctive contribution to the enrichment of human life, we need to see more clearly that the first service of Jesus to mankind lies in the fact that he taught and exemplified a singularly pure and lofty form of religion. It is written of him indeed, that he went about doing good, but it is written again that he was in the habit of spending solitary hours in meditation and prayer. If we would follow him truly and fully must it not be both in prayer and in service, in thoughtful communion with God as well as in unsparing service of man?"[89]

Appendix D

Jesus led men away from the conviction that they were of no avail: "An inspired rebel named Jesus of Nazareth appeared . . . with an idea so revolutionary that the moment he grasped it this aimless well-behaved spectator leaped to his feet with a shout of relief. Man is no puzzling anomaly but the

Son of God; an earthly incarnation of the Holy Spirit; gifted with the talents of thoughts and conscience and idealism which qualified him to be God's instrument and partner in a holy design. He has an indispensable function in this world; to serve as the outlet of that Holy Spirit which resides in him, thinks through his mind, hopes through his vision, builds through his hands. He is no unnecessary spectator whose single task is to keep out of God's way. He is God's Executive Arm, to whom the Father says: Son, I need you. Go work today in my vineyard. His ideal of righteousness is no mere innocence, but the exceeding righteousness of one who knows himself, and has discovered his own power, and can recognize his function, and give himself, an eager volunteer rejoicing in the opportunity.

"Looking back with our perspective of time and distance, we can see more clearly than ever how inspired with prophetic insight Jesus was, how rebellious against the impoverished ideas of his day, and how revolutionary his thought of God and man was destined to be."[90] [Thus] "The Way of Jesus completely abolishes that venerable falsehood: that man has neither purpose nor function in this enterprise of living. Man has both; and to the highest degree. Man is God's Son, Junior Partner, Instrument, Executive Vice President. He is here to act as well as speak for God, a prophet in a double sense. He is to foresee what a thing of beauty this world might be, and then make it that thing. Instantly a brilliant light falls on the landscape, breaking it up into right and wrong, good and bad, shining plateaus of truth and dim valleys of error, gleaming pin points of nobility and black spots of sin. A purpose in life at once reveals the moral topography of life. We can find our moral incentive in our love of life, just as Jesus found it in his love of God.

"To him all this was simple and plain. We shall not find it easy to plant the idea, but the entire drift and trend of modern thought is helping us. All of which means that the Way of Jesus has, among other things, its answer to the puzzle of the ages: Why was man created?"[91]

Appendix E

"God does not want your frail bodies and their temporary words and deeds, but your immortal souls."[92] Specific picayune laws disgusted Jesus; they told the scribes not what to be, but only what to do. "How far may a man walk from home without working [on the Sabbath]? What exactly constitutes home? Having satisfied themselves after long discussions that the Sabbath begins the moment one can see three stars on Friday evening; that a man can walk three-quarters of a mile from his home without doing anything worthy of being called work; that home is any spot where there is a pair of one's shoes, it became possible for a man to plant eight pairs of shoes at intervals of three-quarters of a mile from his home and so prepare for himself a Sabbath day's journey of six miles and return without once breaking the Law: Remember the Sabbath Day to keep it holy; in it thou shall not do any work."[93]

"The Way of Jesus bears an unmistakably adverbial flavor. It is not a WHAT, it is a HOW. He cares nothing that a man is a Romanist, Anglican, Methodist, Baptist or Presbyterian. His only care is: How can I help him to be a good one. If we would put him where he himself would ask to be put, in our own hearts, a best beloved friend, never absent and never failing, then he would speak to us with full force and effect, and lead us in his Way, and make our hearts burn within us by his revelations of God, and also of his revelations of our own neglected, forgotten, unused selves. That is where he belongs."[94]

Appendix F

"What may Christianity be for us today? Just what it was for him; a light upon our path, a song within our hearts, a guide and an inspiration, a hope never failing and a comfort ever at hand. Christianity is not obsolete. If Jesus ever said, 'I am the way, and the truth, and the life,' he spoke words that are just as true today as they were then. If Voltaire ever said, 'Christianity cannot be called a failure because it has never been tried,' he uttered more truth than poetry, because the world's present condition is due to a dearth of Christianity in human hearts, and the world's best hope is the thought, and prayer, and spirit, and action of that immortal Man of Galilee."[95]

Appendix G

"As heredity and variation are but two phases of organic growth, so are tradition and individual initiative but two phases of social progress. In both processes — organic growth and social progress — the primary force is the conservative one, that maintains what the past has secured. If individualism is necessary to healthy growth, associative action is essential to any growth whatever of the social body. In so far as individual perfection can be attained, it cannot be by seeking it as an end in itself; it can be reached only by means of that which conduces to general social progress.

"It may be questioned whether there is any large future for Unitarianism unless all excessive individualism is modified and controlled. Such individualism is in opposition to the altruistic and associative spirit of the present time. Liberty is not an end in itself, but its value is to be found in the opportunity it gives for a natural and fitting association of individuals with each other. Freedom of religious inquiry is but an instrument for securing spiritual growth, not merely for the individual, but for all mankind. So long as liberty of thought and spiritual freedom remain the means of individual gratification, they are ineffective as spiritual forces. They must be given a wider heritage in the life of mankind before they can accomplish their legitimate results in securing for men freedom from the external bonds of traditionalism. Even reason is but an instrument for securing truth, and not truth itself.

"Rightly understood, authority in the church is but the principle of social action, respect for what mankind has gained of spiritual power through its centuries of development. Authority is therefore as necessary as freedom, and the two must be reconciled in order that progress may take place. When so understood and so limited, authority becomes essential to all growth in freedom and individuality. What above all else is needed in religion is social action on the part of freedom-loving men and women, who, in the strength of their individuality, co-operate for the attainment, not of their own personal good, but the advancement of mankind. This is what Unitarianism has striven for, and what it has gained in some measure. It has sought to make philanthropy the test of piety, and to make liberty a means of social fidelity.

"Free inquiry cannot mean liberty to think as one pleases, but only to think the truth, and to recognize with submissive spirit the absolute conditions and the limitations of the truth. Though religion is life and not a creed, it none the less compels the individual to loyalty of social action; and that means nothing more and nothing less than faithfulness to what will make for the common good, and not primarily what will minister to one's own personal development, intellectually and spiritually.

"The future of Unitarianism will depend on its ability further to reconcile individualism with associative action, the spirit of free inquiry with the larger human tradition. Its advantage cannot be found in the abandonment of Christianity, which has been the source and sustaining power of its life, but in the development of the Christian tradition by the processes of modern thought. The real promise of Unitarianism is in identifying itself with the altruistic spirit of the age, and in becoming the spiritual interpreter of the social aspirations of mankind. In order to [achieve] this result it must not only withdraw from its extreme individualism, but bring its liberty into organic relations with its spirit of social fidelity. It will then welcome the fact that freedom and authority are identical in their deeper meanings. It will discover that service is more important than culture, and that culture is of value to the end that service may become more effective. Then it will cheerfully recognize the truth that the social obligation is as important as the individual right, and that the two make the rounded whole of human action."[96]

Chapter 8

A Christ For These Days

We have covered the story of Jesus Christ in American Unitarianism over a period of nearly two hundred years. We found him very much alive well into the second half of the nineteenth century, but we saw, too, that an undermining of his health, which began with Emerson's address to the seniors of Harvard Divinity School in 1838, gradually took an increasing toll. The scope of the virtues and benefits of Jesus Christ, in other words of his vitality for followers, was increasingly curtailed, until by the middle of the twentieth century, as far as a high percentage of American Unitarians were concerned, he was dead. Jesus Christ no longer existed as a live religious force, factor, or figure. He could be kept on or discarded, and the evidence is that he was largely discarded. Even when he was kept on, it was but as a name, a phenomenon in religious history, without significance in terms of anyone's personal religion. Certainly he need not be looked to for help, either as a source himself or as an intercessor with God.

For several years now, however, thousands of persons who had abandoned Jesus Christ, far, far, more in number than all of the Unitarians who killed him with their personal discipline of self-reliance, their religious independence, and their rationalism, have turned back toward him, together with a significant segment of the youth who were born and began to grow up with Jesus Christ already dead. It will be interesting to see to what extent, if any, the Unitarians will take part in, or carry out their own program of, the late twentieth century "resurrection" of Jesus Christ.

Already many liberal religious young people have reflected the current boost for Jesus Christ in popular movements and media. It is not only the youth of orthodox background who have discovered satisfaction in, or at least have responded with enthusiasm, even excitement, to, the musicals "Jesus Christ Superstar" and "Godspell." I anticipate that the cycle of ecstatic reunion with Jesus Christ will make its turn, however, as it did in the nineteenth century. And even from the beginning of this new craze for Christ, undoubtedly some persons, young and old, are bringing to bear a measure of circumspection and tempering rationalization.

In any case, in casting up the prospect of the return of Jesus Christ to the religion of Unitarianism, it may be useful to review the beliefs and views which have been held within American Unitarianism heretofore. Let us endeavor then, to construct a composite Jesus Christ from the components which have been introduced and discussed in the earlier chapters of this book. We may build our figure by using several categories of beliefs regarding Jesus Christ, with alternatives in some instances. Out of this exercise we may discover an outline for a Christ for these days.

The Birth of Jesus Christ

Since Unitarians have not been biblical literalists, the virgin birth has not been an object of belief. Jesus is God's son and so is of divine origin, but his birth was not supernatural. The New Testament account of his birth is a beautiful and useful, even helpful, myth. It is a fact, nevertheless, that God intentionally sent Jesus into the world to perform the specific mission of providing mankind with a religion of salvation.

His Nature (Human or Divine)

Jesus was human, yet more than human. Though he was the son of God, he belonged to the true race of prophets. He was God incarnate, even as each person is an embodiment of God. One sees God in him, yet he possessed two natures, human as well as divine: his person was human, so that he was born, lived, suffered, and died on a cross. At the same time he was intimately united and in perfect communion with the indwelling God. He was man, but more than mere man. He was a religious genius, but he was more than that. He was God's prototype for all other men, a God-man, in whom the divine Spirit and the human soul were in perfect union. God's creation, he yet was free to choose his aim in life, which was to be completely faithful to the will of his Father in heaven. It has been suggested that his own experience of losing his earthly father during his formative years was the paramount influence in his conception of God as his Father in heaven.[1] It must be remembered, however, that God was already referred to as Father in Jesus' own scriptures, which we call the Old Testament.

Jesus' humanness is the ground of his appeal, and it enables us to make a companion of him. As a human being, he possessed temperament. At different times it was fiery, militant, peaceful. He was a normal, emotionally well-balanced man, not given to ecstatic experiences. His sympathetic insights gave him a great influence over persons, and the charm of his personality won their allegiance. This very humanness, brought to light and emphasized in the nineteenth century, belied the Jesus Christ-God of the Middle Ages, who had no flesh, no blood. It appealed to the humble, common folk, who were destined always to live apart from kings and lords, who, for their part, chose to see Jesus as the king of kings and lord of lords. Thus Jesus became a companion for the simplest of people, someone they could walk with and talk with, at any time. While Jesus, for his part, wanted to be where the people were, not hidden in a temple, nor cooped in a monastery cell.

Some have said that, though Jesus was not God, he was the embodiment of God in man; God's word, God's purpose dwelt in him; and, because of his unparalleled sense of union with God, his Father, he was man in God. And an extension of this characterization was that Jesus demonstrated in his life and teachings at once the humanity of God and the divinity, that is, the divine potential, of man. God placed his spirit in the man Jesus without measure, and Jesus was, accordingly, God's great spiritual representative.

Jesus did not regard his experiences as unique. We should say he took the incidents of life in stride, from the performance of miracles to his crucifixion. He felt impelled to do God's will, although he could have declined to do God's will, and therefore was to this extent independent, yet he considered self-sufficiency in man a sin.

Jesus' self-identification afforded him poise in manner, simplicity in behavior, and peace of mind, notwithstanding his realization that devotion to principle and cause may exact sacrifice. His sense of service to his fellow-men and his idealism for man's perfection in God's world can lead one to the conclusion that Jesus' meaning for man lies in social service; but for Jesus himself, his primary preoccupations and intent were the manifestations of his relationship to his Father. Jesus believed in his fellow-men, and though on occasion he would decry their errors, he did not write them off as hopelessly and endlessly lost, as a branch of orthodox Christianity did, later on. A man of peace, he was constantly at war on God's side against the forces of evil which would devour the promise of humankind.

Divine Authority; Appointment by God

As for Jesus' right and authority to behave as he did, or as men later said he did, he was sanctioned by God. "Jesus Christ is the only master of Christians, and whatever he taught . . . we regard as divine authority"[2] Though Jesus himself declared that he came from God, and though he possessed a sense of mission from the outset of his ministry, he thought of himself as the long-promised Messiah only in his latter days. Jesus Christ is the source of our knowledge of God's will, and he was sent by God so to function. Jesus himself was not authority, however. He was God's spokesman, "chosen by God's wisdom, and prepared by God's providence."[3]

Miracles

Jesus' miracles can be accepted or denied. On the one hand, they were the sign of God's acting in and through Christ, and Christ was no ordinary man to be such an agent. The miracles actually occurred, and they were the proof and basis of the Gospels' authority. At the same time, they constituted the original attraction of Christianity for those who learned of them. On the other hand, they can be dismissed on the ground that all of life was a miracle to Jesus, and therefore anything that happened was miraculous. In contradiction: they were not the *proof* of a valid religion, but the exaggerations and misrepresentations of enthusiasts. Persons of this view sought to support their persuasion to follow this religious reformer, who was denied acceptance by the religious authorities of the land, on the grounds of *intellectual* conviction.

A Variety of Observations About Jesus Christ

As God is one, so, too, Jesus Christ is one. He is not two beings, as in the Trinity, nor can he be one with God who sent him. If he was of a higher rank than man, he still was not a part of the Godhead. If he was one with God, his identity was the same as that of all men with God. One must decide whether there is a question of degree or not, that is, of whether Jesus Christ was more at one with God than his fellow human beings were.

Jesus' religion was, of course, pure Christianity. The truth of its doctrines and mandates is verifiable in experience and often finds support in the teachings of other religions.

Whereas it is true that Christ came to this earth, that coming is not the coming related to a new order and the day of judgment. In other words, it is a mistake to speak of Jesus' physical presence on this earth as his coming: that was merely his preparatory advent. His return will be his coming, his first coming, not his second coming; and it will be a spiritual coming, not a bodily one. As a matter of fact, Christ has already come repeatedly, at significant times in man's history, in a spiritual advent. As for judgment, it is the law that judges, not Christ: Christ is the sinner's friend, not his judge.

The Christ of history is a true reflection of Jesus of Nazareth, but the identifying of Christ as the Wisdom of God is a creation of theology, or of Christology.

The limitation of divinity to Christ, denying it to men, is a fault of the Trinitarian doctrine and leads to the creation of the device of transubstantiation through the Eucharist, to effect the union which is really there to begin with. This is an example of the same concealment of Christ of which many writings regarding Jesus are guilty.

Christ's religion emancipated the human heart from the doom of earthly flesh, but enjoyment of this emancipation requires that one desire Christ, reach toward him. It is not a passive benefit. Again, Jesus was raised up by God from death for our redemption, which will come if we achieve a perfect obedience to Christ's teachings.

But Christ also gave man a practical morality, supported by both the teaching and the example of his love. His concept was not of man dwelling forever in the life man knows from day to day, but always he taught against a background of an expectation of fulfillment. It has been said, "The Christian life trudges through the valleys, but its face is set to the hills."[4]

The Death and Resurrection of Jesus Christ

There is a strong and valid appeal to the argument that the *whole* life of Jesus was important for mankind, as opposed to an exclusive preoccupation with the efficacy of his death. His death was, nevertheless, an act of God's love, and the blood of his bodily sacrifice, as it were, draws us nearer to God; and thus God's plan of reconciliation was fulfilled. Those who believe in Jesus Christ will enjoy eternal life. It must be understood that as it was for Jesus, we, too, after death shall not return to life as we know it now, but shall ascend to *reality*. The resurrection was, indeed, a fact, but a fact of the resurrection of the soul in a clothing more perfect than the physical body. But there is no vicarious salvation; each man is responsible for his own salvation. He will carry out his responsibility through availing himself of the advantages of Christ's teachings and examples. The effectiveness of Christ's sufferings on our behalf is to be measured by the quality of a man's life. "The real substitution and vicariousness . . . [is] the transmutation of the sufferings of sin into the sufferings of innocency; . . . the removal of guilt by the labors and sacrifices of goodness."[5]

Christ's Church and the Future

It is commonly believed by the majority of Christians that the Christian Church is the direct and intended result of Jesus' endeavors. This has never been a Unitarian belief. To take a stand in opposition on this point is not, however, to fail to recognize that a new religion did, indeed, grow from Jesus' teachings, and followers did, indeed, identify themselves as persons of like mind and of the same loyalty to Jesus Christ. Recognized disciples, apostles, groups, and churches quickly appeared. Jesus had, in fact, founded a new "empire of inward piety and universal charity," as Channing called it, a spiritual church of friends who kept his commandments, as opposed to the highly organized institution of the Church which was to develop in the centuries ahead. Jesus' informal church can endure forever; it can survive all machineries purporting to hold its identity.

In the same way Jesus' words will stand throughout eternity on their own merit, independent of men's hierarchies and organizations. This is not to say that there is not a practical need for a church, which shall preserve Christ's teachings and facilitate the gatherings and mutual encouragement of Christ's followers of every age. The risk is always present, however, that the church will fall into mis-use as an instrument of preservation and instruction and become a presumptuous power, "a prison for the intellect, and a straight-jacket for the will."[6] The true church of Jesus Christ is a church universal, whose influence undiluted, undistorted, and undirected against its true nature, will purge the cloudy waters of any civilization it encounters, and make it "run clear in the end."[7]

Assurance and purpose, salvation and the kingdom of God, for all mankind, are Jesus Christ's offerings. His ethics deserve the acceptance and practice of the world, and, for the whole, broad arc of experience, the way, the truth, and the life may be found in him.

Here, then, is a summary of American Unitarian beliefs regarding Jesus Christ and his role in the world past, present, and yet to come. How much will you keep and how much will you discard? Will you leave Jesus Christ out of your religious thinking from now on, or will you make him central? Will you have Jesus Christ as only one of a pantheon, so to speak, along with Buddha and Zarathustra and a local Guru, or will you elevate Christ to the Godhead? Above all, will you avail yourself of Christ, if you do avail yourself of him, as an ethical guide and an exemplar of social concern and action, or will you gain from him a spiritual motivation, which goes deeper than recognition and appreciation of the undisputed good qualities of his life and teachings?

It seems to me that for one hundred years Jesus Christ has become increasingly an ethical teacher and in himself a social norm, and that this kind of approach and evaluation, as good as it is, as far as it goes, has, notwithstanding, neither led to the world's salvation nor done aught for Jesus Christ as a *religious* figure, other than to let him die slowly on the cross of rationalization.

No one can fail to observe the phenomenon of a return to Jesus, which has spread through a significant segment of contemporary young people. What is the message of their behavior? Does it tell us anything of a direction for American Unitarianism?

Perhaps the first question to decide is where we need to go. It can be assumed no one is happy where we are. It is never the case that all are happy with their lot at any given period in history. Those who are satisfied almost invariably, and unintentionally, antagonize some of those who are not. The latter, in turn, whether they improve their own lot or not, manage to make the happy miserable; so that both elements must move on to more congenial ground. That is where we are today, stewing in an untenable position of persistent, provoking inequities, and shaken by the race between man's cupidities and nature's resources.

It is high time that America discovers that preoccupation with the material does not bring pie in the sky. There seems to be, for practically all persons, an endless seeking for further material gain, and at the same time, an accompanying sense of frustration of never reaching the goal of enough. It would seem safe to conclude, then, that we must look elsewhere for satisfaction. That "elsewhere" is the opposite, or counterpart, of materialism, namely, spirituality. If material gain is not satisfying us, perhaps spiritual gain is what we must seek. Old wells have dried up. We must find new ones.

The social situation in the beginning of the nineteenth century is recognizable for similarities to ours now. Judge Daniel A. White, a friend and contemporary of Channing, wrote, "When I entered college, the French Revolution had broken up the foundations of religion and morals, as well as government, and continued to rage for some years with its utmost fury, spreading its disastrous influence throughout the civilized world, and pouring upon our country a flood of infidel and licentious principles."[8] Indeed, in Jesus' time, the political situation was corrupt and the religion of the Jews, as it had been subverted, was ineffectual. Jesus himself was seeking a way out. He proved to be the way for his disciples then, and he may well prove to be the way for us, as well, even as he has been rediscovered by countless thousands of Christians, down through all of history since his own time. Channing in his time felt a need which involved Jesus Christ. He did not see that need supplied by Jonathan Edwards' Calvinism, but he did find it in Jesus Christ as the Gospels presented him. The time was ripe for a new approach, not only because of the spiritual need, but also because it was a time in cultural history when old norms could be abandoned and new perspectives elected: Witness the birth of a new country, a democracy, in the New World.

Theodore Parker came along and took Channing's spiritual well, Jesus Christ, and made of him a practical model for social improvement. And others followed who dried up the well by filling it with the dust of rationalism. We are fortunate in our search today, that we do not suffer the ancient strictures which not only psychologically impeded the restive, but socially and institutionally presented formidable barriers to exploring new frontiers. Admittedly, even today such barriers are not wholly eliminated, but those who are already Unitarians are happily beyond the pales which still restrict many others.

Whether American Unitarianism continues is not important, unless it can provide assistance to the society within which it exists. It has done nobly in intellectual and sociological fields. Its opportunity now lies in the spiritual realm. A fresh and enlightened emphasis upon Jesus Christ, who is already in the historical base of its structure, constitutes a means of providing that leadership. All major religions possess a central figure. We have inherited the loftiest and most perfect of them all in Jesus Christ. But an "enlightened" emphasis is no longer to be considered intellectual enlightenment. We are speaking of a spiritual need, and the enlightenment which must characterize American Unitarianism, if it is to fulfill its function, is spiritual enlightenment. Jesus may appeal to some as a radical revolutionary. He may appeal to others as a non-violent revolutionary. He offers to all a prophetic strain which implies hope of progress toward a Godly world. "Liberal" theology has made so many concessions to contemporary culture, however, that by its own practices, it has disqualified itself as a possessor of leadership caliber.

"Honk if you love Jesus" is the admonition of a bumper sticker in current fashion. It has a silly sound. But it has a firm basis. It represents the desires of persons who have found in Jesus Christ a leadership, a companionship, a salvation from the clutches of a crazed world, to communicate with one another and to be in fellowship. The devotion of Jesus freaks and evangelicals to the person of Jesus may be too superficial, too uninformed, to be lastingly or generally profitable, but there is a genuine need for spiritual leadership and fellowship which awaits fulfilling.

I suppose it would be helpful if I were to prescribe the type of Jesus Christ figure who would suit our needs in these times. Malachi Martin has written a lively, witty, and thoughtful book,[9] in which he delineates various types of Jesus which have been fashioned to individual tastes. Included among these types are a wide variety, such as: "Jesus Jew" (*circa* A.D. 50); "Jesus Muslim" (from about 7th Century A.D.); "Jesus Yogi" (19th Century A.D.); "Jesus Goodfellow and Jesus One-of-the-boys" (from about 18th Century A.D.); "Jesus Mystic Gun; Jesus Black, Jesus Femina, Jesus Gay, Jesuschristsuperstar" (all from 20th Century A.D.).[10] These are extreme characterizations, of course, but to some extent I think it is a necessary and defensible practice to provide oneself with a Jesus Christ figure which suits one's individual needs. The truth is that Jesus Christ is no mere historical person, and who is to determine for all persons Jesus' true and effective delineations? If Jesus were an exactly determined person of precise historical documentation, I venture to say he would be inadequate to serve us.

My point is not so much what characteristics we wish to see in Jesus Christ, however, as the recognition of the need for a close, specific, emotional relationship to a Jesus Christ of some sort. It is one thing to cite such a need, of course, and another to bring one's self to fulfill it. I have recalled the various characteristics Unitarians have attributed to Jesus Christ, during the last two centuries. A composite of them pretty well suits my tastes. Intellectually, religiously, and psychologically they are, for the most part, satisfying. To become emotionally involved with Jesus Christ is something else again, however. I believe such an involvement to be necessary: to establish a condition which will take a hold on one and provide purpose, guidance, and, most badly needed, faith and motivation.

Here is the rub: many of us, most of us New England Unitarians, have been brought up in the mold of restraint and moderation. Can I, myself, become emotionally involved with Jesus Christ? I see the need, but can I fulfill it? Possibly not. I once spent a period of time, more than thirty years ago, working closely with blacks in religious services characterized by their enviable spontaneity, and I came to the feeling that I achieved an empathy, even if I could never demonstrate the same degree of spontaneity, in myself. The kind of involvement I am talking about regarding Jesus Christ is not necessarily one of uninhibited emotionalism, like that of early or late ecstatic Christians, but it does constitute something different from my native nature, so to speak. It is a reliance, but not a demeaning dependence, upon a conscious and loving spiritual association with a very real Jesus Christ. At least I can try to make the modification required.

But there is more to think of than that. There is the creation of the religious world of our children, generations now beginning and in the making, which should concern us. When we are busy with their religious indoctrination and instruction, we shall do well to insure that Jesus Christ is "resurrected;" that he is born in them and reborn in our Christian society. He must be no mere intellectual figure in religion, about whom we read, but a soul with whom we dwell, in a constant integrity, sometimes in our awareness, sometimes not, but in the habit of our thought always. We need him to contribute to our wisdom, to our concern, to our tenderness, to our love, to the immeasurable dimension of our self, to the soul within us, as we carry out our relationship to the world and the people about us. The faddish styles of Jesus Christ are not to my taste, nor to the general and lasting benefit of mankind, I believe, but a spiritual Christ, the mythological figure conjured up in our minds by Gospel accounts, who inspires our enraptured devotion, this is the Christ for these days.

In summary, then, declarations of man's sufficiency are not enough. Bold assertions that God is dead, and a denial that Jesus Christ is either fitting or essential to a contemporary man's religion, only mock those who make them. Salvation lies now not in mind alone, nor in materialism, but in spirituality, in a sense of the holy. It lies not in the laws of nature as sciences define them, but in an awareness of and a reliance upon that which is above physical nature. It is not an intellectual affirmation of the validity of Jesus which now is our way out, but an emotional espousal of his way of life, an unabashed reliance upon him as intermediary between us and God, and as intermediary between us and our stumbling world. He is at once our staff, on whom to lean, and our light upon the way. Indeed, he is the way, the truth, and the life, and the composite Jesus Christ of American Unitarianism created thus far in this nation's history is the instruction book for our understanding of him and the guide to our involvement with him. The "resurrection" of Jesus Christ to an effective place in American Unitarianism is not a sure thing, but it is a possibility. I would go farther and say that the "resurrection" of Jesus Christ in American Unitarianism is essential, both to an adequate living of life in these times and to a purposeful continuation of the American Unitarian Universalist Association.

Appendix A

Jesus Figures of Malachi Martin in his

Jesus Now.

   I Jesus of Nazareth

  II The non-Christian Jesus figures

      A. Jesus Jew (From about A.D. 50)

      B. Jesus Muslim (From about 7th Century A.D.)

 III The great historical Jesus figures (From about 4th Century A.D.)

      A. Jesus Caesar

      B. Jesus Monk

      C. Jesus Pantocrator

      D. Jesus Doctor

      E. Jesus Torquemada

  IV Jesus Protestant (From A.D. 1521)

   V Satan: Anti-Jesus figure

  VI Some Jesus figures for the emotional man (From about 19th Century A.D.)

      A. Jesus Jehovah's Witness

      B. Jesus Christian Scientist

      C. Jesus Original Gospel Movement (OGM)

      D. Jesus Pentecostalist

      E. Jesus Jesusite

      F. Jesus Yogi

 VII Some Jesus figures for the reasonable man
(From about 18th Century A.D.)

      A. Jesus Apollo

      B. Jesus Goodfellow

      C. Jesus Prometheus

      D. Jesus Anthropopithecus.

      E. Jesus One-of-the-Boys

VIII Some Jesus figures for the social liberationists (From 20th Century A.D.)

      A. Jesus Mystic Gun

      B. Jesus Black

      C. Jesus Femina

      D. Jesus Gay

      E. Jesuschristsuperstar

  IX Jesus Take-My-Marbles-and-Etc.

Bibliography

Allen, Joseph Henry. *Our Liberal Movement in Theology.* Boston: American Unitarian Association, [1883?].

———— *Sequel to "Our Liberal Movement."* Boston: Roberts Brothers, 1897.

Bellows, Henry W. *Re-statements of Christian Doctrine.* Boston: American Unitarian Association, 1867.

———— *Twenty-four Sermons.* New York: Russell and Bellows, 1886.

Bolam, Charles G.; Goring, Jeremy; Short, H.L.; and Thomas, Roger. *The English Presbyterians: From Elizabethan Puritanism to Modern Unitarianism.* London: Allen and Unwin, 1968.

Bowen, Clayton R. "Christianity as a Dynamic." *The Biblical World,* 53 (March 1919).

———— *The Gospel of Jesus.* Boston: Beacon Press, 1916.

———— "Jesus and the End of the World." *Meadville Theological School Quarterly Bulletin,* 16 (January 1922).

———— "The Last Supper and the Lord's Supper." Lecture at the Meadville Summer Institute, June 29, 1914.

———— "The Task of New Testament Interpretation." Reprinted from *Meadville Theological School Quarterly Bulletin,* 6 (October 1911), in *Studies in the New Testament.* Edited by Robert J. Hutcheon. Chicago: University of Chicago Press, 1936.

The Works of William E. Channing, D.D. One volume edition. Boston: American Unitarian Association, 1875.

Channing, William Henry. *The Life of William Ellery Channing, D.D.* One volume edition. Boston: American Unitarian Association, 1904.

Christie, Francis A. "The Historical Element in Christianity as a Spiritual Religion." An address reprinted from the Report of the Proceedings of the Twenty-fourth Meeting of the General Conference of Unitarian and Other Christian Churches held at Washington, D.C., October, 1911.

———— "One Body in Christ. Romans xii, I Corinthians xii." *Journal of Biblical Literature,* 16 (1897), 118-130.

Clarke, James Freeman. *Orthodoxy: Its Truths and Errors.* Boston: American Unitarian Association, 1894.

Commager, Henry Steele, ed. *Theodore Parker: An Anthology.* Boston: Beacon Press, 1960.

Cooke, George Willis. *Unitarianism in America.* Boston: American Unitarian Association, 1910.

Emerson, Ralph Waldo. "Theodore Parker: An Address at the Memorial Meeting at the Music Hall, Boston, June 15, 1860." In *Miscellanies.* Boston: Houghton Mifflin & Company, 1888.

Fenn, William Wallace. *The Christian Way of Life.* London: Lindsey Press, 1924.

———— *The Theological Method of Jesus.* Boston: Beacon Press, 1938.

The William Wallace Fenn Journal. Privately published by Dorothy Fenn Duncan, 1973.

Gatell, Frank Otto. *John Gorham Palfrey and the New England Conscience.* Cambridge: Harvard University Press, 1963.

Hedge, Frederic Henry. *Reason in Religion.* Boston: American Unitarian Association, 1865.

———— *Ways of the Spirit and Other Essays.* Boston: Roberts Brothers, 1877.

Lathrop, John Howland. *A Memorial to Francis A. Christie, D.D.* Edited by Robert Dale Richardson, Concord, Mass., 1959.

Martin, Malachi. *Jesus Now.* New York: E.P. Dutton & Co., 1973.

Norton, Andrews. *A Statement of Reasons for not Believing the Doctrines of Trinitarians, Concerning the Nature of God and the Person of Christ.* 2d ed. Boston: American Unitarian Association, 1856.

Park, Charles Edwards. *The Way of Jesus.* Boston: Starr King Press, 1956.

——— *Christianity: How It Came to Us; What It Is; What It Might Be.* Boston: Beacon Press, 1948.

Parke, David B., ed. *The Epic of Unitarianism.* Boston: Starr King Press, 1957.

Parker, Theodore. *Experiences as a Minister.* Boston: Rufus Leighton, Jr., 1859.

Peabody, Francis Greenwood. *Jesus Christ and the Christian Character.* New York: Macmillan Co., 1905.

Ware, Henry, Jr. *Discourses on the Offices and Character of Jesus Christ.* 2d ed. Boston: David Reed, 1826.

Wilbur, Earl Morse. *Our Unitarian Heritage.* Boston: Beacon Press, 1925.

Wright, Conrad. *The Beginnings of Unitarianism in America.* Boston: Starr King Press, 1955.

——— *The Liberal Christians.* Boston: Beacon Press, 1970.

Wright, Conrad, ed. *Three Prophets of Religious Liberalism: Channing, Parker, Emerson.* Introduction by Conrad Wright. Boston: Beacon Press, 1961.

Yates, James. *Vindication of Unitarianism.* Boston: Wells and Lilly, 1816.

Introduction

[01]Conrad Wright, *The Beginnings of Unitarianism in America,* p. 3 f. The full citations for principal works named in footnotes are found in the Bibliography, p. 147.

[02]Wright, *Beginnings of Unitarianism,* p. 221.

[03]Quoted in Wright, ibid., p. 221. from Jonathan Mayhew, *Christianity Sobriety,* p. 65.

[04]Quoted in Wright, ibid., from Samuel West, *A Sermon Preached at the Ordination of the Reverend Jonathan Newell* (Boston, 1775), p. 6.

[05]Quoted in Wright, ibid., from Samuel Webster, *Justification by the Free Grace of God, through the Redemption there is in Christ* (Boston, 1765), p. 12.

[06]Quoted in Wright, ibid., from Thomas Barnard, *The Power of God, the Proof of Christianity* (Salem, 1768), p. 18.

[07]Martin Green, *The Problem of Boston* (London: Longman's Green & Co., Ltd., 1966), p. 81.

Chapter 1

[01]Judge D. A. White, quoted in *The Life of William Ellery Channing,* p. 30 f.

[02]Ibid., p. 431.

[03]Ibid., p. 433.

[04]Quoted in Charles E. Beard and Mary R. Beard, *New Basic History of the United States,* (New York: Doubleday and Company, Inc., 1960), p. 67 f.

[05]Green, *The Problem of Boston,* p. 24.

[06]William H. Channing, *Life of William Ellery Channing,* p. 15 f.

[07]Ibid., p. 18.

[08]*Life of Channing,* p. 32.

[09]Ibid., p. 33.

[10]Ibid., p. 42.

[11]Ibid., p. 53.

[12]Ibid., p. 71.

[13]Ibid., p. 91.

[14]Changed about 1956, I understand, to "In devotion to truth . . ."

[15]*The Works of William Ellery Channing,* p. 381.

[16]Ibid., p. 382.

[17]Ibid., p. 368.

[18]Ibid., p. 367.

[19]See Appendix A of this chapter on page 24 for a summary of all nine points.

[20]*Works of Channing,* p. 367.

[21]Ibid., p. 371 ff.

[22]Ibid., p. 402.

[23]*Works of Channing,* p. 402. See Appendix B to this chapter for an extended summary of "Objections to Unitarian Christianity Considered."

[24]Ibid., p. 378.

[25]*Life of Channing,* p. 212.

[26]*Life of Channing,* p. 170.

[27]*Works of Channing,* p. 312.

[28]Ibid., p. 302.

[29]Ibid., p. 304.

[30]*Life of Channing,* p. 169.

[31]*Life of Channing,* p. 170.

[32] *Works of Channing*, p. 221.
[33] *Life of Channing*, p. 211 f.
[34] Ibid., p. 230.
[35] Ibid., p. 230 f.
[36] *Life of Channing*, p. 305.
[37] Ibid., p. 306.
[38] *Works of Channing*, p. 306.
[39] Ibid., p. 309.
[40] *Life of Channing*, p. 70.
[41] *Works of Channing*, p. 375.
[42] Ibid., p. 378.
[43] Ibid., p. 380.
[44] Ibid., p. 304.
[45] *Life of Channing*, p. 323.
[46] *Works of Channing*, p. 381.
[47] Ibid., p. 310.
[48] *Life of Channing*, p. 170 f.
[49] *Works of Channing*, p. 316.
[50] Samuel Eliot Morison, *Three Centuries of Harvard* (Cambridge: Harvard University Press, 1936), p. 258.
[51] *Works of Channing*, p. 307.
[52] Ibid., p. 310.
[53] *Life of Channing*, p. 171.
[54] *Works of Channing*, pp. 387 through 398.
[55] *Works of Channing*, pp. 403 through 408.

Chapter 2

[01] Andrews, Norton, *A Statement of Reasons For Not Believing the Doctrines of Trinitarians, Concerning the Nature of God*, p. 16 f.
[02] Ibid., p. 58.
[03] Ibid., p. 60 f.
[04] Ibid., p. 66.
[05] Ibid., p. 229 f.
[06] Ibid., p. 424.
[07] Ibid., p. 421 f.
[08] Ibid., p. 425.
[09] Ibid., p. 272.
[10] Ibid., p. 235.
[11] Ibid., p. 238. The six other pre-world creations were: The Garden of Eden, the Law, the Righteous, the Israelites, the Throne of Glory, and Jerusalem.
[12] Norton, *A Statement of Reasons*, p. 244.
[13] Ibid., p. 246.
[14] Ibid., p. 252 f.
[15] Ibid., p. 393.
[16] Ibid., p. 412.
[17] Ibid., p. 177.

[18]For example, Norton was familiar with contentions of liberal German theologians and scholars, but he would not go so far as they did on some points, such as the regarding of Jesus "merely as a human teacher." Ibid., p. 252, Cp. later U.S. "Humanism".

[19]Quoted in *Heralds of a Liberal Faith,* edited by Samuel A. Eliot. Boston: American Unitarian Association, 1910, vol. 2, p. 230 (footnote).

[20]Cp. *Stream of Light,* edited by Conrad Wright. Boston: Unitarian Universalist Association, 1975, p. 47 f.

[21]Henry Ware, Jr., *Discourses on the Offices and Character of Jesus Christ,* p. 10.

[22]Ibid., p. 11 f.

[23]Ibid., p. 13.

[24]Ibid., p. 13 f.

[25]Ibid., p. 15 f.

[26]Ibid., p. 16.

[27]Ibid., p. 17 f.

[28]Ibid., p. 19 f.

[29]Ibid., p. 21.

[30]Ibid., p. 33.

[31]Ibid., p. 39.

[32]Ibid., p. 49.

[33]Ibid., p. 52.

[34]Ibid., p. 52 f.

[35]Ibid., p. 53.

[36]Ibid., p. 54.

[37]Ibid., p. 55.

[38]Ibid., p. 58.

[39]Ibid., p. 60.

[40]Ibid., p. 63.

[41]Ibid., p. 63 f.

[42]Ibid., p. 64.

[43]Ibid., p. 65.

[44]Ibid., p. 66.

[45]Ibid., p. 67 f.

[46]Ibid., p. 77.

[47]Ibid., p. 84.

[48]Ibid., p. 85.

[49]Ibid., p. 89.

[50]Ibid., p. 92.

[51]Ibid., p. 91.

[52]Ibid., p. 93.

[53]Ibid., p. 97.

[54]Ibid., p. 98.

[55]Ibid., p. 99.

[56]Ibid., p. 101 f.

[57]Ibid., p. 102.

[58]Ibid., p. 109.

[59]Ibid., p. 113.

[60]Ibid., p. 115.

[61]Ibid., p. 118.

[62]Ibid., p. 120 f.

[63]Ibid., p. 130.

[64]Ibid., p. 136 f.

[65]Frank Otto Gatell, *John Gorham Palfrey and the New England Conscience,* (Cambridge: Harvard University Press, 1963), p. vii.

[66]Ibid., p. 43.

[67]Ibid., p. 43.

[68]Ibid., p. 65.

[69]G. W. Cooke, *Unitarianism in America,* p. 157 n.

Chapter 3

[01]Henry Steele Commager, *Theodore Parker: An Anthology,* p. 21.

[02]Ralph Waldo Emerson, "Theodore Parker: An Address at the Memorial Meeting at the Music Hall, Boston, June 15, 1860," in Ch. XII, *Miscellanies,* (Boston: Houghton Mifflin Company, 1888).

[03]Theodore Parker, *Experiences as a Minister,* p. 36.

[04]Conrad Wright, ed., *Three Prophets of Religious Liberalism,* p. 114 f.

[05]Ibid., p. 38 f.

[06]Commager, *Theodore Parker,* p. 39.

[07]Ibid., p. 40.

[08]Ibid., p. 49.

[09]Ibid., p. 51.

[10]Ibid., p. 53 f.

[11]Ibid., p. 56.

[12]Cp. Channing's view of the Bible as the seal of authority in religion.

[13]Commager, *Theodore Parker,* p. 58.

[14]Ibid., p. 48.

[15]Ibid., p. 60.

[16]George Willis Cooke, *Unitarianism in America,* p. 157.

[17]Ibid., p. 157.

[18]Ibid., p. 168.

[19]Ibid., p. 170.

[20]Ibid., p. 171.

[21]Ibid., p. 171.

[22]Ibid., p. 171.

Chapter 4

[01]Cooke, *Unitarianism in America,* p. 418.

[02]Joseph Henry Allen, *Sequel to "Our Liberal Movement," cf26 p. 100.*

[03]*Ibid., p. 99.*

[04]*Clarke, Orthodoxy,* p. iii.

[05]Ibid., p. 205.

[06]Ibid., pp. 206 through 208.

[07]Ibid., p. 208 f.

[08]Ibid., p. 223.

[09]Ibid., p. 290 f.

[10]Ibid., p. 305.

[11]Ibid., p. 308. Cp. John 11: 25, 26 "I am the ressurection, and the life: he that believeth in me though he were dead, yet shall he live: And whosoever liveth and believeth in me shall never die."

[12]Clarke, *Orthodoxy,* p. 291.

[13]Ibid., p. 314 f.

[14]Ibid., p. 323.

[15]Ibid., p. 319.

[16]Ibid., p. 323.

[17]Ibid., p. 329 f.

[18]Ibid., p. 331 f.

[19]Ibid., p. 333.

[20]Ibid., p 335.

[21]Ibid., p. 338.

[22]Ibid., p. 340.

[23]Ibid., p. 350 f.

[24]Ibid., p. 226.

[25]Ibid., p. 227.

[26]Ibid., p. 231 f.

[27]Ibid., p. 233.

[28]Ibid., p. 291.

[29]Ibid., p. 259.

[30]Ibid., p. 262.

[31]Joseph Henry Allen, *Sequel to "Our Liberal Movement,"* p. 64.

[32]Ibid., pp. 65 through 74.

[33]Ibid., p. 88 f.

[34]Ibid., p. 89 f.

[35]Ibid., p. 93.

[36]Ibid., p. 94.

[37]Frederic Henry Hedge, *Ways of the Spirit,* p. 336 f.

[38]Ibid., p. 331 f.

[39]Ibid., p. 335.

[40]Ibid., p. 338.

[41]Ibid., p. 339.

[42]Ibid., p. 348 f.

[43]Ibid., p. 349.

[44]Ibid., p. 350.

[45]Ibid., p. 350 f.

[46]Ibid., p. 351.

[47]Ibid., p. 352.

[48]Ibid., p. 353 f.

[49]Ibid., p. 354 f.

[50]Ibid., p. 355 f.

[51]Ibid., p. 341.

[52]Ibid., p. 92.

[53]Ibid., p. 93.

[54]See text above, p. 91

[55]Ibid., p. 93 f.

Chapter 5

[01]H.W. Bellows, *Restatements of Christian Doctrine*, p. 118.

[02]Ibid., p. 119.

[03]Conrad Wright, *The Liberal Christians*, p. 83 f.

[04]Ibid., p. 89.

[05]Ibid., p. 90.

[06]Ibid., p. 91.

[07]Ibid., p. 104.

[08]Bellows, *Restatements of Christian Doctrine*, p. 89. See Appendix A of this chapter, p. 93, for an eloquent espousal of reading the Bible intelligently and as a cure for the eclipse currently being suffered by "God's Word, and God's truth, and Christ's cause."

[09]Bellows, *Restatements of Christian Doctrine*, p. 275.

[10]Ibid., p. 275 f.

[11]Ibid., p. 279.

[12]Ibid., p. 282.

[13]Ibid., p. 285.

[14]Ibid., p. 285 f.

[15]Ibid., p. 290.

[16]Ibid., p. 295.

[17]See Appendix B of this chapter, p. 94, for Bellow's fuller statement on this theme and on God's predestination of the soul.

[18]Bellows, *Restatements of Christian Doctrine*, p. 290.

[19]Ibid., pp. 304 through 306.

[20]Ibid., p. 306 f.

[21]Ibid., p. 309.

[22]Ibid., p. 310 f.

[23]Ibid., p. 315.

[24]Ibid., p. 318.

[25]Ibid., p. 327.

[26]Ibid., p. 332.

[27]Ibid., p. 333 f.

[28]Ibid., p. 334 f.

[29]Ibid., p. 335.

[30]See Appendix C of this chapter, p. 95, for Bellows' fuller statement contained in *Twenty-four Sermons*, p. 287 f.

[31]David Parke, Quoted in *The Epic of Unitarianism*, p. 123 f.

[32]E. M. Wilbur, *Our Unitarian Heritage*, p. 456.

[33]Ibid., p. 458.

[34]Parke, *The Epic of Unitarianism*, p. 127 f.

[35]Wilbur, *Our Unitarian Heritage*, p. 463.

[36]Parke, *The Epic of Unitarianism*, p. 130.

[37]Wilbur, *Our Unitarian Heritage*, p. 462.

[38]Parke, *The Epic of Unitarianism*, p. 130.

[39]Francis Greenwood Peabody, *Jesus Christ and the Christian Character*, (New York: Macmillan, 1905).

[40]Peabody, *Jesus Christ and the Christian Character*, p. 40 f.

[41]Ibid., p. 54 f.

[42]Ibid., p. 62.

[43]Ibid., p. 64.

[44]Ibid., p. 67 f.

[45]Ibid., p. 69.

[46]Ibid., pp. 5,6.

[47]Ibid., p. 22 f. For the fuller statement of Peabody on Jesus' "practical morality," see Appendix D of this chapter, on page 96.

[48]Ibid., p. 113.

[49]Ibid., p. 194 f.

[50]Ibid., p. 205.

[51]Ibid., p. 210 f.

[52]Ibid., p. 224.

[53]Ibid., p. 233.

[54]Ibid., p. 227.

[55]Ibid., p. 234.

[56]Ibid., p. 258.

[57]Ibid., p. 258 f.

[58]Ibid., p. 261. A further discussion of this aspect of duty-doing, with an extended quotation from Frederick Robertson, is contained in Appendix F of this chapter, on page 97.

[59]Peabody, *Jesus Christ and the Christian Character*, p. 265.

[60]Ibid., p. 271.

[61]Ibid., p. 275 f.

[62]Ibid., p. 293.

[63]Ibid., p. 196.

[64]Bellows, *Restatements of Christian Doctrine*, p. 93.

[65]Ibid., pp. 295 through 297.

[66]Bellows, *Twenty-four Sermons*, p. 287 f.

[67]Peabody, *Jesus Christ and the Christian Character*, p. 22 f.

[68]Ibid., p. 194 f.

[69]Ibid., p. 260 f.

Chapter 6

[01]Other percentages were Tufts, 13; Starr King, 10; St. Lawrence, 10, in *UU World*, Vol. 6, No. 14, Oct. 1, 1975.

[02]J. Howland Lathrop in *A Memorial to Francis A. Christie, D.D.*

[03]Christie, "The Historical Element in Christianity as a Spiritual Religion," an address delivered in 1911.

[04]In *Journal of Biblical Literature*, (reprint of the article, no date or other reference available).

[05]Clayton R. Bowen, *The Gospel of Jesus*, (Boston: Beacon Press, 1916).

[06]Ibid., p. 212.

[07]Ibid., p. 212 f.

[08]Ibid., p. 213.

[09]Bowen, *"The Last Supper and the Lord's Supper"*.

[10]Bowen, *The Gospel of Jesus*, p. 208 f.

[11]Ibid., p. 209.

[12]Ibid., p. 209

[13]Ibid., p. 210.

[14]"Go ye therefore, and teach all nations, baptizing them in the name of the Father, and of the Son, and of the Holy Ghost."

[15]Bowen, *The Gospel of Jesus*, p. 217.

[16]Bowen, "The Task of New Testament Interpretation," p. 7.

[17]Ibid., p. 23.

[18]Ibid., p. 25.

[19]Ibid., p. 23.

[20]Bowen, *The Gospel of Jesus*, p. 136. Bowen points out that some of John's converts, late in the first century, claimed Messiahship for John!

[21]Bowen, "Jesus and the End of the World"

[22]Bowen, "The Task of New Testament Interpretation," p. 27.

[23]"Jesus and the End of the World"

[24]Bowen, "The Task of New Testament Interpretation," p. 8.

[25]Ibid., pp. 9,11.

[26]Bowen, "Christianity as a Dynamic"

[27]Ibid.

[28]Ibid.

Chapter 7

[01]Walter F. Greenman, "Memorandum on William Wallace Fenn" in *The William Wallace Fenn Journal,* privately published by Dorothy Fenn Duncan, 1973, p. 67.

[02]*The Fenn Journal*, p. 103.

[03]Cp. Bowen: "Jesus was not in any sense a theologian," p. 105 above.

[04]W. W. Fenn, *The Theological Method of Jesus*, p. 12.

[05]Ibid., p. 14 f.

[06]Ibid., p. 24 f.

[07]Ibid., p. 26.

[08]Cp. F. G. Peabody's ascent to God through ethical behavior.

[09]Fenn, *The Theological Method of Jesus*, p. 28.

[10]Ibid., p. 28.

[11]Ibid., p. 38 f.

[12]Ibid., p. 42.

[13]Ibid., p. 41.

[14]Fenn credits this point to Wernle.

[15]Fenn, *The Theological Method of Jesus*, p. 43.

[16]Ibid., p. 45.

[17]Ibid., p. 46.

[18]Ibid., p. 51.

[19]Ibid., p. 57.

[20]Ibid., p. 63.

[21]See Appendix A of this chapter, p. 129, for additional excerpts orom Fenn's writings on this subject.

[22]Jesus, *The Theological Method of Jesus*, p. 64.

[23]Ibid., p. 65.

[24]Ibid., p. 67.

[25]Ibid., p. 67 f.

[26]Ibid., p. 71.

[27]Ibid., p. 72 f. See a fuller statement on Jesus' "Kingdom" in Appendix B of this chapter, p. 131.

[28]Fenn, *The Theological Method of Jesus*, p. 74.

[29]Ibid., p. 90 f.

[30]Fenn, *The Christian Way of Life*, p. 54.

[31]Ibid., p. 55.

[32]Ibid., p. 56.

[33]Ibid., p. 57.

[34]Ibid., p. 59. For a fuller statement on Christ and Christianity in terms of social service, see Appendix C of this chapter, on p. 131.

[35]Parke, *Epic of Unitarianism*, p. 134.

[36]Ibid., p. 135.

[37]Ibid., p. 137.

[38]Ibid., p. 140 f.

[39]Weekly Calendar of First Church in Boston, June 2, 1946.

[40]Charles Edwards Park, *The Way of Jesus*, p. vii.

[41]Ibid., p. viii.

[42]Ibid., p. ix.

[43]Ibid., p. 3.

[44]Ibid., pp. 4 through 8.

[45]Cp. Francis G. Peabody on this same point and on the characteristics described in paragraphs 6 and 8 immediately following. p. 88 above.

[46]Park, *The Way of Jesus*, p. 9 f.

[47]Here we find Dr. Park using the term *a fortiori* reasoning, which had been introduced by Fenn in his work on Jesus.

[48]Park, *The Way of Jesus*, p. 17.

[49]Ibid., p. 20.

[50]Ibid., p. 26.

[51]Ibid., p. 30.

[52]Ibid., p. 38.

[53]Ibid., p. 60 f.

[54]Ibid., p. 62 f.

[55]Ibid., p. 70.

[56]Ibid., p. 69.

[57]Ibid., p. 68. For a fuller view of this subject, see Appendix D of this chapter, p. 132.

[58]Park, *The Way of Jesus*, p. 76 f.

[59]Ibid., p. 81 f.

[60]Ibid., p. 90.

[61]Ibid., p. 109. For a fuller statement of Jesus' place and purpose, see Appendix E of this chapter, p. 133.

[62]Park, *Christianity: How It Came to Us; What It is; What it Might Be*, p. 119. For a further statement on Christianity for today, see Appendix F of this chapter, p. 134.

[63]Cooke, *Unitarianism in America*, p. 442 f. For a fuller statement of Cooke's evaluative foresight, see Appendix G of this chapter, p. 134.

[64]Green, *The Problem of Boston*, p. 196.

[65]Cooke, *Unitarianism in America*, p. 443.

[66]*Unitarians Face a New Age*, p. 3.

[67]Ibid., p. 6.

[68]Ibid., p. 33.

[69]Ibid., p. 54.

[70]Ibid., p. 65.

[71]Ibid., p. 69.

[72]Ibid., p. 150 f.

[73]Ibid., p. 170 f.

[74]Ibid., p. 183.

[75]Ibid., p. 326.

[76]Adopted in Syracuse, New York, 1969.

[77]Parke, *The Epic of Unitarianism*, p. 147 f.

[78]Ibid., p. 149.

[79]Ibid., p. 152.

[80]Ibid., p. 153.

[81]Ibid., p. 153.

[82]Ibid., p. 154.

[83]Unitarian Universalist Pocket Guide, p. 13.

[84]Ibid., p. 31

[85]Ibid., p. 36.

[86]Ibid., p. 51. In December 1972, Dr. Greeley, now minister of the First Parish in Concord, Massachusetts, delivered a sermon entitled "The Varied Views of Christ."

[87]*The William Wallace Fenn Journal*, from an article which appeared in the *Chicago Journal* April 16, 1900, Section IV, p. 86 f.

[88]Fenn, *The Theological Method*, p. 73 f.

[89]Fenn, *The Christian Way of Life*, pp. 56 through 59.

[90]Park, *The Way of Jesus*, p. 68.

[91]Ibid., p. 70.

[92]Ibid., p. 101.

[93]Ibid., p. 102 f.

[94]Ibid., p. 109.

[95]Park, *Christianity: How It Came To Us; What It Is; What It Might Be*, p. 120 f.

[96]Cooke, *Unitarianism in America*, pp. 441 through 443.

Chapter 8

[01]Park, *The Way of Jesus*, p. 15 f.

[02]*Works of Channing*, p. 367.

[03]Clarke, *Orthodoxy*, p. 208 f.

[04]Peabody, *Jesus Christ and the Christian Character*, p. 259.

[05]Bellows, *Restatements of Christian Doctrine,* p. 309.

[06]Ibid., p. 333.

[07]Ibid., p. 332.

[08]*Life of Channing,* p. 30 f. Quoted also in chapter 1 above, p. 14.

[09]Malachi Martin, *Jesus Now.*

[10]For a longer list of these types, see Appendix A of this chapter, p. 145.

Index